FOOD FOR SOLITUDE

For My Mother and Father

FOOD FOR SOLITUDE

Menus and Meditations
to heal Body, Mind and Soul

Francine Schiff

ELEMENT
Rockport, Massachusetts • Shaftesbury, Dorset

© Francine Schiff 1992

Published in Great Britain in 1992 by
Element Books Limited
Longmead, Shaftesbury, Dorset

Published in the USA in 1992 by
Element, Inc.
42 Broadway, Rockport, MA 01966

Frontispiece photograph by Beverly Hall
Cover design by Max Fairbrother
Cover illustration by Barbara McGavin
Typeset by Burns & Smith Ltd, Derby
Printed and bound in the United States of America

British Library Cataloguing in Publication Data

Schiff, Francine
Food for solitude.
I. Title
155.92

Library of Congress Cataloging-in-Publication Data

Schiff, Francine.
Food for solitude/Francine Schiff.
Includes index.
1. Spiritual life.   2. Solitude–Religious aspects.
3. Food–Religious aspects.   4. Cookery–Religious aspects.   I. Title.
BL624.S34   1992
291.4′4–dc20 91-36856

ISBN 1-85230-181-3

Appreciations

I will always be grateful to all the people who trusted in me and this project, a solitude journey that began more than a decade ago. Thanks to your loving support I was able to research, write and complete this book. Some of you were there at the very beginning, others came along the way, and others were there at the end to help me to let go. Through many many layers, many weavings and unweavings, each of you were there in your special way when I needed you the most.

I am especially grateful to my godfather, Britton Chance for all the confidence he had in my creative process. His continual encouragement and generous support on all levels helped to make this book possible. Thank you Brit for holding the faith all the way!

Angela Cox, my initial editor and good friend put special time and effort into the original manuscript. Her patience, persistence, and creative insights contributed a great deal to this work. Angela, I will always appreciate our collaboration.

Mother Serena, my godmother, was a giant source of inspiration. I wish she was here to see the fruition of many seeds she helped to plant. I will always appreciate all her blessings, grace, wisdom, and love.

Special thanks to all my friends in healing circles and contemplative communities all over the world. Your understanding, devotion and prayers helped me to continue the work, especially during my years of truly hermitizing. I deeply appreciate all the sanctuaries, and secret sacred places that gave me refuge, and allowed me to just be me, so I could continue this work alone, but not alone.

Appreciations to my ''Cathedral sister'' photographer Beverly Hall. Her friendship and understanding throughout the entire process was an inspiration. I spent many peaceful hours looking through her *monastary window*, the photo she so graciously lent to open up the book.

Thank you Krista for all your years of offering everything from soup to prayers. Thank you Joshua for understanding. Thank you Ella for all your kindness and generous grant. Thank you Rosemary for listening. Thank you Bill for helping me to let go.

I feel fortunate to be part of the Element family, and I appreciate all their effort on behalf of Food for Solitude. I am most grateful to my publisher Michael Mann, who deeply understood all the nuances of the manuscript. His vision and guidance helped to shape the final destiny of this book.' Also, many thanks to Annie Wilson for all her effort and care.

I also want to acknowledge the many people not listed here who helped me to continue and complete this work. To all my friends, family and collaborators: Thank you. Thank you. Thank you. I'll always appreciate your participation in this journey.

Contents

Introduction

How I found my food for solitude, how it found me, is a story in itself, perhaps to be told in another incarnation. But for now, what I really care about is how you will discover your own food for solitude, how you will learn to transform what could be boring lonely hours alone, into the most creative and fulfilling experience possible. This is a book of unusual ingredients. Eclectic, contemporary, contemplative, creative, spiritual and, most of all, fun.

Like the nature of solitude itself, there are many foods and moods. As you will see, food is on all levels. As metaphor it nourishes us in realms beyond our normal perceptions. As ingredients from our mother earth it nourishes us so we may be grounded enough to go a bit higher. Without the soup we couldn't say our prayers, but without the prayer what good is the soup? We need both — both the soup and the prayers. The soup in itself is a prayer. The prayer in itself is the soup to nurture our hearts and souls.

If you already enjoy your solitude, then I hope you will find new and inspiring ingredients to make your time alone even more meaningful. If you are shy about being alone, especially about eating alone, then I know the recipes — gourmet food for one — will change all that. If you care about what other people have to say about their food for solitude, about their solitude journeys, their hermitizing time, their solitude moments, their fears and needs to be alone, then here you will find insights and perceptions that will confirm what you may already feel, and tell you things you never heard before.

Above all, I hope these ingredients inspire you to be alone creatively, happily, and with complete permission to give up all the guilt about being truly alone on all levels. If I accomplish anything, I want to give you that permission to feel good about *being alone*, to encourage you to celebrate yourself, however you choose, so you can continually discover your own kind of food for solitude.

The process of getting all these ingredients together was indeed a long and wonderful journey for me. It started with my own need to learn to be alone, rather than lonely, to learn that yes, the answer is within, and that no matter how many Prince Charmings we find along the way, in the end we all are alone but not alone. On our own we are already complete. But along the way there are many circles to fill in, along the trail there are many trials. No matter who we are, there is no way to escape rites of passage that lead from pain to healing, from fear to love, from negative thinking to an attitude of gratitude.

Letting go of loneliness and all our concepts about being alone — eating alone, working alone, playing alone and so on — dissolve gradually as we ever more accept and realize that solitude is in truth an inner grace. Once we realize that the answer is within, we can create the kind of life we desire. We no longer blame our loneliness, disconnection and 'bad luck' on our family, our enemies, our jobs, our lost loves… We truly can change, and transform our loneliness into the healing we deserve.

For solitude is an attitude, an attitude of gratitude. It is a state of mind, a state of heart, a whole universe unto itself. The early contemplatives in all traditions knew this secret of happiness. The anchorites and hermits and saints and mystics always knew that being alone was the greatest gift. And whether or not we sit upon mountain tops or kitchen stools, whether we seek sacred ashrams or simply stir the soup, the message is the same. For what does it mean to be alone, if not to be all *one*. To be who you are already — in your deepest self, to *be happy*.

So let the light be kindled. Get your pot of soup simmering, and in the midst of your everyday life you will discover your food for solitude. Perhaps it will be a song coming from the wind, perhaps a sunset, a smile, a seed to be planted, a bread to be baked. Perhaps it will be a source from long ago, or a tradition about to be formed through your own ceremony alone. Just look inside your heart, and ask — what do I need today? Whatever it is, it will lead you to the inner peace and harmony you deserve. Look inside this book with the eyes of a child, and you will play forever in your own solitude mood. Flip through according to taste, begin at the end, begin in the middle, begin at the beginning, but please *begin*.

Blessing and Peace
To All my Solitude Mates

Francine

Before beginning...
A note to the reader

Through what became the *food for solitude conversations*, I was blessed to be able to reach into the hearts and souls of remarkable people from all walks of creative and spiritual life. From soup to silence we shared a whole diversity of ingredients and each time the flavor and nuances of solitude were ever more enhanced.

Essentially I asked everybody the same initial question: *What is your food for solitude?* And out of that came the most wonderful stories of transformation, of creativity, of healing and, most of all, celebration. Each person shared their own unique food for solitude story, and in the truest sense this is a gift, a sharing of creative solitude at its best.

Someone asked me, what is the most important ingredient of this collection. I thought about that for a while, then I said to her, YOU! You are the most important element of all these ingredients – to be nurtured, to be healed, to be transformed. And now I say to you, my dear solitude mate, you too have your own food for solitude story.

You are the *one* to participate!

Do You Believe
the Answer Is In You?

Solitude is an Attitude

If someone asked, "Do you believe the answer is in you?", how would you reply? This is an odd question because it covers all grounds. It's one thing to ask what time it is, and then look at a clock. You know the position of the sun will determine your answer. But what about the light within? What about your inner time and space, a realm where boundaries blend into expanding amorphous states, cycles where questions and answers become one. Who is determining the answer here? Whose question is it?

Diving deeply into yourself doesn't mean you are no longer interested in outside sources, or that you plan to go on an isolationist cruise of no-return. It simply means that you are ready and willing to confide in yourself. Literary legend, Frances Steloff, once said, "Solitude means that you can think about the things that are important..." And then with a twinkle in her eye, she said, "It reminds me of a poem." I wish you could have seen her reciting it, laughing in between each and every line, but meaning every word as she said:

> "I'm the best friend I ever had
> I like to be with me.
> I like to sit and tell myself
> things confidentially."

But what if you can't confide in yourself? Perhaps the worst kind of loneliness is not being able to be in touch with yourself. It's that feeling of restlessness that doesn't allow you to simply sit with yourself. So you look elsewhere for nourishment and support. You run around trying to find the 'perfect solution' to satisfy you, and of course you never find it. In the end you always have to come home to your true self, to experience your own kind of confidence.

In *The World of Zen* compiled by Nancy Wilson Ross, there is a chapter by Akihisa Kondo entitled, 'Zen in Psychotherapy: The Virtue Of Sitting.' Here he elaborates on the Zen approach to getting in touch with yourself.

> In Zen practice ... one can know the meaning of sitting only by practicing sitting. The answer must come out of oneself, by one's own experience. Single-mindedness is just single-mindedness and leaves no room for interrogation. It is a sheer act of faith in oneself. It implies, therefore, total respect toward the real Self. 'What is real self?' is not to be intellectually understood, it is to be experienced. Enlightenment, the realization of the true Self, comes out of the practice of sitting, out of the 'sitting' state of mind.

Indeed, this is a confidence that comes from solitude, but it's also because you bother to be alone that this confidence grows. It takes many many solitude moments to cultivate an inner solitude that gives you the confidence to be alone wherever you may be. Then you don't need to go anywhere special. You just have to remember to check into that internal center, the one that lives inside of you. As Job in the Old Testament says, ''Is not my help in me?''

For dormant within each of us is a ray of brilliance, sometimes shaded, sometimes about to be awakened, but always ready to be called upon. It is what Mother Serena calls ''a divine spark of God.'' This is the treasure within each of us, a world beyond definition and boundary, yet always open to new forms and ideas. This is the ever constant yet always changing remarkable answer within.

DO YOU BELIEVE THE ANSWER IS IN YOU? Most of the people I talked with answered this question either directly or indirectly, because that rare creature called inner solitude is the basis of their creativity. I hope these highlights from our conversations give you a new perspective or confirm what you already know.

We were at the NBC news studios when EDWIN NEWMAN and I talked about his food for solitude, and in the middle of our conversation, he had to break to do the noon news. While he was doing the news, a sort of minor crisis came up, and he had to shift gears in the middle of his presentation. On the air, he had less than two minutes to make a decision that could shape the consciousness of how events seemed to turn out that day. He had to throw out one story, and put in another. He had to choose the right ingredient. But how did he decide?

When we came back from the studio to his office, he said, ''I think that I can relate solitude to this whole business of being a broadcaster.'' He then went on to talk about the distinction between being on 'automatic pilot' and his idea of the 'internal editor':

''To some extent, doing a news story has something to do with solitude, because at the moment when you are making a decision of that kind, you are alone. Up there, a few minutes ago, I was making a decision alone. The news editor brought me the story and said, 'Do you think we ought to use this?' Now, I could have said to him, 'Do *you* think we ought to use it?' and I know I would have gotten a competent answer. In which case the solitude would be his, he would be deciding. So, I said, yes, I want to use that story. And there I was with about a minute and a half to decide how to get that into the news summary we were doing.

But where do those decisions come from? I had the idea years ago, of what I used to call 'the internal editor.' I knew that there was something in here that said, say it or don't say it, something that dictated taste for me. It was my conscience for broadcasting. This is different than being on automatic pilot, which is a skill you have that enables you to know what to do in a given set of circumstances, on the air let's say, or in putting a program together… But in addition to that automatic pilot, it seems to me, one ought to have an internal editor that tells you: 'say this, don't say that.' If you don't have that internal editor, that's when the trouble sets it.

Although television is very much a team job, there are times when you are alone. There are times when you have to decide what to do and what to say inevitably… Sometimes, you may find that you're on the air, and you have to make very quick decisions, particularly when you're ad libbing… I remember once resisting an impulse to say something because the news wire was feeding in a certain bulletin that I thought was very distasteful, due to the current circumstances. I wanted to comment on that, but something else said to me, don't say it, which I think was the correct decision.

This is where solitude comes in, because at that time, no matter what was going on, I had to behave as though I were alone, as though I had solitude. No matter how much noise there is, how much activity, no matter how many people are thinking and talking and planning, to good effect, you still have to have solitude in your head, in order to think. To do your job, you have to be able to think, and to be able to think, you have to be alone.

When you are alone, you are turned into yourself. You are at peace. You have a sense of satisfaction, a sense that you're not being cheated. And then you know, the answer is in you. You don't need to go out to find what you're missing, because you know it's all there… Essentially, we are always alone, even with other people… Either we exercise our free-will to make decisions or we let other people do it for us. Solitude and the process of deciding are intimately linked.''

BUCKMINSTER FULLER:

"When I was a young man I had a series of business failures where I lost everything, and I felt like a complete loser. I was so depressed that I went to Lake Michigan with the idea of getting rid of myself. But in a moment of revelation something changed my heart. I started thinking about all the consequences of suicide, how it would affect my family, how it would affect the entire universe. I realized quite clearly that each life is born of two lives, and either I throw myself away or consider myself no longer belonging to me, but belonging to everybody. The only way I would keep myself alive would be to use me for everyone else and forever.

I also realized that if I were to continue to live, for the first time in my life I would be doing my own thinking. I would have to do what pleased me to *earn my life*, and not take a job just to please others. And I knew I had to do it all alone, on my own. For the first time in my life, standing over that lake, I faced real solitude. I was overwhelmed by God. In a moment of choosing life or death, I knew I had to choose life.

I was on trial then, and I feel that all humanity is on trial right now. Every precious second counts. Each and every action of love will make a difference. The examination is for everybody. Every individual has to face this love of truth. The planet depends on this, on how each individual behaves, on how you behave, on how I behave. We are all in this together, alone, but not alone.

Solitude is when you discover God firsthand. You don't need any intermediary. It is when you commit life to everyone else."

God gives the lonely a permanent home.

Psalm 68:6

DIANA VREELAND could have just as well been quoting the Psalmist when she talked about her feelings concerning God. ''I suppose I am a religious person,'' she said, ''but not in the typical way.'' She then enthusiastically exclaimed:

''Certainly I believe in God. My God, if I didn't believe in God, you have to! Atheism may be interesting, but how lonely it must be. Now *that's* a lonely life. If you believe in God, you never lose the connection. It's simple. You are connected to life and all it contains. You are connected to yourself. If you don't believe in God or whatever you want to call it, then you have to be lonely. Because things finish and there's no future, there's an extinction like a candle.

There's a difference between being a solitary person and a lonely person, and believing in God makes that difference. Choosing to be alone with God gives you that connection. And in the end, there aren't that many people who you want to be with, who you can share God or solitude with, but do you want that many... all you need is a few.

I don't understand how people cannot believe in God. I suppose it comes from how one is brought up. We were never taken to church. We never went to a Sunday School. Our family never talked religion. We simply were people who believed in God, very simply, that's all, no more no less... I guess that's where my real confidence came from. It was my real foundation.

Your position in the world is related to confidence, and that is related to God. It makes no difference what you do, as long as you do it well and with all your heart. Everyone in the world, in their own way, can be a king or queen. In their own way, everyone can be in the highest position of all.

Everything you do has to do with your standards. You have to have your standards. It is essential. And standards come from yourself. You can say from education, but I had a very poor education. I think my solitude was my education. Being alone, and being with God, gives you the highest standard of all.''

DO YOU BELIEVE THE ANSWER IS IN YOU? is a tricky question to ask at all, and to ask it of Anthropologist/Philosopher GREGORY BATESON you have to be prepared to have him tell you what you really wanted to ask. Finally, after a long lunch, lots of questions, and a lot of laughter, I said, okay, so where do you get your ideas from? And in his aristocratic English accent he answers, ''From the point of a pen!'' All right, Gregory, and what's directing the pen? ''The fingers.'' After that there was a long silence.

To probe Bateson about his inner journey is like trying to put a square peg in a round hole and make it fit. To analyze the inner process of someone else is very difficult, and probably impossible. As he said, ''You can't really talk about insight. Insight is the one thing everyone wants to know about, but insight is where YOU are going!''

When Bateson wrote *Steps to an Ecology of Mind*, he was writing about the process of getting ideas, but getting him to talk about this was not easy. Finally he took pity on me, because I refused to let him avoid answering the question, so he put down his fork, started to wave his hands around, and pointing to his forehead, he said, ''You want to know about all this insight stuff, well of course that's all nonsense... it tisn't in there... it tisn't in there!''

So where is it? Could the new physics of quantum mechanics, and how it was probing into the tiniest aspects of the atom, via hadrons, quarks, and gluons give us a clue? Did Bateson believe in all the connections between inner and outer processes? If the answer was not within us then where was it, besides definitely being inside the great bowl of couscous we managed to enjoy in between everything else. After this very long discussion, Bateson said:

''I don't think atoms have in their insides any of the criteria of mental process problems. I don't think we start from that level at all... People such as Teilhard de Chardin like to bring in God from the underneath, that way... Even Samuel Butler wanted to do that, but I don't go that path. I think asking where the answer is in terms of inside or outside is a result of split-thinking. We put the line in there, but there is no difference between inside and outside...

For example: You've got a man doing things. Experiencing. Doing. Cutting down the tree is the figure I usually use. He's got an ax. He's got a tool. And there's the tree. And the information going around. You can have principles in that – the man, and the tree and the ax. And if you want to go and look at how a tidepool is organized, you will find similar principles. And you don't really need to go to the tidepool, in a sense. Or, having gone to the tidepool, you don't need to look at yourself with an ax...''

He continued on to say that all these principles help each other, but there wasn't one place that could be an answer to solve all problems, "because you don't know any one of them well enough." The idea that meditation could reveal everything to you simultaneously, and that through a mystical experience you could know it all, did not appeal to Bateson. "It doesn't help me much, it is interesting," he said, "like anything in the tidepool is interesting."

Though the source be obscure, still the stream flows on.

Poincaré

The Fourteenth Dalai Lama, His Holiness TENZIN GYATSO

''I have never felt lonely in my life. I feel blessed with the attitude of solitude... Solitude always depends upon one's own attitude. If you are suspicious of others, and you don't have the correct attitude, then even if you remain with people, side by side, you still feel loneliness. But if your mental attitude makes you feel warm towards other people, and you have a very sincere motivation towards other people – if you truly care about other people's welfare and are concerned with their suffering, and you share as much as you can – now this is a real remedy for isolation or loneliness.

Solitude is always a deliberate choice. With this kind of motivation, with this kind of attitude, no matter who I am, whether I am an Easterner or a Westerner, a believer or a non-believer, a scientist or a religious person, it doesn't matter. As long as I am a human being, and I feel compassion for my other brothers and sisters, as long as I can empathize with my other brothers and sisters, then there is no feeling of loneliness.

Thus it is one's own attitude that makes a person lonely or makes solitude creative. The altruistic attitude, a genuine sense of brotherhood/sisterhood makes you forget your own loneliness. Then you don't feel cut off or isolated. But it's not easy to be completely selfless and that is why we have our spiritual practice. However, let me add that no one has to be completely altruistic. Even if we practice peace, we cannot be completely selfless. Of course desire or concern for one's own future is right, along with a concern and compassion for others too. That's fair.

So basically, our own attitude toward others determines whether or not we will be lonely or not. In the end it doesn't matter whether you are alone or with other people. It makes no difference; it all has to do with how you think...''

JOHN LILLY

"One important discovery I made in solitude is that all the barriers are in me. As long as I can keep that in the forefront, I don't get too involved in anything, or I get involved enough depending on what is required... If I get upset about somebody or some situation, I suddenly pull away and think, "That's your own barrier," allowing that emotion to start interfering with your thinking. It is 'you/me'. It isn't anybody out there, even if they're shouting and angry or whatever it is. A lot of what we do is the demand of our culture to give a certain kind of response. It is to put on a face, put on a body-motion, put on clothes or put on whatever!"

JULIE NEWMAR

"When I was growing up I thought there was something wrong with me because I was so tall. I felt like some sort of freak. But now when I meet other women who say they look up to me and can relate to me because they too are tall, I realize how important it is not to worry about being accepted by society. You have to begin to accept yourself as you are. I've learned that the answer *is* in me. We keep learning this as we continue to grow, and this is on all levels of body, mind and soul. In our culture there seem to be gurus and experts for everything, especially when it comes to taking care of our body. They have all the answers that we'll ever need, so we never bother to question them. But I don't buy that stuff... Someone once said the finest drugstore in the world is contained in your own body... It could be the body is perfect. I really believe that, so I use no drugs whatsoever, not even aspirin. One pays for not knowing. I would rather find out who or what is paining me than suppress this important information my body is giving me. I never hurt my body. I will stretch, run, exercise to the point of good feeling, but no excess over the age of thirty-five. I'm so sensitive to my body, that it can tell me: I need milk, ascorbic acid, etc... It knows what is lacking and it tells me. I pay attention because I love to feel good. I'll miss my body when it dies..."

IRA PROGOFF

''I learned that I could think for myself quite early. I remember sitting in a junior high class when some question about history came up. Some kid gave an answer, and the teacher said, 'That's right.' I remember feeling, 'Well, that's not the real answer.' I remember the sense that there were answers that pass muster for the people; they are accepted by the consensus. So, the teacher says you're right, and gives you an *A*. But, it's not right.

At that point, I had the sense that something was wrong. I had two thoughts. One was that there is an inner truth they don't know. They see the world the way they want to, but there's another way and that's an inner truth. At the same time, I also knew I couldn't tell them, because they wouldn't understand.

Not everyone knows they can think for themselves, but at some point or other, a person realizes that, if they're ever going to realize that. It takes time to develop a trust between yourself and your intuitional powers. You can't trust those inner voices all the time. In working with my inner voices, I have learned when to trust them, and when not to trust them. Not every lead in from my inner voice is the final truth. You have to learn to be silent and to listen to the messages within. And even though I worry about it sometimes, I do it anyway.''

BRITTON CHANCE

"The ability to enjoy your creative solitude just has to come from an inner self-confidence and self-reliance... But to be able to be satisfied to be alone is an achievement that you don't easily attain, except perhaps by understanding your own nature a little bit better than you might have as an adolescent. I think that ability to separate yourself from the clamor of other human beings is more achieved than granted. There isn't a magic turning point that serves you confidence on a platter. You gather self-confidence that you're doing the thing you want to do, that you're doing it well, and that it's adequately appreciated by one's peers, or if it isn't appreciated you don't care! I think you gather these attributes over the years of life."

...Faith in oneself. Few people have faith in themselves. Of these few, some are endowed with it as with a useful blindness or a partial eclipse of their spirit (what would they behold if they could see to the bottom of themselves!) while the rest have to acquire it. Everything good, fine, or great they do is first of all an argument against the skeptic inside them. They have to convince or persuade him, *and that almost requires genius. These are the great self-dissatisfied people...*

Friedrich Nietzsche

K<small>YGONGLA</small> R<small>ATO</small>

''There are many wise people who are not Buddhists... one can learn without a teacher... We all can become God... the perfect Buddha. One man can then create mountains and clouds and do what God did before... Eventually everyone will have solitude.

The Buddhists say that everybody will become Buddha whether they believe it or not. The more and more you realize the nature of things, the more you will see things perfectly and then you will become Buddha...

As for my solitude, I don't have solitude, maybe one day... I don't have any answer, everything is answered already!''

POLLY BERGEN

''The most difficult thing, I think, one has to do in one's life is to finally once and for all take the responsibility for one's self on all levels. It took me a long long time, when I could finally say to myself, *alright, no more fairy tales*. I'm not going to write any more scenarios. I am going to be responsible for myself the rest of my life. I am going to take care of myself, which means I will not depend on external help as my only alternative. I can't depend on marrying some fellow who's going to take care of me, and I wouldn't want to. And that's the whole point: the day you arrive at that moment in your life when you can say, 'I'm going to take care of myself.'

I learned this in solitude, but it wasn't easy. I used to have this incredible defense mechanism that gave me the appearance of being totally and completely self-sufficient, strong, capable, all those things that were not necessarily who I was. There was a part of that in me, but a lot of it was make-believe. I mean I was playing Rosalind Russell in all those films.

I first realized who I really was in my mid-thirties, after playing the part of a schizophrenic in a film. This was about a woman who never allowed herself to be vulnerable. After doing this part, I realized that no one who knew me, knew *me*. I knew who I thought I was, but I didn't want anybody to know about *her*.

Then I played another part, in which the woman was like a walking open wound. And by the time I finished doing that film, there was no way I could put all the stuff that I had used to play the part back inside. I had brought all the things out that no one had ever seen in me – all the fear, the anxieties, and the insecurities. I had used them, and when the picture was over, there was no way I could stuff them back inside. So, I went through several very very difficult years trying to deal with myself, and trying to allow other people to deal with me as I was. Those first three or four years I was terrified.

The way I finally became alone and not lonely was the realization that I just simply had to. *I had to learn to be alone*. I realized that what I was doing had no meaning. I was just filling time and space. It was hard and painful, but when the loneliness changes into solitude, you know it's all been worth it!

Now I'm open to anything and everything that happens. There is no scenario. I may meet a wonderful man tomorrow, and I may not meet a wonderful man tomorrow. It so happens that my life will be fine one way or the other, because I'm not depending on external realities. I'm counting on me and only me for all the right reasons, and now I can reach out to others for all the right reasons.

I think most women have been conditioned to reach out for all the wrong reasons. I know that all my life I wanted to marry some man who would take care of me. But what I really meant was a man who would hold me and love me, and always be there, and he would make me feel safe... I guess I would marry my father, which is basically the image. But a very large part of that taking care of is financial. It's material, even though we don't think of it that way. I believe all women were basically conditioned to be dependent. I was guilty all my life, because I obviously had the ability to take care of myself. But to others it seemed odd and so I rejected it. It was unacceptable. Today it is different for women. And today, I know the answer is within... the gold is within, and there is no more guilt.''

Externals are not in my power, choice IS!

Epictetus

JOAN FONTAINE

''One has to learn to overcome the pain of loneliness,. There has to come a time in your life, when you can face solitude and enjoy it. When I was a child, I was sick all the time. I had pneumonias and rheumatic fevers. I was six months a year in bed, and that is solitude. So I learned to live in a total fantasy world. I had my own friends, all totally imaginary of course. In the day time I read, and at night I fantasized when the lights had to go out. I had all my playmates, and everything was entirely in my own imagination. So that when I got to be eighteen, acting was more natural than being real.

As a matter of fact, when my mother went to the premiere of *Rebecca*, Louella Parsons said to her, 'What do you think of your daughter, Mrs Fontaine? Isn't it a marvelous thing she's an overnight star!' And my mother said to the columnist, 'Joan has always seemed rather phoney in life, but she's quite real on screen!'

It was a strange remark for mother to make, but I had no external personality. I mean, talking with people and being with people was unreal. *Being alone was not unreal*. That was me; the whole other world didn't exist. Not until I was fifty was I able to say, I'm alive. I'm here, and I can deal with other people on a face-to-face basis. I had always dealt with them as an external person, because my real person was in my dream world.

I am grateful for having all my dreams. They gave me strength. When I was a child I needed it. My father deserted my mother when we were tiny children. He gave her no child support and it was very hard. But something inside me knew I could take care of myself. Something in me knew I had to be responsible, and so I've been totally independent all my life.

What is important is the inner person. And how you make out, and how you exist through all the external things that happen to you, will relate to what happens to your insides as you go along. The inner world is more important than what's outside.''

Peace is your natural state... Happiness is the Self, the Self is All. There are no others... Once you realize the Self, it becomes your direct and immediate experience. It is never lost... For whom is the inside or outside?

Ramana Maharshi

Because of the absurdity of the Swedish tax system, actress BIBI ANDERSSON found herself in prison one night. She spoke about her loneliness and her freedom, and unlike Brother David, who said for a hermit to be in a solitary cell might be heaven, Bibi Andersson shared a totally different perspective:

"The night I spent in prison was the most crucial night in my life. It sounds dramatic to say that, but it's true. Yes, what I went through was like being in a hotel, for that's what Swedish cells are like. It was comfortable. There was nothing dangerous about it, superficially. But I was locked up, and it was a terrible discovery for me to realize that there are things in life that I cannot escape from. It was awful to feel that other people's power over me can be greater than my own possibility to just walk away.

Before this night, I've never been in any situation where I've not been able to walk away. Even on opening nights when I hate to go on stage, and I'm so nervous I can die, I can always collapse and have a doctor take me to a hospital. I'm still hanging in there out of my own free will. But this was the first time I had no will. I had no power. I learned that to be taken away from yourself is the most scary thing that can happen to anybody. They took away myself from me. I was just nobody. It was awful. They took away my will, but maybe because I let them.

This experience taught me a lot about freedom. To have your freedom taken away is awesome. Even if we don't really have free will, we still have the illusion that we are acting out of our own free will. Even if it's an illusion we believe it… So maybe they just took away my illusion. I think because of that night in prison, I got stronger. I got stronger in the sense that I really realized that either my nerves are too weak for this, or I'm strong enough for this. And I just made the decision that I was strong enough for this.

There was another time that I had the same sensation that something was happening to me that I was not in-power-of. I was literally drowning in Brazil. I was dragged out by waves, and the person I was with started to run away from me, to get help. When I saw that person run, I knew that I was totally on my own. I felt I was totally alone, and then I felt a strange sensation within me. I decided, NO. It's not time. I'm not going to die. I will have the strength, even though I don't know how to get it. Then a voice said, THINK! and I suddenly remembered what somebody had told me. Whenever you are caught out in a water stream, never try to aim straight ahead to shore. Try to throw yourself to the side, so you get out of the circulation. And so, I took all my last powers and I threw myself to the side, instead of trying to swim in. And that's the pure panic, you try to swim in, and you just go further out. And instead of doing that, I was going to the side and the wave took me up.

In a sense I saved my own life by saying, no, it's not time. That was almost the same decision I made that night in prison, when I said to myself, 'I'm collapsing. This might very well be the end of my capacity to survive, to survive as me, so I can exist as a person. I will start to be obedient. I will start to be scared. People will be able to dictate my life, and I will just give up something.' I still don't know what I felt I was giving up, but I knew it was inside me, and that it belonged to me. And then I went out of the prison, and I said, No — no newspaper, no person, nothing — is going to do that to me, not yet.

It is during a crisis that you discover your freedom. Sometimes it's a learning, growing, shocking experience to realize we are alone and free and then it becomes funny and even fun. In one way, being detached saves you from all the fear of being alone. Yet detachment is not what you want from life. That's only a temporary state to get you through the pain, so you can grow."

The mysterious magical power of creativity is fascinating, and the child's world of being alone teaches us a lot about our own creative solitude. "If you're talking about the peace of solitude, then my six-year-old daughter Jenny understands that," said Bibi Andersson. "She loves to go out to the forest in Sweden for long periods of time, because she really loves the peace there, whereas I feel lonely if I stay there too long. She knows much more about solitude than I do. In that sense she is the grown-up and I am the child."

JENNY'S MR NOBODY

"I always have a friend to walk with when I'm alone, because I have my heart to walk with, and I have my feelings... In my heart there lives a little man who's called 'Mr Nobody', because he is nobody, he is just living in there. No one can see him, and no one can feel him, except me. That's why he's called Mr Nobody, because nobody knows about him except me.

He's lived in me since I was born, but I never gave him his name. Everybody has a lady or a man inside them. Everyone has this person, but there is no name. It's just someone you know about, and think about. If you ask this friend, what is your name, he says, I don't have a name, my name is nothing, but I'm always with you.

Mr Nobody talks to me all the time, especially when I walk by myself to school. He tells me what to do. If they're teasing me in school, he helps me. Sometimes he tells me what to say, so I can tell others, just like I'm telling you now... He tells me what kind of soup my dolls will like. He tells me not to cry when I'm all alone. He's the one who told me about the light. The light can be bad, if it burns you, but it can also be good. The light makes people live. If the sun wasn't here, everything would become snow and ice, and we would have no food. If the sun should just stop, and just go away, we wouldn't live. It feeds the plants, and it feeds us. I love the sunlight. I don't like it when it's rainy. My dolls also love the light. And when it's a nice day, I take them for a walk.

Sometimes it's sad to be alone, and sometimes it's funny. When you can be alone with Mr Nobody and your dolls, it can be happy. I love to cook food for my dolls, sometimes it's soup, and sometimes it's other stuff. I make it all by myself, but I wouldn't eat it. I take salt and pepper and whatever else is around, put it into the water and just stir it around, then I let it cool and serve it to them. For a person this wouldn't taste so good, but they like it!''

MOTHER SERENA has her gentle way of explaining why the answer is within each of us, "that divine spark, a little piece of perfection within you, waiting to transform and grow." She spoke about *silence*, and as she talked, a beautiful peace filled the room.

MOTHER SERENA

"How can you explain an experience that involves peace and that involves silence? These are two of the most spiritual experiences that a human being can have, and strangely enough, both these experiences are motivated by love... You may ask, what is the difference between peace and silence? Silence brings peace, and peace brings silence. They are two opposites according to the two laws of Hermetic philosophy... If you are at peace, usually you are silent.

Silence means you are under complete control of all your emotional reactions, which are conquered in silence. Everything that happens in our body happens in complete silence. And when you start hearing from it, then you know something is wrong! The principle of healing is to invoke silence — going into the silence.

Inspiration always comes from within ourselves. Remember this, that even God can't make you change. He can guide and inspire you, but you have to do what needs doing yourself, otherwise there would be no purpose to living, we would be just like robots.

The Divine in you makes you grow and change. God is not out there, he is with you, within us... A spark of God is with all of us and that's why he placed it there, so that he'd be accessible all the time."

The only essential thing is that we strive to have light in ourselves. Our striving will be recognized by others, and when people have light in themselves, it will shine out from them...

Then we get to know each other as we walk together in the darkness, without needing to pass our hands over each other's faces, or to intrude into each other's hearts.

Albert Schweitzer, *The Light Within Us*

Menus And Meditations

Treat Yourself Like Company

One of the nicest ways to settle into 'Menus and Meditations' is to step into your kitchen and treat yourself like company. This is the ideal time to truly pamper yourself, to let the child in you say YES to whatever your heart desires. Being kind to yourself in the kitchen can very well be an initiation into solitude at every level. All you need is the willingness to try, and the time to give yourself the same care you would lavish on your most honored guest. Think about it — wouldn't you like to have beautiful flowers just for you and your dinner table? Maybe you'd treat yourself to a plant, but fresh flowers! Or what about buying that caviar, the kind you so readily offer guests? Don't you also deserve it? And what about taking the time to fix yourself the most exotic gourmet feast for one. Would you bother, or do you feel it isn't worth the effort? A lot of people feel like that, simply because taboos about eating alone make most of us feel guilty. But isn't it time to trade in all those taboos for treats and truly celebrate!

Psychologist Rollo May admitted that he wished he could learn how to eat alone with the same gusto as he's worked alone. ''Why not lobster for one?'' he said, ''But would I dare!'' Then he added: ''To me food means sharing with another person, and that is true for most people. If only we could learn to share food with ourselves, realizing that it isn't selfish, then we would be linked to the cosmos on another level.'' And he's right. Eating alone can be a great way to make friends with yourself. Then solitary dining takes on a new meaning.

Of course, how you entertain yourself all depends on who's doing the inviting. Everybody has his or her kind of treat. Columnist Eugenia Sheppard, who wrote about all the famous 'beautiful people' parties said, ''When I dine alone, I always have a party. I dress up, sit in the dining room, light candles, and have fresh flowers on the table. I have a party for one.'' Gloria Steinem, on the other hand, likes shuffling around in her slippers, and for her, junk food is the greatest. ''I can chain-eat six milky bars at a time, or eat a quart of ice cream and not even notice it,'' she said. Treating yourself like company is a very personal experience, and all that matters is that you're the one having a good time.

I remember the first time I tried to make pancakes. For me, they were the sort of food I would never make only for myself. Just the thought of eating them as a child, and my mother fixing breakfast for us, conjured up such strong communal feelings, that the idea of fixing them just for me seemed selfish. But that morning my cravings for pancakes overcame any hidden taboo I might have had and so I tried my first batch. And it was a wonderful flop. Okay, so now I know that woks are great for everything else except pancakes. But it didn't matter. For this was a long and leisurely morning when I had given myself permission to experiment in the kitchen, and best of all no one was there to have to impress, including myself! It's not every day I whip up pancakes, so doing this was *exotic* for me. Maybe you do this all the time, then your sort of treat would be different.

Of course if cooking turns you off, you can still treat yourself like company. There's no excuse. There is always the best gourmet shop in town to turn you on. And when you come home with all your goodies, you can eat with your hands or use the finest silver and china. You can play soothing music, take out the linen napkins and all the finery that goes with it, or simply lounge around, open the box and get into that fabulous pizza you've finally ordered after weeks and weeks of cravings. All that is important is that you feel comfortable.

But remember, being comfortable doesn't only mean snuggling in your favorite chair; it also means snuggling into the right attitude. So get comfortable inside your thoughts and feelings. Make yourself at home, as the saying goes. Remember you deserve this treat and you deserve to feel good about it.

And the next time you find yourself alone and hungry, you'll share a meal with a friend – YOU!

Actress POLLY BERGEN touches upon the essence of what I think treating yourself like company is all about. As she said, ''Solitude is being able to do all the things for oneself, that you would do for someone you really cared for.'' Once you get into the spirit of this, you'll discover all sorts of seductive treats that make being alone your kind of party for one:

''For me solitude is doing my nails and not caring. It is definitely a luxury. It's doing all those things that I'd never do otherwise. I tell every woman that she should do them, but I forget. I've written books and given hundreds of lectures that have said,you know that every time you get out of the bathtub, you should always rub down your entire body with a nice body moisturizer, and you should do this and that, and I never do any of it; who has time! Most of us spend our time catering to others, but don't spend time alone being kind to ourselves, because we don't think that we're worth it. That's the reason that solitude is my time for me, and that's why it has nothing to do with work. It's only play and luxury. It's when I treat myself like company.

The most important thing about being alone is being as kind to yourself as you would be to a guest. I think it's very important to stuff my refrigerator with all sorts of wonderful things, and to fix myself a marvelous meal.

I always fix myself a bed-tray, because I love to live in my bedroom. I get up in the morning and prepare the most wonderful, enormous breakfast of eggs and bacon, juice, coffee, and croissants. I put a beautiful porto mat and napkin on the tray, and maybe even a rose. Then I enjoy carrying it in. I get back in bed, and put the tray down. I'm waiting on myself. I'm being good to myself.

I'll turn on the TV and watch the morning news or some old Abbott and Costello film that makes me howl with laughter over something that's just terrible. I read the newspaper or do the crossword puzzles. The joy of sitting down and reading every article in the Sunday *New York Times*, including the things I don't understand, is really great. It takes all day, and it's wonderful. Of course I don't do this every Sunday, but when I'm on a 'be good to oneself spree,' then I do it, because for me, that is what solitude is all about.''

Treats

I'm a party of one
with tea for two
so I treat myself like company
until I'm through!

Some sweets and such to accompany you

Peaches and Cream

...On the subject of prayer, Henry Ward Beecher wrote in his *Life Thoughts* (1858): "It is not well for a man to pray cream, and live skim milk" — unless, of course, one is on a diet. Then yogurt shakes are the best way to believe you are tasting cream while drinking the skim!

Peaches and Cream Yogurt Shake

2 cups plain yogurt	2 cups sliced fresh peaches
6 fresh peppermint leaves	1 tbspn. honey
1 tbspn. sesame seeds	

Put all of this into your blender for a minute or so and ENJOY!
If you are trying to lose weight, omit the honey and sesame seeds. If you're trying to gain, then include them, and if you are neither trying to lose or gain, then add some more peppermint leaves, they make you feel even more okay.

With this basic blender recipe you can create the best 'ice-cream' in town, without even using a machine. Here is how to make your own frozen yogurt:

Home-made Frozen Yogurt

This is a variation on the peaches and cream shake. All you have to do is omit the sesame seeds, add some more peaches to thicken it up, a bit more honey to sweeten it up, and then put it into the freezer. To cream it up again, re-blend, and you'll have the peachiest, best frozen yogurt you ever tasted...
If you don't care for peaches, then just follow the basic blender shake recipe, using the fresh fruit of your choice — blueberries, strawberries or bananas.

Try *Mango and Ginger*... Instead of peaches substitute two mangoes, a bit of fresh ginger that you can press in a garlic press, yogurt, and honey. You can live without the peppermint leaves, but they do add a special zing to this creamy mixture.

Here is a healthy sweet treat, highly nutritious, full of soul and wonderful energy... For the perfect food combination, try the Plantain Special with a giant salad made of endives, arugula, fresh peppermint and your favorite dressing...

A plantain is a tropical fruit that looks like a giant banana, and tastes like an exotic kind of potato. It is the perfect starch snack for any time of day or night. For dessert, you sweeten it up by adding some shredded coconut and raisins. Or spice it up with garlic and you have the ideal side dish. And just as they are, plantains taste like the sweetest home fries you ever made. Here is one of my favorite variations:

The Plantain Special

1 plantain	3 mushrooms
1 tbspn. peanut oil	a splash of tamari sauce
1 scallion	a slice of red pepper
2 sprigs fresh coriander	a few olives

Slice the plantain and stir fry in wok with oil, turning over once. Add chopped scallion, coriander and mushrooms and stir fry some more, adding tamari. Cut up red pepper and add to plate with a few calamato olives.

...Soon her eye fell on a little glass box that was lying under the table: she opened it, and found in it a very small cake, on which the words EAT ME were beautifully marked in currants. 'Well, I'll eat it,' said Alice, 'and if it makes me grow larger, I can reach the key; and if it makes me grow smaller, I can creep under the door; so either way I'll get into the garden, and I don't care which happens!

Lewis Carroll, *Alice in Wonderland*

Sesame and Banana Candy

3 tbspns. organic honey	1 tspn. fresh ground cloves
1 banana	¼ cup blackcurrants
½ cup sesame seeds	1 handful shredded coconut

Pour honey into a warmed-up wok or skillet, and stir over a low flame until it starts to bubble. Make sure you use a wooden spoon. Slice banana into bubbling honey and stir until all pieces are covered with honey. Let this heat for a few minutes. Then add the sesame seeds and stir well. Stir in the cloves. Now you should be able to make different shapes, squares, balls, or whatever you like. Play around with this and then as a finishing touch add the blackcurrants and coconut and finalize the form you like. Then spoon onto a plate and let cool. Cover with saran wrap, and keep in refrigerator. It only takes ten minutes to make this natural sweet snack without refined sugar, and they live almost indefinitely in the fridge — almost indefinitely; that's if you can resist eating them all at once!

Something Seems Fishy!

There is sole for feet
and sole to eat
and sol to heat
and then soul which is something else again.

There are as many ways to serve sole as the souls who seek solitude. And just like the fish recipes that follow, definitions of solitude vary according to taste. Page 404 of the Oxford English Dictionary uses a lot of space describing the classical meaning of solitude. We learn that the word solitude was not in common use in English until the seventeenth century. In poetry of the eighteenth century, solitude personified ''the state of being or living alone; loneliness, seclusion, solitariness (of persons)... Vaughan mystics 1850 — 'Solitude brings no escape from spiritual danger' or 1887 — Ruskin-Practertia II, 237, 'I was not, I suppose born for solitude.' ''

Words like solitary, soulful, and sole first pertained to lonely places, as well as to celibate, unhappy, unmarried, single people. And that's when you know that something seems fishy! With the exception of a few mystics who knew all along that solitude was not loneliness, the word was commonly used to signify bad news. But exploration in the dictionary only uncovers a few roots and variations into the meaning of solitude. The best definition of solitude is the one we live by. And eventually all the meanings come together with a lot of soul, a lot of sole, and with sol, which means the center of all things.

A basket trap is for holding fish; but when one has got the fish, one need think no more about the basket. Words are for holding ideas but when one has got the idea, one need think no more about the words.

Taoist Book of Chuang Tzu

The following thoughts and wonderful fish recipes come from three people who truly enjoy their solitude.

Solitude... is when you marry your thoughts.

Julie Newmar

If JULIE NEWMAR had not won a Tony Award for her Broadway performance with Charles Boyer and Claudette Colbert, in *The Marriage-Go-Round*, she could have easily been teaching philosophy instead. She is a rare mixture of beauty, brains, patience, and humor. Her insights on solitude and creative cooking for one, come from a long-standing performance of living their truths.

''Solitude is a portion of something. It's when you marry your thoughts. It's when you start off on the wrong leg and end up on the right. It's peaceful. It's not languid. It can make your guts feel as if they are consuming you. It can be the highlight of the tension which challenges a former truth.

I love clichés. They're so true. Solitude is when I park my car on the second floor garage... It's rare to experience real solitude. The ocean brings it to me. I've had transcendental experiences at the ocean. Solitude is the moment before greatness! I no longer cry on Sundays. That wasn't solitude.''

''The first best thing in the world for you is fish, and I never in my life have had a fish as good as butter fish. Butter fish beats lobsters and oysters. Think: the word butter fish. It melts in your mouth. It's perfection all by itself. It tastes of richness and delicacy and sweet freshness. You can get this fish on the east coast in any fine fish market, but for me there's nothing like my California butter fish. I love to go to the farmers' market in Los Angeles, to Tusquellas, and there you find the finest fish in America. I choose my butter fish, take it home, and prepare it right away.''

Julie's California Butter Fish

1 tbspn. sesame oil	2 scallions
Butter fish	onion
Spanish mild green sauce	3 crushed almonds
salt, pepper	2 tbspns. dry white wine

''Take a skillet and pour in some sesame oil, which is very good for health and also your sex life. Put the butter fish in and on top of it you can put a Spanish mild green sauce, which is not too hot. Put in some salt and pepper, some scallions, some onions or onion salt, and almonds if you like. Then add a couple of tablespoons of wine. Cook the fish only for four minutes on each side, because you want it to be very tender, so tender that you can eat it with a spoon. You could die from this dish it's so good!''

For me ... solitude is delicious!

Mary Hemingway

MARY HEMINGWAY, the last wife of Ernest Hemingway, was a woman who enjoyed long stretches of solitude. Her writing and her research transformed what could have been loneliness into creative solitude. When you lose someone you love you can't pretend that life without your partner is perfect but Mary Hemingway's positive attitude allowed her to transcend and go on. She talked about her relationship with Ernest, and her feelings about solitude:

''I absolutely believe in solitude, but for me it cannot be defined as something in which I feel, 'Ooh, I am by myself and there's nothing around.' There's always a thousand things around, so that I don't really feel solitary. Ernest left me enough work to do the rest of my life. I'm responsible for all his manuscripts that haven't been published, so I'll never be lonely.

Books are my constant companions. It's delicious to just do nothing but read for days and days. If I were to describe solitude I would say there are an enormous amount of stimulating things, mostly paper, letters, and books which are all saying: 'Pay attention to me.' Very often they are much more interesting than people because people talk back. Things can't.

Solitude means heaven to me. In the mountains of Idaho, near Sun Valley, I have a comfortable house. I frequently have house guests, but I love it when I am alone. Here is this great big lovely empty house with wonderful views and birds outside. I can go for three or four days at a time absolutely by myself.

Then I forget about work, and just enjoy the retreat. I love being outdoors climbing in the sage brush, listening to the birds, looking at the chipmunks. It's all very simple. I can climb a hill behind my house and get a view of the whole valley, and there it is — wonderful sky and space and fresh air and SOLITUDE. I think solitude is a marvelous companion.

At home it's wonderful to have time to read and just lie in my hammock and muse. I let my mind wander into various areas of the past, present, and future. It could be places, things, events, or conversations. Sometimes it's just remembering my favorite pictures, scattered all over the world in the various museums I know — the Prado in Madrid, the Academia in Venice, and the Louvre, and the Tate. Then I like to remember streets that I've loved at one time or another. It's all very relaxing.

Ernest didn't feel the same way about solitude as I do. Most writers love solitude, but Ernest hated it. Whenever I was away from Havana, visiting my parents in America, he would yell and scream for me to come home. He tried to be generous and would say stay with your family as long as you like — but! He was seldom solitary because he had so many friends in Cuba, or wherever he went. He pretended vividly that I was necessary to his feeling of well-being and that makes me feel very good.

It would be deceptive if I didn't say that I miss Ernest. I miss his judgment, I miss his wit, his jollity, his companionship. As I say, I don't go around weeping, but I do miss him, I can never find another substitute.''

Mary Hemingway's Cuban Fish Recipe

Seviche (cooking with lime juice)

Broad bill swordfish or haddock (¾ lb. filets)
2 fresh limes
red hot pepper
dash of salt

"When I am working alone, I like to make myself something simple like Seviche, which is a Cuban raw fish recipe. Seviche, a dish I learned to prepare when I lived with Ernest in Cuba, makes a marvelous first course, when you are having a dinner party. But, it could be the main course if it's dinner for one. Seviche is raw fish, sliced but not shredded. It requires using a very firm flesh fish like haddock or broad bill swordfish. When I first buy the fish it's translucent. Then I slice it into bite-size pieces, the thickness of a one-inch flat ruler or thinner. I put it into the refrigerator for at least half an hour, but it's better if you have time to let it be for five hours. This makes the fish turn white.

Next, I arrange the fish in the bowl or dish I plan to eat from. When I'm ready to eat it, I cut the limes in half and squeeze them over the fish. It's important to cut the lime right before squeezing, otherwise the air takes away its important properties, and changes the flavor. I add some red hot pepper and salt, and its ready to serve."

Environmentalist BARRY COMMONER enjoys eating alone as much as he enjoys puzzling out scientific problems. His solitary lab evenings might be spent working on some intellectual problems as well as creating a gourmet fish feast for one:

"For me solitude means being linked to a process of historical events. This has an enormous emotional impact. It means you don't feel isolated. I've enjoyed all the environmental and energy work I've done because I have seen history happen — I've felt linked up and in tune with a process larger than myself. This is the kind of solitude in which I feel at one with the world.

I enjoy being by myself when I'm engaged in intellectual creativity. I enjoy walking alone to the laboratory. Then I have a chance to puzzle out things. I get the time to find the answers to creative problems. I feel good about being alone, when my thoughts are productive and lead somewhere. When I puzzle something out, I feel as though solitude has served me well. I admit I am very result-oriented, but I find that the process is closely related to the product. I believe in doing things for a purpose. If you want to call that religion, fine, but most of what I do is for the purpose of social change. Your own personal change is obviously part of this process. Yes, on the way I've grown and changed, but I haven't done it consciously."

Barry Commoner's Solitary Fish Feasts

"I always eat a great deal of fish, at least three or four times a week. I prepare it by either poaching or broiling. This, accompanied with a giant salad and a good European beer, makes my solitary lab dinners something to look forward to.

I don't follow recipes. My recipes are a kind of abbreviated version of things I see in cookbooks. Poaching fish is simple the way I do it. If you follow those fancy French cookbooks, you make a fish stock with vegetables, and that takes a long, long time. I like to give myself the luxury of an hour to cook, then I don't feel as though I'm neglecting my work, so I do a variation on the vegetable broth.

I always use the whole fish. A whole fish is very important because it's the only way you can tell it is fresh. One of the things my mother taught me, is how to tell fresh fish. The eye has to be very clear and not sunken back into the head. The eye is very sensitive to drying out, so I never buy fish without the head. I always buy fish with the best looking eyes."

Poached Trout

2 carrots
1 onion
few cloves of garlic or to taste
2 or 3 scallions

salt and pepper to taste
herbs of your choice
1 whole trout
wine (cooking)

"First you put some water into a large pot, throw all the vegetables, herbs and seasoning into the pot, and bring to a boil. Next, lay a fish rack over the vegetables, and put the fish on the rack. Let it all simmer for a half an hour, and when the fish is almost steamed, pour the wine over it. Then it's ready to serve."

Barry's Special Garlic Sauce

2 cloves garlic
peanut oil (a spoonful)
salt and pepper to taste
tarragon
thyme

"I tend to use an enormous amount of garlic. I'm very fond of garlic, and I use it all the time in salads and everything I prepare. For all my broiled fish dishes I make my garlic sauce and spoon it over the sauce as it broils. It's very easy. All I do is cut up a clove or two of garlic. I just slice it and then mash it with a spoon; then you don't need a garlic press. I add some oil to it, preferably a cold-pressed oil like safflower or peanut, because they don't smoke when cooking. Then I add some salt and pepper and herbs, and mash it all up. Then I spoon this over the fish as it broils."

Barry Commoner's Broiled Pompano

"My favorite fish is pompano, and that I always broil. I have a standard recipe for broiling fish, and you can use this for the pompano, as well as for shrimps and scallops. The secret is my special garlic sauce.

I broil the pompano under the flame of the oven. You can use a Pyrex dish, or a flat stainless steel pan. You put the fish flat on the Pyrex dish, and after it's heated a little bit, you spoon the garlic sauce over it as it's broiling. You turn the fish over a few times so it absorbs the sauce. It takes about fifteen minutes at the most to be done..."

Broiled Scallops and Shrimp

"I cook scallops and shrimp the same way as I broil the pompano. But with the scallops, I first put the garlic sauce over them, and let them sit for about fifteen minutes before broiling. This marinates them. Then I put the pan under the broiler, in an oven pre-heated at 350°. The shrimp and scallops only take five to seven minutes to broil."

According To Taste

Thoughts and feelings about being alone have many flavors and nuances. There is essential solitude and luxurious solitude, and everything solitude in between. What is necessary solitude for one is indulgent for another, what is gourmet solitude for some may be leftovers for someone else. Yet with all these variations on the same theme, there really isn't one recipe of how to be alone, because ultimately solitude itself cannot be defined. As Lucretius once said centuries ago, "The universe cannot impose on itself set restrictions."

JOAN FONTAINE

"My private moments are absolutely crucial... I need to let go of everything and everyone. Not many public people know how to escape from all of that, but that's when I can be a private person. I can *be alone*. It's important to learn how to shuttle between your public and private moments without getting shocked. You have to learn how to un-wind and re-wind. You have to know how to be where you are as you are ... I feel fortunate that I really love to be alone. I think that's why I survived so well.

When I am traveling for my work, I am alone almost every night in various hotels. And when the interviews stop, I go home alone and I am just thrilled. I go into a strange hotel, go up to my room, lock the door and say Wow — alone at last — now I am *alone*! What I love most of all is the *silence*. It's the silence that works. Silence is marvelous... Whew! It's gorgeous. No sounds... nobody... no touching... I walk through the door, and there it is waiting for me in the room. I have instant silence!"

ROLLO MAY

"Solitude comes mainly when you are by yourself, but it also comes in moments when you are with others, if you have the capacity to be instantaneously alone even though you are in a crowd of a thousand people. Some people can be in solitude no matter where they are, all the time. But I need to alternate between the market place and the mountain, and then my creative process comes together.

The mountain is where I get my visions, it is my most cherished solitude spot. It is where I experience a sense of significance of various creative ideas. This takes place more on a feeling level, than on a thinking level. Solitude is essentially a right brain function. It puts the imagination, insights, and perspective into the data learned by the left brain when in the market place.

Usually, I like to walk by myself, or I listen to music as a background for my thoughts. I spend my solitude time opening myself up to possibility. This involves letting my imagination roam. I use solitude to play with visions, possibilities and ideas. Solitude gives me an incredible sense of peace, that gives the ideas I play with a sense of worth. They aren't rushed or pushed. And it is out of those times of being alone that I receive my most important ideas."

GLORIA STEINEM

"For me it's a great luxury to spend time alone. Solitude means freedom, no pressure, nobody knowing what you're doing or expecting you to do anything... Solitude has a nice sound to it. Loneliness is a value judgment, but solitude is a perfectly good positive word. Women respond to it more than men, probably because they haven't had it. They don't have a room of their own, as Virginia Woolf would say.

For most women, facing solitude has been related to a lack of choice. Sometimes it's accidental and sometimes it's arbitrary. Some women have too much solitude, and others not enough, but both groups share a lack of choice. In other words, there are many women who have never had a room of their own because they lived in their parents' house and then they got married. They never had a space of their own. It means a great deal to have that space. But on the other hand, some women have been isolated in their houses all by themselves all day long in the suburbs or some place, all of their lives and have too much solitude. But the shared problem is lack of choice."

PAOLO SOLERI

"Solitude has to be seen as a position, like a recoiling in order to spring. You take a step backwards in order to spring better forward. Solitude is that condition which is necessary to move into the other position, a position of social and cultural interaction.

If you want to be alone a lot, in order to create, you have to be very careful about the situation in which you put yourself. If doing your own little trip is the ideal goal, you defeat the best of yourself. You have to be very careful that you are not going on an ego trip.

Solitude is the incubator where you develop the critical pressure to generate something that is hopefully going to be of universal value."

JERRY BROWN

"Solitude is when you've let all the noise quiet down and you're just there, looking and seeing. Solitude is clarity and caring."

ROSALYN TURECK

"Solitude to me means the whole inner self. There isn't a beginning. There isn't an end. It's just there. Solitude has a very dense meaning. It covers so many areas of being. It covers so much. I don't think it can be defined or confined. It can't be limited. It exists within you, with whatever you are doing. That's why I say it's so dense. It's like the creative process itself. Creativity can exist only inside.

The wellspring source, of which there is never a beginning nor end is like an underground river, and this is going on within one all the time. It has to do with creativity and your work. It has to do with creativity in every aspect of your life. For me, solitude has to do with every personal emotion you have…"

GREGORY BATESON

"Solitude is a state in which you cannot be interrupted from seeing the patterns, the patterns that connect."

JOSEPH CAMPBELL

''The whole Indian tradition of yoga and the power of the *sadhu*, comes from solitude... The whole idea of the holy man, the *sadhu*, comes from being alone. He has gained that power through solitude. And then a journey like that of Odysseus is like a solitary journey. Even though he starts out with twelve ships, he loses eleven of them, and then he loses the last ship. But all the ships are part of him, it's really a solitary journey. He never talks to anybody on those ships.

My favorite mythological solitude hero is Parzival. I think that the myth of the grail quest as rendered in Eschenbach's *Parzival*, is the great myth of the European soul. It is mythology of love, the inner journey. For the classical world it was the Iliad and the Odyssey. But, for classical Europe, and I think that for the later Gothic and post Gothic Europe, the great legend is Parzival. I don't know anything greater that matches it. For me, he is the great solitary hero.''

JOHN LILLY

''Solitude is freedom. It's an anchor, an anchor in the void. You're anchored to nothing, and that's my definition of freedom. Freedom is when you are anchored to *nothing, nobody*. The void is more the territory of woman than man. Men have to put form into everything, women are able to accept more. I've reduced my solitude to a profound rest in the void.''

TOM WOLFE

''*Fantasy is my food for solitude, and the fantasy is of applause*. And I'm being honest with you — a lot of people would lie to you, they wouldn't tell you the truth. It's a problem I have. I tell all the truths. I suppose that if I'm in real solitude, I'm almost always working, or simply fantasizing. I sometimes fantasize about a *frieze* I'm going to make called *Third Avenue*. It's going to have all the great people I see on Third Avenue, which I dearly love. But, I think what sustains me throughout the whole fantasy is the idea that people will say, 'WOW, out of sight! You should see the *frieze* that Tom Wolfe has in his living room.'

But I must admit, the fantasy only carries you so far; that's *brain candy. The fantasy is kind of brain candy*. And it's like candy. You can go for so long and you get a little sugar high, but it doesn't take you very far. Fantasy without my work makes me lonely.''

WILLIAM IRWIN THOMPSON

"Historically solitude becomes increasingly important when you live in an overpopulated world, but ironically there is a paradoxical kind of love/hate relationship that goes on. Man feels a need for solitude, but when he really confronts it, there's an aspect of boredom, an aspect of undernourishment of the self. There's nothing really inside he can attune to. Therefore, he ends up bringing in all the junk of society along with him. He takes snowmobiles into the quiet Canadian landscape, or he takes dune buggies into the desert, transistor radios into parked caravans along the side of glacier lakes.

Everywhere industrial man goes, he takes all of the junk of the cities with him. Finally he ends up having a painful confrontation with solitude. To be really solitary, one has to have a very rich internal life.

Most people want solitude because they want to discover their unconditioned freedom, where they are free of all definitions. When you take away definitions as father, as brother, as son, and even those deeper roles, you are reaching for a kind of unconditioned self. This is where people confront their absolute freedom. Some people discover the complex dance of freedom within their solitude. When you live in a collectivizing society of great institutions and noise, then the way you discover your freedom is to assert it through solitude.

You have to have the ability to unplug – from the telephone, from the television, from the compulsive drinking, from the compulsive entertainment, and even from society and conviviality, and say I'm going absolutely away. But freedom is more than just escaping to unplug.

Freedom for me is not having to do anything and delight in that. It's an interesting relationship of opposites, because at the one time you're moving with a larger pattern, as if you're swimming in a stream that's historical and there's a current to it. You have the freedom and the power to be able to swim to the side and get out, or even if you want to be slightly neurotic and heroic, swim in the opposite direction. Maybe sometimes asserting one's freedom is discovering all those options and then deciding to accept the joy of it, of swimming with it and adding one's particular energy to the general kind of collective flow."

NANCY WILSON ROSS

"In solitude... there was nothing to learn, I was happy!"

Slowing Down

Imagine the olden days when there was time. Time to spend all day long preparing the evening meal. Time to make wooden wheels for the carts carrying hay for the livestock. Time to walk down the road to get the meal pitcher of water from the well. This was time to live, time to appreciate, time to know that your time was short.

SENATOR EUGENE McCARTHY knows about that kind of time and he savors it. He has a farm in Virginia where, as he says, "I never have more than two or three guests; otherwise it gets cluttered up." Then Gene McCarthy the poet speaks, "But mostly I have it as a solitude retreat so I can just simmer my thoughts and just be." He shared his thoughts about the significance of solitude and slowing down. A long time ago, he felt, it was very different:

"Life used to provide solitude, not just for reflective poets. There were times in almost everybody's life when there was quiet. Imagine the kind of satisfaction it must have been for a small group of workmen putting together a wagon, selecting the wood, heating the iron, doing all those things. There was a separateness and a personalness about it, which is important. Human nature is basically the same. Some people may be more sensitive and more concerned, but the need for that kind of individualization and personalization is universal. It is everyone's concern. If you don't have it you develop a mass state of distraction and over-stimulation, and I think we suffer from this.

Slowing down is important. We all need solitude. People who don't even reflect need solitude. There are different ways we can express this solitude. Cooking is one way of slowing down for me. On my farm I don't do a lot of fancy cooking, but I like to cook Irish oatmeal, which takes forty minutes. I enjoy the process of taking time in even just cooking oatmeal, instead of just throwing the instant cereal and saying it will be ready in three minutes.

There's really nothing to Irish oatmeal. You put it in the pot, and let it boil, and then simmer. But it takes forty minutes! And while it's simmering, well, you do a lot of things. You can think about it, you can go out and see if the garden is growing..."

Porridge for One

The following traditional recipe for Irish oatmeal will serve you one very hearty portion:

Into two cups of bubbly boiling water sprinkle one half cup of oatmeal, and a half teaspoon seasalt. When porridge begins to thicken, reduce heat and simmer for thirty minutes, stirring occasionally. If you use a double boiler, only the preliminary stirring is needed.

Traditionally, Irish oatmeal is served with fresh buttermilk, with a bit of honey and butter... I like to fix it with vanilla yogurt, a bit of nutmeg, and some maple syrup. Also, when initially simmering it, I skip using salt, and later on sprinkle on some cinnamon or nutmeg. Fresh milk or cream is also nice to stir in before serving... Enjoy!

Ceremony Alone

I celebrate myself, and sing myself
And what I assume you shall assume,
For every atom belonging to me as good
belongs to you.

Walt Whitman, *Song of Myself*

Ceremony, true ceremony, comes from an inward spiritual grace. And once you realize this, you know that even though you are alone, you are connected to the whole universe. Each and every ritual has its own way of centering an individual. Through unique and sometimes mysterious powers, its enactment imparts a distinct sensibility on the inner form of a person. It can make you feel worthwhile and part of something important. And it doesn't matter what ritual you perform, it only matters that you give yourself totally to it.

Walt Whitman knew this firsthand when he wrote *Song of Myself*. Through the ordinary everyday concrete things, he was able to feel a universal resonance. Out of a true love for the cosmos he saw himself in a blade of grass. In his solitude he felt an interconnection to the earth, the stars, and all that is worth celebrating. He constantly called upon his higher self, the one that is within each of us and joined to one and other through the power of solitude itself. Whitman proved it: to be truly alone is always a ceremony.

I have selected tea, bread, grace, and meditation as themes for ceremony alone, because to me they mean communion. In their own special way they each offer an intimacy that truly links doing and being.

A Pot of Tea

There is an old Zen saying:

tea is nought but this
first you make the water boil
then infuse the tea
then you drink it properly,
that is all you need to know.

Rikyu

When you enter the tea hut in Japan, you remove your shoes and remove the world outside. You sit down, you bow to your host, your host bows to you, and you wait. The tea is served. You sip. You enjoy. All the cluttered company within you leaves. Your thoughts evaporate with the steam as it rises above the teapot.

Zen ceremonies are truly beautiful because of their simplicity. Elegance is innate. In the austere tea hut, one perfect flower creates an aura of love. A touch of gentle incense blends into the aroma of the green whipped tea taken in beautiful ceramic bowls. It is going back to basics. You can spend your whole life learning how to have a cup of tea, and then one day, you and the tea become one. You have stopped trying to be ceremonious. Now you simply surrender to it.

When you depart from the hut you put on the robes of the world once again, but something has changed. The whole idea is to be in the center of yourself always. Sipping tea is peaceful and you create that peace. As you walk along the path leading from the tea hut back into the world, you bring the grace of this ceremony with you.

Traditionally, ceremonious tea is reserved for two or more. The host and guest sip tea together as a way to join energies, to be *one* in spirit. So doesn't it make sense to sip tea alone and just be the *one* you are already!

The Ceremony of Tea ... Just For Me?
YES

You don't have to be in Japan, or wear ceremonial robes of a Zen Roshi to enjoy the ritual of tea. The solitary person who decides to create a personal space of solitude, inevitably invents a whole system of unique customs. What could be simpler than boiling a kettle of water, and while it's boiling adding your favorite herbs to the teapot? This is the most fantastic blend; even Paracelsus would be impressed. But you don't need to be an alchemist to brew this solitude special — just yourself.

I call this tea... *I am going to put me all together*. Why not? It works. And by the time you put it all together, you will be ready for another special ceremony alone.

A Pot of Tea
with
11 Herbs

dandelion leaves	skullcap
hibiscus flowers	foenugreek seeds
rose hip	golden seal
star anise	lemon grass
rosemary	camomile

and a bit of rose geranium

Get together your teapot, your boiling water and a pinch of each of the herbs.

Let brew for twenty minutes. Pour into your favorite cup, and enjoy...

Some Other Niceties

A honeypot, with a swirler, a few wedges of orange or lime, and lots of patience mixed with humor . . .

Bread Is What You Knead It To Be!

There is a sense of comfort in knowing that your ceremony alone means something to the universe. A relaxing ritual like baking bread can stir up feelings that unite you with ancient sacraments. Ceremonies long forgotten become familiar once you begin to make bread.

Bread making as a ritual, goes way back to Old Testament times. By 1500 BC the art of making dough was known all over the Middle East and the baking of bread was considered a sacred rite, a way of participating in the whole process of change. Imagine being in the Nile Valley when the oven was first invented and the process of leavening discovered. The bread is rising, and you are there to watch it. The magic of transformation is within this mysterious moment.

Or consider the farmer working in the land nourished by the Tigris Euphrates River of the Fertile Crescent. Like other Mesopotamians of the time he is thinking about storing grain in the special shrine built as an offering to the agricultural deities. For this farmer, this is not just an ordinary temple, or a storehouse to unload grain. It is where his ancestors have performed all the ancient agricultural rites, and for him, this is a holy place. It is a place of true devotion.

This farmer understands deeply that there is bread to feed the spirit as well as to nourish the body. He feels a strong connection to his past, to all the workers of the land who gave their life for the lives of others. He is aware that before anyone can begin to enjoy the gift of bread, the seed must be planted, cultivated, and harvested. He looks up at the sky, but it is dry. Without the rain there is no grain. Yet without the sun there is no fire and no bread. All these elements must come together to create the magic of bread, so appropriately called the staff of life. And so our farmer prays for rain.

Today it is easy to take a loaf of bread for granted. We pick it up at our local supermarket, pop it into the toaster and then pop it into our mouth, and that's it. How often do we consider all the elements that went into making it? How often do we appreciate it in the way our farmer could? That's why you need to give yourself time…

As you begin to relax into the ritual of baking bread you start to remember. It's as if the memory of making bread is deep inside your fingertips. Even though you might have forgotten, they remember. 'Hands to work, hearts to God,' so say the Shakers, and as you start to knead the dough, the whole ritual of making bread seems very familiar.

Heaven Bread

A simple pear bread recipe was called Heaven Bread by someone I love, and after that it grew into its name, and became ever more heavenly. The most important ingredient, of course, is all the love you pour into it, then others always taste the difference. Then there are the little tricks that also make it heavenly, like grinding whole wheat berries to make your own fresh flour, or using a garlic press to crush almonds. Once I even tried playing music for it, and believe me those vibrations mixed into the bowl along with all the other ingredients. When you are having fun and doing it just for the sake of doing it, anything and everything is the right way to do it, because when you're not having fun, rituals turn into ordeals, and that's a different sort of bread.

Every time I bake Heaven Bread it's like making it for the first time. I like the feeling of really losing myself in it, just doing it, forgetting everything else, being with it. There is a silence that comes as you work; your hands chopping, stirring, molding. It becomes so quiet that you can hear the sound of almonds as you crush them into the mixture. All that matters is the whole universe inside that giant bowl where you add and stir until finally, after all the ingredients are lost inside the whole wheat flour, you pour some maple syrup and cassis all over it. Then you add a touch of coconut as an afterthought — snow on the mountain.

Real ceremony and ritual give you the basic recipe so you can be spontaneous and free. You just have to measure a few things like the two cups of flour, the one cup of yogurt, the one tablespoon of baking powder, the two eggs. The rest is up to you. You sprinkle on a little nutmeg, throw in a few raisins, add a bit of dried papaya, whatever pleases you. And when the whole house takes on the atmosphere of Heaven Bread, it smells better than any incense. You know that heaven and earth have joined energies in these quiet moments. You know that bread is happening.

It may take lifetimes before we truly change, but in these few hours a bread appears. Is it not miraculous, the mystery of transforming a dry seed into grain, into flour, into soggy dough, just a first step before it is touched by fire, when it is warmed and transformed. We wait with it, and watch, until it's time to take it out to cool. Then once again we begin to break bread.

Heaven Bread

2 cups whole wheat flour	1 cup chopped walnuts
1 cup yogurt	1 large pear chopped
2 eggs	1 tspn. nutmeg
1 tbspn. baking powder	1 tspn. vanilla
1 tspn. walnut oil	1 handful organic raisins
2 tbspns. honey or maple syrup	3 tbspns. butter

First pre-heat your oven to 350°. Then grease your Pyrex baking dish (standard bread size) with butter until you no longer see the shine in the glass. Then into a large bowl, add the flour, yogurt, eggs, baking powder, and walnut oil. Mix very well, using a large wooden spoon and your hands. Add the honey, or maple syrup if you prefer, the walnuts, pears, nutmeg, vanilla, raisins, and butter. Mix again very well until you can pour it into the Pyrex dish. Add a touch of nutmeg to the top, and then bake this for about an hour and a half, or until your whole house is full of heavenly aroma. Stick a knife into the bread to see if it's dry. Once the bread cools, turn it upside down onto a plate. If you wrap it well with aluminium foil, it will remain fresh for two weeks in your refrigerator. Heating it for a few minutes before serving enhances the flavor, and adding some more honey and butter is also very good.

Grace Before Meals

Do you not know it is the Divine you feed,
the Divine you exercise?

Epictetus

Saying grace is a ritual rooted in a deep reverence for life. It is a simple way of acknowledging an appreciation of the interconnection of all forms of being. We acknowledge in our hearts that we are a part of this great life chain of love. One form changes and dissolves so another may be fed, and that which is fed also becomes the food. This goes on and on without ever stopping. Life gives life. Consider the salmon which instinctively swim all the way upstream to where they were hatched in order to lay their eggs. It is a long and hard journey, and those who make it lay eggs and then die immediately. They deserve our grace.

There are many ways of expressing gratitude. There is no rule that we have to say a traditional prayer, and sometimes we are better off saying nothing. Silence is a wonderful way to begin a meal. Or we can create our own prayer using words that are meaningful to us. What really matters is that we feel a sense of connection and interdependence. Most important is the feeling of communion between ourselves and the food and all the energy that worked to create it.

There is a traditional Zen grace that captures this essence. Nancy Wilson Ross, who wrote *The World of Zen*, shared it with me before we began a meal together. It says:

> *We venerate all the great teachers*
> *And are thankful for this food*
> *The work of many other people*
> *And the suffering and sharing*
> *of other forms of life*

Like the traditional tea ceremony, saying grace is another way of removing our worldly shoes before entering into our world of food for solitude. It can be the most intimate moment of our day. These moments of grace are as much a gift as the food itself. We are reminded that now is the time to be re-energized, to be taking in, rather than to be giving out. This is our chance to slow down, so we can truly benefit from the nourishment we are about to receive. This is why the word *grace* is our key, because just saying grace isn't enough. It's how we continue to eat gracefully that matters. It's enjoying and loving each and every morsel. What could be a better prayer of gratitude?

A disciple once asked Epictetus, a Greek philosopher who lived in the first century AD "How is it possible to eat according to the Divine acceptance?" Epictetus answered, "If you eat with justice, and with gratitude, and fairly, and temperately, and decently, you eat according to the Divine acceptance." He understood instinctively why grace was essential. It was not a ritual of empty gestures, for him it was a deep feeling in his heart:

You are a distinct portion of the essence of God, and contain a certain portion of Him within yourself. Why then are you ignorant of your noble birth? Why do you not consider whence you come? Why do you not remember when you are eating, who you are who eats, and whom you feed? Do you not know that it is the Divine you feed, the Divine you exercise?

Meal Prayers

Zen, with its teaching of reverence for life, offers us many beautiful prayers of gratitude. The following Meal Chant is a longer variation of the prayer shared by Nancy Wilson Ross:

BEFORE THE MEAL
The Five Reflections

First, let us reflect on our own work and the
effort of those who brought us this food.
Secondly, let us be aware of the quality of our
deeds as we receive this meal.
Thirdly, what is most essential is the practice
of mindfulness which helps us transcend
greed, anger and delusion.
Fourthly, we appreciate this food which sustains
the good health of our body and mind.
Fifthly, in order to continue our practice
for all beings we accept this offering.

Sutra Book
The Zen Studies Society, New York

Feasts For The Heart
Sources On Ritual

For your ceremony alone, you may choose to read and reflect. For this you need lots of uninterrupted time to feast your eyes and mind with food for the heart.

If you are interested in the meaning and use of ritual as it applied in ancient customs, then pick up a copy of *The Analects of Confucius*, translated by Arthur Waley (Allen and Unwin). Here you will find a very useful interpretation about the purpose of ritual as viewed by Confucius and ancient Chinese sages before him. Arthur Waley's introductory chapter offers amusing anecdotes and helpful information about ritual in general. You will also understand a little more about yourself, and all the unconscious ceremonies you perform:

> *The difference, in respect of 'attitudes' between us and the ancient Chinese is that we learn them unconsciously; whereas with the Chinese they were a subject of conscious interest and attention...*
>
> *The commonest method of symbolizing one's own 'smallness' as contrasted with the 'greatness' of another is to shrink oneself. Even we, with our impoverished vocabulary of attitude, maintain various forms of ceremonial 'shrinking,' such as bowing, nodding, kneeling. The Chinese* chunt-tsu *knew a far wider range of bendings and contractions, many of which (but by no means all) are mentioned in Book X of* The Analects... *(page 57)*
>
> *The domain of Chinese ritual, of obligatory acts and abstentions was a vast one. Three hundred rules of major ritual and three thousand minor observances had, according to the usual computation, to be mastered. The expression 'to know' used by itself, means 'to know the rites,' and he who lacked this savoir faire could not be regarded as a gentleman. (page 67).*

If you want to get into traditional realms of ritual and ceremony, then read Mircea Eliade's classic book on mythology, *The Sacred and the Profane* (Harcourt Brace and Company). His section on Rites of Passage will offer you lots of food for thought:

> *To become a man in the proper sense he must die to this first (natural) life and be reborn to a higher life, which is at once religious and cultural. One does not become a complete man until he has passed beyond and in some sense abolished 'natural' humanity, for initiation is reducible to a paradoxical experience of death and resurrection or of second birth...*

It is important to note this, for it shows once again that religious man wants to be other than he finds himself on the 'natural' level, and undertakes to make himself in accordance with the ideal image revealed to him in myths. (page 187)

There are many transitions in one's life that are dramatically played out in one ceremony or another. But perhaps most dramatic of all is when it's your turn to come through that door of solitude. After that, you'll never be the same. As Eliade points out, rites of passage are always a radical change in ontological and social status:

Initiation is equivalent to a spiritual maturing. And in the religious history of humanity we constantly find this theme: the initiate, who has experienced the mysterious, is he who knows:

The ceremony everywhere begins with the separation of the candidate from his family, and a period of retirement in the bush. (pages 188, 189)

Meditation ... The Ultimate Ceremony Alone

Experiencing meditation can be the ultimate ceremony alone. Immersed in deep meditation, one is linked to the entire cosmos, dining on the infinite source of all nourishment. The universe becomes your food for solitude. This is a state beyond hunger, for there is nothing left to fulfill. It is like a dance between aspirations and accomplishments, where all dreams become true. It is as if a portion of fate has been arranged for this very moment.

Meditation is both universal and personal. There really isn't one recipe that promises to be the perfect path for everyone. Some people prefer sitting formally in sacred spaces; others meditate all the time in their own way, no matter where they are. Not everyone needs the ritual of saying mantras, watching mandalas, or sitting in a Zen monastery to practice zazen. In fact, many people I talked with said the same thing — that for them, "All of life is meditation." Scientist, Britton Chance, believes creative discipline is part of his meditation, and he doesn't limit this solely to his work. As he said, "My spiritual discipline is enhanced by science, so if you ask if I meditate, I think it's a semantic problem. If one sits quietly, I think one is meditating. I like to sit quietly, on the beach, in my boat, or in the laboratory."

No matter where you are, meditation helps you to solve problems and to open that door into creative solitude. But you need to know how to begin, and the way to begin is inside yourself.

As psychologist, Ira Progoff, said: "If you want to find the answer within, then meditation is the way. It gives you clues that your conscious knowledge may miss. Everyone has a different idea of what meditation means, for there are many ways of asking questions and waiting for answers."

I hope the following thoughts inspire you to meditate in your own way:

IRA PROGOFF believes meditation gives one inspiration to go on with all the externals of daily living. He sees meditation as an on-going process to help the person living amidst the pressures of the modern world. You don't need to run off to sit on the nearest mountain top in order to make peace with yourself. If meditation is working, it will work any place for anyone who sincerely seeks solitude. For Progoff, meditation is a continual dialogue between all levels of consciousness, and through this meditation there is an integration of body, mind, and spirit:

''Meditation with its various disciplines and methods progressively deepens the level of one's consciousness and attention. I see *meditation as mediation*. It involves building a sensitivity that enables a person to mediate between the outer phases and deeper sources of his or her life, so that it becomes possible to go back and forth as though up and down a ladder.

Let's say I'm working on a problem, and I've only gone a certain distance with the problem. I need something that my rational mind can't give me. That's when I move deeper into my own source, one that's beyond all my conscious ideas, and I just listen. This is where meditation helps… For me meditation has to be an inter-action between the invisible and visible world, and it has to do this in a continuous working way, that is in terms of the unfolding life history of each person. And further, it has to do this in terms of the personal experience without reference to particular doctrines and teachings.''

For MARY HEMINGWAY, analyzing the meaning of meditation isn't as important as living its message:

''I meditate a couple of minutes a day when I'm taking my morning shower. It keeps me clean. The meditation wipes away the little small problems. Instead of thinking what am I going to have for lunch, I think, ''How can I perform better today than I did yesterday? How may I be kinder to friends?'' For me, meditation is something simple like that…''

Actress BIBI ANDERSSON talked about how she spent her time alone to relax:

''I think a lot when I'm alone. Sometimes I'm embarrassed about this, I call it my daydreaming. Now, you can say you meditate, it sounds nicer, but to me it's my daydreaming… I let my thoughts wander. I let them wander where they want to and I go with them. But, sometimes, I may sort problems out, or start to think — what should I have done, or what didn't I do, or why did that person react like that? I think of different situations, and see them in a new perspective, that's what I do in solitude, that's how I meditate.''

Senator EUGENE McCARTHY, contemplative by nature, doesn't find it necessary to restrict his meditation to an appointed moment. Eight years with the Benedictine Order as student and teacher gave him a spiritual foundation that has shaped his solitude and love of poetry. He talked about his experience there, and his favorite food for solitude, reading poetry as meditation:

"The Benedictines are primarily a social order, but they make time for meditation and reflection. I remember how they used to keep the great silence from about 9.30 at night until 7.00 in the morning. You didn't talk to anybody. You could read and think and sleep. I was only one year at the monastery, and not a hermit like Brother David Steindl-Rast, but the experience certainly affected my solitude.

Do I meditate? I don't really work at it that hard. I think that after you've been around as long as I've been, that your meditation sort of comes and goes. You don't need the discipline of saying, now I'll set aside an hour for meditation. You can meditate while you're waiting for that oatmeal to cook.

If you asked me what my favorite food for solitude was, I guess more than real food, reading poetry is the most satisfying. For me, reading poetry is a meditation. Poetry is the best and most intensified form of language, and that's what meditation is really about. It's a concentrating process, not a diffusing one. You have to really concentrate to write poetry, and so there you are…"

I promised EDGAR MITCHELL that I wouldn't ask him anything more about the moon since I figured he had talked enough about that. But I couldn't resist asking, is going inside yourself as romantic as going to the moon? And for astronaut Edgar Mitchell who was part of that historical landing of the first earthlings ever to walk on the moon, the journey inside the human psyche is just as challenging.

''My meditation desires to be a meeting with God. It isn't always because we do it imperfectly, but that is the goal. Of course there is the idea of having to overcome one's ego in order to do that... I think we find as we delve deeper into our psyches that we have layers of egomania that we never dreamed we had. We think we've gotten rid of that, and it's under control, but the deeper we dig, the more we find. It's like peeling away layers of an onion, there's always one more layer beneath.

For me meditation is food for solitude. I think for a human entity to really understand his inner workings, he must first want to find a state of tranquility. Inner joy, inner bliss, inner comfortableness is not achieved from chaos, but is achieved from a state of tranquility. The question is how do we find it.

I've gone through a lot of changes since I've been on the moon, and these changes have been deepened by my learning how to get to the quiet. For me, it's a matter of finding time and attempting to do it. I use any time I can to be alone, whether it be on an aircraft traveling from one spot to another, or early in the morning when I wake up. I use the time just to be quiet and listen. And what I am listening to is the inner direction. Sometimes I may find a question in my mind that needs answering. Then I just have to be quiet and listen to the answer. There is also a constant cleaning, a filtering out of the whims and the train of thoughts that tend to invade our minds continuously.

People meditate in different ways. What may work for you might not for me. But I don't think there is anything we figure out totally on our own. We gather different pieces of information from someone else's experiences, and then we try it for ourselves. I've tried a number of procedures to quiet my mind and the one that works for me is an imaging or visualization technique. This is a system that I've devised for myself and it works. You could say it's my recipe for meditation.

I see mental space as a wind-whipped mill pond. I liken the mind to a pool of water or a pond, and when the various disturbing thoughts go running through my mind, the pond becomes wind-blown with white caps and waves on it. I can actually see all of this in my mind's eye, although in the beginning it wasn't so

clear to me. I have had to make myself more visual, because being visual is quite an asset to this whole process. You have to constantly clear the negative thoughts away.

My approach is to imagine that my thoughts will become quiet and still, and just by thinking that, they do. I allow them to settle down, and because that is the goal I set, my inner thoughts follow along. I keep the analogy in my mind of the mill pond getting quiet, and as it quiets down so does my mind.

Doing something like this takes time and practice. I have used this technique about three years, so at this point, when I become tense or agitated, I can just tell my mind to relax and become quiet, and it responds. Yet, sometimes it's very difficult, because the mind likes to be agitated. You have to train yourself to remember that if you are going to get angry or agitated, you are destroying yourself. The process of quieting down your mind has to become a way of life.

Meditating has changed my life and my attitude toward life. I am more able to cope with stress, and I take a far more philosophical view of the craziness that seems to happen in the environment around me... Meditation feeds me my solitude, and for me, solitude is not aloneness at all. I think the ultimate idea is to grow, learn and find greater self-satisfaction, and to experience a totally more satisfying way of being. I find solitude in its inner complexion as a vital part of that process. To me it is the ultimate practice if it works. Solitude becomes oneness, and in proper meditation you are in communion with the entire universe tapping into the ultimate source of reality.''

The dance between the myths of the past and the not yet dreamed images of the future create a convergence of art, science, and religion and it is within this tapestry that cultural historian, WILLIAM IRWIN THOMPSON, sets his loom. When he left the academic world in order to start the Lindisfarne Association, he had hoped to link his sense of planetary consciousness with the culture at large. Could a contemplative community with ecological consciousness work in the real world, so that it becomes interwoven in a practical way? This question is always an ongoing experiment.

The links between inner and outer environments fascinate Bill Thompson, and in his quest for solitude he seeks all those patterns that connect. For him, meditation is highly personal, yet also something to be shared with others. Meditation is a way to share solitude. He talked about how a contemplative community could work as a retreat right in the middle of a noisy New York street:

"Lindisfarne is a contemplative community right in the heart of the city, and so we are, therefore, dealing with solitude paradoxically while we live in community. The way we do this is to base our day on meditation. There is a shared silence, but each person is going into his own internal solitude.

I think one can have as deep and profound and intense meditations here on the corner of Sixth avenue and Twentieth street, as in the Hebrides or in the Himalayas or in the desert. There's a romantic notion that solitude can only be achieved in extreme horizons, or extreme exotic places. That's a romantic fantasy, because when you get there you find that you brought everything inside you along. It just doesn't work.

For me, meditation and solitude is a daily thing. I refuse to live the office life of Manhattan from nine to five. Our offices don't open up until one o'clock in the afternoon. So every morning is devoted to individual private scholarship. Every morning I begin the day with meditation and silence, and then the rest of the morning is devoted to writing. So, I'm alone; I'm alone with just the stream of thoughts in a creative kind of process.

Meditation for me is very personal and very different than it used to be. I don't believe in technique anymore. Meditation is definitely not reciting a mantra, or running a pipe cleaner up and down my spinal column unlocking chakras. Meditation is just absolute silence and absolute suspending of breath and thought. It's a position of complete simplicity, of just sitting at the edge of your own being, as you would sit at the edge of a continent watching the waves of the ocean. If there's a time where I've been rushed or something of that sort, I might use a simple breath method, where I watch my breath until it stills. But basically I just float on the top of my head.

I don't go on trips. I don't get into fantasies, because that's a form of thought. I just sit at the edge of my being and watch the relationship between my being, and that which is larger than my being. In this state, I don't see anything. I just feel. I move beyond thought. It isn't a thinking process.

It's just like the interval between each heartbeat which is outside of time. It is almost as if there is a gateway outside of time in the interval between each heartbeat. As you center in, and as you become very silent, the interval between each heartbeat expands and expands and expands until the heart stops beating, and the breath goes away and thought goes away. You just *are*. There is no description for it. There is no technique. It's just very simple.

Sometimes I will listen to music in my meditation. I think Bach or Beethoven can be the closest we can come at one level to higher states of consciousness. But on one particular retreat I took in Iona, I wanted to get away from music too. So, I didn't listen to music. I just listened to the waves or the wind, since there's a lot of wind on Iona. There I had the opportunity to meditate five or six hours a day, to be with the essence of meditation, pure and wonderful silence.''

Emptiness cannot harm emptiness.

An old Tibetan saying

When I first met THE FOURTEENTH DALAI LAMA, I was impressed with the quality about him that made him seem much more like a solitary monk than someone who is the spiritual leader as well as a political king of all Tibetan Buddhists in the world. It was inspiring to realize that despite all the fanfare and fuss surrounding his position, at heart he was just a simple soul evermore seeking to deepen his own spiritual practice. Even he yearned for more time alone in order to meditate and develop his already advanced spiritual consciousness.

For the Dalai Lama, meditation is definitely the ultimate ceremony alone. Consciousness, spirituality in itself, is the highest expression of creativity. As he said, ''If you have a real and sincere practice you'll never feel lonely. I've never felt lonely — alone, yes — but I've never felt separated or isolated from the rest of the world. Even in my exile from my homeland of Tibet, I felt my inner solitude and not isolated. I am grateful for my meditation practice that gave me this inner strength.''

In the following thoughts, HIS HOLINESS TENZIN GYATSO talks about his own personal practice and the importance of solitude for spirituality:

''Being alone is very important for my spiritual practice. My daily practice is in early morning and also in late evening. This is very much my kind of solitude. It is a practice of a certain way of thinking; a specific kind of meditation I practice without other people. This is important for my concentration. I need this time alone.

Of course, meditation practice with or without others depends on one's inner development. For some people, once they reach a certain experience, then consciousness can work in two ways simultaneously. While talking, one part of consciousness meditates on certain things and another part can continue chatting. But that depends on one's inner experience. At the moment, I cannot do that. So that's why I get up every day in the early morning when I'm able to be free, and I spend three to four hours in solitude. This is usually between 4.30 or 5 until 9 or 10, something like that. I find this very creative and useful.

I feel that consciousness and meditation is the basis of creativity. Meditation sharpens your mind and develops strong motivation. It creates more alertness and builds up inner strength. And this is the foundation on which you create. Without this basis it is confusing; if you really want to create something you cannot. How can anyone with a dull or discouraged mind create?

If every day in the early morning you have some meditation or some practice, it will have a very strong influence during the rest of your day. When you meet with people, or if you hear some bad news or good news, your mind somehow has become stabilized, due to the early morning practice. There is less excitement or reaction as a result. There is less attachment, less anger. It is very useful.

In Hinayana Buddhism teaching, the main emphasis is on self-liberation. In this practice, social activities and social service are of little interest. Here solitude is very much related and useful to spiritual development. Whereas in certain practices of Bodhisattvayana, complete isolation can be very necessary and helpful; there the main emphasis should be toward service for other people. In either case, one obviously needs special times to cultivate the solitude within.

Right now, I feel that I don't have enough solitude. I would like to have more time alone in order to nourish myself spiritually. Then I would have more time to study the Buddhist scriptures, to read the wisdom of the great metaphysical Buddhist books. More than anything I love to read these kind of sources when I am alone. This enhances my meditation. If you have more knowledge it helps you to think, to investigate, to probe more deeply into your mind.

In some kinds of meditation, investigation is very important and in others not important. But it is necessary to practice in both ways, so that all these things are included. In Buddhist practice there is both wisdom and altruism (compassion). These two things are most important. Without wisdom you can't improve altruism, and without altruism the wisdom cannot be useful. They must go together.

I once visited the famous Spanish monastery of Montserrat near Barcelona. (It's where the Holy Grail was supposed to have been kept). There behind the monastery on the hill is a small hut where one Catholic monk stays. When I visited that monastery, this monk would come especially to see me, and we spent a lot of time talking. He explained to me how for five years he remained in that small hut in complete solitude. He rarely had hot meals, only vegetables and some fruit. Then I asked him, during this period what he meditated on, what was his practice. And he said, 'Love. I meditated on love.' And although his English was even worse than my English, we had a very very good companionship. We used to sit together, face to face, sometimes just looking into each other's eyes and face, and then we shared some real feeling. I told him, 'You are a modern Milarepa'* ...His was a very meaningful solitude practice.

There is a part of me that is like that hermit. One day I would like to have more solitude, then I would read and meditate. But even if I wanted to go off to a natural cave I still have to consider my physical condition. Somehow it's already spoiled due to certain circumstances. So I couldn't now become a true hermit and live altogether alone in some isolated environment, though I would want some kind of solitude. Every serious Buddhist practitioner needs that. At heart, I am just a simple Buddhist monk. This is my true inner self...''

---

* 12th century Tibetan poet-saint-yogi, famous for *The One Hundred Thousand Songs of Milarepa*, one of the founders of Kagyudpa sect of Tibetan Buddhism.

Spend An Evening With The I Ching

Someone once said, "Ask the right question and the universe will reveal itself!" My first experience with the I Ching was just like that. I had gotten together with some friends who made me a fabulous Chinese feast, and then for dessert, served the I Ching. "Ask it any question you like," they said. "Ask something really important concerning your future, and let's see what it has to say." It sounded like the perfect fortune cookie, but it was much more. That night was my first taste of a treat I discovered was not just a fortune teller, but an oracle full of spiritual nourishment. Since then, spending evenings alone with the I Ching has grown to be one of the ceremonies I cherish the most.

The I Ching is considered by scholars to be among the most treasured books in world literature. They all agree that it is one of the great spiritual classics of all time. Older than the Egyptian Pyramids, it goes back 5000 years when it consisted of only sixty-four hexagrams, based on the universal principle of change. Each image meant something special to the seeker who considered it an oracle capable of bestowing wisdom. The commentaries regarding each hexagram were added thousands of years later, combining the best insights of both Taoist and Confucian philosophy.

It is interesting that this teaching of 5000 years ago, based on the principle of change, has its modern parallel in quantum mechanics theory, which includes Heisenberg's uncertainty principle. Long ago, the I Ching understood that if you were certain, there could be no change. It doesn't really matter whether or not the same question is asked over and over again, and you get a different response each time, or the same response is given again and again to different questions. Because, when you consult the I Ching, you are capturing a moment of destiny in relation to the whole. Within the ever changing, expanding but orderly universe, no matter where you are, you are always in transition. Life is your journey and this is your opportunity to change, to transform, to grow as part of the whole.

Consulting the I Ching is very much like asking your own insight a question. The whole process has its way of unlocking and opening your heart, and there you discover many questions hiding deep inside you. For instance, sometimes you may get a reading that does not correspond to the question you asked. Instead the I Ching gives you a deeper answer. When you come to it totally from your heart, it is amazing how it always understands what you truly need to know. It becomes a meditation in that learning how to ask the right question deepens your sense of inner concentration. You are able to focus in on what is really essential, and by doing this you are on your way to answering your own question.

The I Ching is definitely right brain food, for it silences the chit-chat of left brain logic that keeps asking questions, going everywhere yet nowhere. It teaches how to get to the root of your problems, rather than looking for short term solutions. So maybe you will not get an easy solution to a difficult problem, but you may discover something revealing about yourself, that will prevent the same pattern from occurring. Asking the I Ching a question can be like spring cleaning your karma. It opens a new window into your universe by helping you to look inside, where you see simultaneously the root of your problem and the opportunity to transform it. The Book of Changes is clearly a book of hope. And if the day ever comes when you no longer need it because you can rely upon your own heart and intuition, the I Ching will have done its work for you.

GETTING YOUR FIRST READING — THE METHOD OF COINS

If you are spending your first evening with the I Ching, I recommend getting the Bollingen translation to learn how to use it. Of course if you are already devoted to it, you know that you could spend the rest of your life learning something new each time. But basically this is one way to get your hexagram, using the method of coins. The special I Ching coins, inscribed on one side and plain on the other are available, but you could also use tokens or any other kind of coin. The Bollingen edition describes the process of using the old Chinese coins with a hole in the middle and an inscription on one side this way:

Three coins are taken up and thrown down together, and each throw gives a line. The inscribed side counts as yin, with the value 2, and the reverse side counts as yang with the value 3. From this the character of the line is derived. If all three coins are yang, the line is a 9; if all three are yin, it is a 6. Two yin and one yang yield a 7, and two yang and one yin yield an 8... (6 and 8 give a broken line, while 7 and 9 give an unbroken line.

Throwing the coins is a special ceremony in itself. Each time you throw the coins, it helps to repeat the question, to truly hold it in your heart. Asking your question in this way is like making a wish six times. This sort of inner concentration is important if you sincerely seek a real answer.

When you are ready to get your hexagram, throw the coins six times, and then you will come up with six broken or unbroken lines. The combinations vary, so sometimes you have six straight lines, or six broken lines, or combinations of the two. Just remember to start your lines on the bottom and work your way up the ladder. Then look up your hexagram in the Book of Changes and treat yourself to its reading. Here is an example:

A Reading from the I Ching:

27. I/The Corners of the Mouth (Providing Nourishment)

```
——————————————
————— —————          above KEN KEEPING STILL, MOUNTAIN
————— —————
————— —————
————— —————
——————————————     below CHEN THE AROUSING, THUNDER
```

This hexagram is a picture of an open mouth... Starting with the mouth, through which we take food for nourishment, the thought leads to nourishment itself. Nourishment of oneself, specifically of the body, is represented in the three lower lines, while the three upper lines represent nourishment and care of others, in a higher spiritual sense.

THE JUDGMENT

THE CORNERS OF THE MOUTH

Perseverance brings good fortune.
Pay heed to the providing of nourishment
And to what a man seeks
To fill his own mouth with.

In bestowing care and nourishment, it is important that the right people should be taken care of and that we should attend to our own nourishment in the right way. If we wish to know what anyone is like, we have only to observe on whom he bestows his care and what sides of his own nature he cultivates and nourishes. Nature nourishes all creatures...

THE IMAGE
At the foot of the mountain, thunder:
The image of PROVIDING NOURISHMENT.
Thus the superior man is careful of his words
And temperate in eating and drinking.

This is an image of providing nourishment through movement and tranquility. The superior man takes it as a pattern for the nourishment and cultivation of his character. Words are a movement going from within outward. Eating and drinking are movements from without inward. Both kinds of movement can be modified by tranquility. For tranquility keeps the words that come out of the mouth from exceeding its proper measure, and keeps the food that goes into the mouth from exceeding its proper measure. Thus character is cultivated.

page 107 and 108, *The I Ching Bollingen series*

Solitude And Soup

Stir yourself. Banish fear.
Use the natural talent
God gave you.

Epictetus

There is a fairy tale I read as a child, about a princess who breaks the spell of the wicked witch, by emptying all the water from a pond with a spoon. I can still remember wondering how she had the patience to sit there by the pond facing such an impossible task. But she had the faith that it could be done and, spoonful by spoonful, the pond began to empty. And of course, as in all fairy tales, she got her due reward.

Sometimes stirring the soup is just like this fairy tale. There are spells to be broken, and blessings that come together, and in between the stirs there are many moments of quiet discovery. The soup comes to a boil, then it simmers, and then it cools. Patience is required. And as you wait for the soup to transform from the solid substance of vegetables into a clear broth, your mind also changes. Hidden thoughts come to surface. Old trouble-making ideas disintegrate. New thoughts emerge, and you know they are new...

It is within this process that demands both patience and devotion that the seeds of solitude have a chance to grow. They have been in the making a long time, longer than it took to make one pot of soup. Who can say exactly when the soup stopped being a bunch of separate ingredients? "To separate, in order to combine," according to the I Ching, "that is the nature of change." That is also the essence of real love. Sometimes things seem together, and sometimes they seem far apart, but deep within, beyond the image, the substance of solitude is never anything but oneness. So, now we have a few ingredients floating on top of the soup, and now they are moving toward the center, and soon they will completely disappear to become soup.

The transformation of energy is a very refined process. This is what consciousness is all about, to change one form of energy into another. We each experience our inner stirrings, waiting and watching as all our hopes and dreams become a wish fulfilled. We live partly in our deepest desires, and partly in the actions that will make it all come together. We stir the soup of our imagination and in between, when it is least expected, it stirs us. And this is when we realize that whether or not we stir it, the soup will change. It has to, for that is its true nature.

*... In the beginning the universe was a soup consisting
mostly of gluons and hadrons... so they say.
And seasons and cycles fall over the wayside
Stopped in mid-air
They are caught in nothing.
Could a black-hole have eaten them for lunch?*

Pick a flower and trouble a star, so say the ancient mystics, which gets us into the bowl of parsnips and quasars. When we see the cross section of a parsnip, and a photograph of a synthesized radio map of a quasar, it is apparent that the mandala maker of the universe created them with the same design in mind. Parsnips and quasars are both roots. One grows in the earth, and the other emanates from unknown places in the universe.

At this point we know more about parsnips than quasars, but astronomers are beginning to put together their quasar cookbook which offers new ingredients of tantalizing proportions. Black holes may dine upon these superstars, but who consumes whom isn't exactly clear. Astronomers consider these extraordinary patterns of light to be the most powerful sources of energy in the universe. Is it an accident that both these roots have the same pattern?

When you eat a parsnip, are you connected to the original light of a quasar? Who knows, but it's fun to think about — especially when you have time to hermitize. Here is a simple soup recipe that lets you enjoy soup and solitude for a week. I call it Root Soup: the quasars are optional.

A Recipe of Mostly Roots

4 carrots	2 turnips
3 potatoes	1 onion
1 leek	1 bunch carrot greens
1 parsnip	3 cloves garlic
1 celery stalk	1 sprig fresh dill

The whole idea of this soup is to have lots of carrot greens. One bunch of carrot greens works well with a six quart pot. Use four or five carrots, three or four potatoes, one leek, one parsnip, a couple of turnips, and one giant onion. Clean and dice all the vegetables, add to the water, bring to a boil, then let simmer for about an hour. Remove the greens, then add the garlic and fresh dill, wait until cool, then add to your blender. This is the most delicious purée of legume you ever tasted. It keeps well in the refrigerator for a week, and tastes better cold. Drink it like juice... Enjoy!

Decay is the beginning of all birth... the midwife of very great things... It brings about the birth and rebirth of forms a thousand times improved... And this is the highest and greatest mysterium *of God, the deepest mystery and miracle that He has revealed to mortal man.*

Paracelsus

Soup, like solitude, often consists of isolated fragments that seem like nothing on their own, but put them all together, and watch their energies become the ultimate essence, a purée of the finest ingredients. It's amazing how many weeds and roots and scraps are left behind. But here is the soul of the soup, the stuff that really makes soup a soup.

Salmon and watercress is essentially a scrap soup, a fish bone with a few vegetables thrown in. It came to be quite by accident. I bought some beautiful filet of salmon at the fish market, and was ready to leave with just my filets, when the woman helping me said, "Don't you want your bones? You've paid for them, it's part of your fish!" Why would I want the bones, I thought. What could I possibly do with them? She must have heard my thoughts, because she took some extra bones from the bin and said, "Now go home and make soup!" From that day on scraps took on a new meaning to me.

So the next time you go to your favorite fish market, ask about their extra scraps. As long as they are fresh, they will be suitable for either freezing or using the same day for your soup.

Salmon and Watercress Soup

salmon bones	1 celery stalk
1 bunch watercress	1 potato, with peel
1 turnip, chopped	few sprigs parsley
1 carrot, chopped	a few cumin seeds

Put all the above ingredients in a 2 quart pot and fill almost to the top with water. Bring to a full boil, then reduce heat and simmer for one and a half hours, stirring occasionally. Whenever you feel like it, you can fish for bones and remove them with a fork. If you don't feel like fishing for bones, then you can wrap them securely in a cheesecloth before you place them in the pot. I was impressed with the infinite structural beauty of the backbone of the salmon. It looked like an ivory crystal necklace. But since I'm not a collector, I didn't keep it, even though I was tempted to save it for a day or two. Anyway, if you manage to overcome the artistic glow of this experience, you'll be careful about not letting the soup boil over. After an hour and a half, let the pot cool on the stove and then refrigerate.

The same night or the next day, remove all the bones and pour the soup into a blender. Now you have a purée of salmon and watercress soup. This will last up to two weeks in the refrigerator.

You can add more filets of fish, watercress, celery and parsley. It tastes excellent as it is, but you can also add sesame seeds and a splash of tamari sauce, or some marsala wine when reheating the mixture.

This is a wonderful fish soup base for anything you want to create. If you add some fresh clams, tomatoes, garlic, and onions, you are closer to a Manhattan clam chowder. Or add some fresh cream, a bit of sherry, and a few scallions, and you are somewhere else...

Who can be the enemy of alchemy, since it bears no guilt? Guilty is he who does not know it properly, and who does not apply it properly... For alchemy means: to carry to its end something that has not yet been completed... It can separate the useful from the useless, and transmute it into its final substance and its ultimate essence.

Paracelsus

There is nothing more comforting at certain times, than to see a beautiful bowl of hot steaming soup, sitting there, elegant, inviting and home-made. I still remember my grandmother's chicken soup. It was full of magical ingredients and lots of love. Only she could make it that special, and if my grandfather was home we got to hear one of his famous stories to go along with it...

Whenever I find time to make real chicken soup, I sit back for a moment, and truly appreciate the many moments I spent with my grandparents, moments that will never be the same without them. Yet somehow when the soup starts to simmer, and you can smell it all over the house, they are alive again. I know that they know I am making chicken soup.

Here is the recipe handed down from my grandmother, to my mother, to you...

Chicken Soup

1 chicken	1 parsnip
4 stalks celery & leaves	2 or 3 bay leaves
2 onions	1 clove garlic
4 carrots	1 tbspn. salt
2 leeks	¼ tspn. pepper
8 sprigs parsley	

Cooking out all the energy from the scraps is mother's chicken soup secret. She recommends using the pressure cooker for the same reason John Cage likes to use it for his brown rice. It saves time, and captures the energy of all the precious vitamins and minerals contained in the food. If you use a pot, be sure that it has an airtight cover, so the steam can't escape along with the nutrition. The following is what to do for either method of cooking the soup. Cover the chicken with water. If you use a large pot, then bring to a boil and let simmer for an hour. Then add the vegetables and spices and more water if needed, and let simmer another 15 minutes.

If you use a pressure cooker, also cover the chicken with water, and heat for 15 minutes. Then add the vegetables and spices and heat for another minute.

To remove the fat: Let the soup cool, then skim the top of the soup by blotting the fat off with paper napkins or towels. Another method is to refrigerate the soup, and then scoop off the fat when crystallized.

To store: After the soup is completely simmered and cooled, remove the chicken and/or scraps and refrigerate broth separately. Bone the chicken and put it into another container... You can add this later when you reheat the soup. Also, you can remove the vegetables, and purée them in the blender for another variation of soup. You will have a great chicken broth, plus a purée of vegetable.

Foods and Moods

My hunger has astonishing moods. Often it comes to me only after mealtimes, and today it did not come at all: where has it been?

Nietzsche

When I think about foods and moods, I think of magic potions and aphrodisiacs and how incredible it is that one cup of camomile tea could turn a headache into peace of mind. And who can forget our friend Alice in Wonderland and all her transformations, just from eating and drinking a bit of this or that... Remember? ''...Oh dear! I'd nearly forgotten that I've got to grow up again! Let me see – how *is* it to be managed? I suppose I ought to eat or drink something or other; but the great question is What?...''

Yes, the great question certainly is What, but just as important is How? For now we realize that we are *how we eat* as well as *what*. And what we ingest is not only our morning bowl of porridge, but all the impressions surrounding us the rest of the day. The food of the universe comes to us in many forms. Sometimes subtle, sometimes gross, these vibrations are part of our life. Consciously or unconsciously we take them in as well as dish them out. People are beginning to seriously consider the karmic idea that each and every action, from the simplest to the most complex, affects the way we live. Each and every mood affects our food, and of course, the food affects our moods.

The Zen sages always say, ''Eat when you're hungry, sleep when you're tired, and when you sit, just sit.'' But somehow this advice gets lost amidst all the distractions of life. Sometimes simple truths like eating slowly and chewing is good for your digestion, seem too simple. And so we forget. But our entire relationship with food — how we treat it, how we respect its preparation, the ingredients we choose, the time we take to digest it — all this connects with the rest of our life patterns. You may not believe this, or maybe you just haven't noticed, so you think it doesn't matter. But it does. It matters in very real ways and sometimes it can even mean the difference between feeling lonely and being happy.

Imagine getting up in the middle of a meeting at the UN and asking each person what they ate for breakfast that day. Did they leave their home in peace or were they still mad at the pot of oatmeal for boiling all over their stove! Maybe we don't need to always do grandiose things to 'save the planet'. Maybe we just have to trust that the peace of the whole world may very well depend on how we eat that bowl of porridge each morning.

The ancient sages knew it was better to not eat at all than to eat in aggravation... Agni Yoga Teachings from the way of the Heart give the following advice:

> 534. It is wrong for people not to pay attention to the effects of eating during irritation and agitation. Very strong poisons are formed by this unwise procedure... It should be remembered that hunger is far better than harmful food... The silence of the ancients during the meal had a sacred significance. But the understanding of sacredness also comprised the cure.

The stomach is the seat of all wisdom

An old Chinese proverb

For some people, eating alone is a ceremony of fun. Food is comfort and company. For others, it is simply something to avoid. As Edwin Newman admitted, ''I hate it sometimes, that feeling of being cheated pops up. When I'm alone, I don't dine, I eat; and in a sense I don't cook, I heat.''

Do you feel like that? Do you eat just to get it over with and is food only a ''fuel for your engine'' the way it is for Edgar Mitchell? Or do you believe that food has a sacred meaning, that eating is a kind of tai chi, a way to flow through life… However you feel, one thing is for sure: *How* you eat as well as *what* you eat could affect the rest of your life… So why do you eat the way you eat?

I hope you find the following attitudes about solitude and food instructive as well as amusing…

ROLLO MAY

''What I prefer to think of as food for solitude is the accent on solitude, and not on the food. But that's because of the way I was brought up. I had nothing tasty until I was eighteen years of age. I was eighteen before I could taste anything. My family was poor, so we ate mostly cornflakes for breakfast, lunch, and supper. My mother, with six children, never had enough time to cook anything, and if she did cook, she fried potatoes. On special occasions we had fried eggs and things like that. We did not eat terribly well.

When I got to Oberlin College, it was a great surprise to me that everybody could eat like a prince. We had decent meals at the boarding house and that is where I first discovered food. Then I went to Europe to teach, and that is where I learned what food really was. I remember being twenty, and teaching in Saloniki, Greece. There I learned about a whole dimension of food and drink and wine. I learned very much to taste it, to taste it excessively, as a reaction from my childhood of cornflakes three times a day.

But being in Greece awakened a whole new attitude about food and dining. Food was special. It was something you tasted and savored. It was part of the art of living. I remember those days with great joy, because that's when I realized what food could be. There the ceremony of preparing it was something sacred. You sat under the stars in Saloniki, dining for hours and hours. It was all very romantic.

When I came back from Europe, while still in my twenties, I would prefer to take women out to dinner rather than to a movie. Of course, in the town where I was then working in East Lansing, Michigan, this was never heard of. There, dinner was something you got to by seven o'clock, and finished shortly thereafter. Dinner in Europe was something you began at eight and ended at midnight. It was a wonderful way to converse. It set the conversation of warmth and emotion.

Today I really enjoy a good meal with a friend, but I prefer not to eat alone. Even though I do it often enough because of my work, I still haven't gotten to the point where I look forward to it. But we all can change, if we understand why we're avoiding what we avoid. I'm sure my attitudes about food and eating alone were shaped a good deal by the fact that we were poor and that my mother and father were semi-American practical Puritans. They believed you shouldn't pay much attention to food. Of course, I think this is complete nonsense. As a matter of fact, it's harmful.

Food is related to all the aspects of your life. Food and sex are the two things that have to do with survival of the individual as well as survival of the race. How you deal with food and eating alone may very well be related to your sex life. If you don't like eating alone, you may not enjoy sex alone. But on the other hand, if you are celibate, eating alone may be a gratifying way of sublimating those desires. You transfer all your feelings to the food, and it becomes your company.

I would really like to learn how to eat alone with the same gusto as I do with others… If you want to really make friends with somebody, the best way of all is to take them to dinner. Making friends with yourself and taking yourself to dinner is an idea that I think I have to take into consideration…''

IRA PROGOFF

"Whenever I get a sore throat I eat quarts and quarts of ice cream to soothe my throat, knowing very well that being quiet is even greater food for solitude. But even eating ice cream matters. It matters because it satisfies my immediate nutriment needs. It's a passing food that pleases my passing mood, and then I can concentrate on other food that is inherently important, that I believe matters to the universe, like reading something spiritual like Lao Tse. But, if you really put it all together, then I guess you could say that even eating ice cream is holy."

DIANA VREELAND

"For me, everything is great in solitude except eating. That's the end of the line. Food is conversation, jokes, fun. Eating for me is a social occasion, and by social I mean one other person. I'm not talking three or four or twenty. I just don't like to eat alone. I can't imagine anything in the world more ghastly than cooking your meal, and then sitting down and eating it. I'd go without it. I'd drink water all night and eat bananas, because I couldn't stand all the fuss — and for what? To eat alone! Of course, everyone has another perspective. Everyone is entitled to the food of their choice when alone, but for me it isn't real food."

GLORIA VANDERBILT

"I really like to work at a stretch, so when I'm painting, I may go for eight hours without stopping. To me it seems like ten minutes and I can really just forget to eat, because it isn't important to me then. But you do have to get something into your stomach, and what I do is keep some cottage cheese in the ice box. I just eat it out of the carton.

But when I'm alone without working, that's a very different mood of solitude. I love to make myself very special solitude foods. These are marvelous solitary snacks that are all sorts of children's food, and mostly white...

I love things like junket made with milk, with nutmeg sprinkled on it. I absolutely adore rice pudding and tapioca pudding. It's creamy white on white color appeals to me as much as the taste. Another kind of treat would be cold wild rice, with heavy cream over it, and brown sugar on the top. It's heaven. I don't eat this stuff all the time. But once a year it can't hurt you, and then it's a real treat. The wild rice isn't white, but it has heavy cream on it. I'm sure all this is Freudian, but I enjoy it."

DOROTHY NORMAN

"For me the meal is an offering of beauty. If it's not beautiful it shouldn't be given. A civilization is judged by the beauty it creates. Each object, each act should be sacred, beautiful, and dedicated to the gods."

LEONARD NIMOY

"I have thought to myself, why do I rush through preparing a meal, throwing it down and then going on to something else, as though that was a time consuming event. Why do I do that? Those are times that I feel the food is a real bother, or else I just feel guilty that I'm eating.

I guess it's because my parents always forced me to eat a lot. I used to get the thing about starving kids in Europe all the time: 'You better eat your food!'

When I was a kid about nine or ten years old, I remember distinctly one day saying to my mother, 'What's hungry, and what does hunger mean?' And she laughed. She was so proud to hear me say that because I never went hungry. But the point was that she always anticipated. She was always laying on food, before there was a need, because it was her need to feed. She was the typical Jewish mother. I still hear her saying, 'Sit down and eat!'... You walk into the house and the first thing you hear is, 'Sit down and eat!' You know, she still sends me food."

BARRY COMMONER

"There are many taboos about eating alone, and when you begin to confront that problem, there are all sorts of social and psychological pressures... I used to think I should eat out, and not feel sorry about having to cook for myself. Then I started doing it but I was trying to get it over quickly. Pretty soon, however, I noticed that was a mistake. So I began cooking for its own sake, and I really began to enjoy it. I can't analyze why, but I do find that it's a striking departure from the hustle-bustle of the day. And I just enjoy doing it.

I think my background has something to do with my appreciation of food, and the whole process of preparing it... When I was a boy, my mother used to let me watch her as she prepared all the food, and it was a time of joy. Unlike other people of my generation, I had no feelings of guilt about being in the kitchen. I never associated working in the kitchen as a chore. I actually enjoyed washing dishes.

Cooking has become a way to relax for me. In the first place, it's working with your hands, which I've always liked to do. And it's a quick way to get gratification. After all, in an hour's time you end up with a product that's worthwhile. But, more important, meals are an essential natural break, it's a real relaxation. Food is a very important psychological element in the whole day, and I don't like to mix it up with work. I hate working lunches.

Eating is important to me. It is part of my life. It is very valuable in and of itself as an activity.''

JIM JENSEN

''Eating alone doesn't bother me. But if other people see me coming out of a restaurant alone, they say, 'Oh, we saw you wandering around alone.' It is as if there was something strange about eating alone. It is as if there was something strange about eating alone and being alone, when I'm perfectly happy to do both… I always liked to eat alone. When I go to a restaurant by myself, the meal is a way for me to sit and watch people. I can watch the comings and goings, and observe and think. It's very comfortable.

When I don't go out, I like to cook creatively for myself. I ad lib as I go along and I really enjoy the whole process. But this isn't any ritualistic meditation. I try to make it as quickly as possible. But even though I can't wait to finish the mess, I do enjoy the creation.''

JOSEPH CAMPBELL

''Dining alone for me is a little like the old story of the Englishman in the Congo. He dressed for dinner and he ate alone. While I don't dress for dinner when I am alone, I do enjoy the ceremony of a meal. I enjoy every detail, and I make a thing of it. In the morning when I have breakfast alone, I have a regular meal: a couple of boiled eggs, some toast and coffee. But I don't eat standing up, walking around, just chewing on the food.

I set the table, bring the food out, and sit down and have it. There's no decor, just the food. That's it. And I enjoy the food. I enjoy eating it. I enjoy cracking the egg, taking it out of its shell. I enjoy the whole darn thing. It's a physical act that I enjoy performing.''

GEOFFREY HOLDER

"Chewing is a bore. Like sex, it's hard work. To eat alone is a ceremony I don't like... I can be alone, if I know someone is coming later."

BIBI ANDERSSON

"For me, food is comfort and company, that's what it is. It's like something I just use as a friend when I'm by myself at home, or on the road with a play. The thought of preparing elaborate food especially for my solitude sounds like too much ambition and that bores me. So, I eat what I like to eat. I eat the things which I think are good. I eat in bed. I eat while I'm reading. I don't make a fuss about it. As far as I'm concerned we should eat for pleasure and without restrictions.

I have no real rules, just to do what pleases me, and sometimes not. Sometimes I have anger food. Coffee has to do with anger. When things are upsetting, I just take a cup of coffee, and that aggravates me even more. I'm not angry very often, but sometimes I get very angry during rehearsals, or while shooting a film. Then I need to put something in my mouth and I drink coffee because it's always around. I wouldn't bother in a state of anger to say, 'Could you hand me a little yogurt with a little molasses and a little honey?' I don't get into healthy things then. I just want something, and I follow my cravings.

The whole idea of fasting and doing all kinds of experiments is a little corny to me. It might be very healthy and so that could be good. But, to me it's like you're substituting other things that are sort of psychological hang-ups. You think that food solves everything — like if you're unhappy in your love affair, or you're unfulfilled in your work, you turn to food as a savior. A lot of people turn to food as a substitute for love, they think it's a solution, but then it becomes a very narcissistic thing. How much they eat, or how little becomes important. Their functioning becomes the most important worldly event. Who needs that! I like myself, I love to eat and I don't like to be obsessed with the internal workings of my body. I like it to function, and I like to keep out of its way!

I am probably a good bad example for you. I'm definitely not a good example of eating habits. Yet, I'm not so sure my eating habits are bad, even though a nutritionist might think so... Once I saw this woman who told me I had to change the speed of how I was eating. Now, to tell me to change this is like telling me to

change my whole temperament, the way I talk, the way I walk, the way I eat, the way I make love, the way I live! Who says it is right for me to sit down and eat slowly with knives and forks, if it just makes me nervous! Maybe it's very healthy for me to grab food from the fridge and eat. If that makes me feel good, this is all that matters. Of course there's nothing wrong with changing your habits, but then you have to change all the way and really change your whole life. Then, starting with one thing like changing eating habits can help…"

Treating The Romantic Blues

A ship ought not to be held by a single anchor,
nor life by a single hope.

Epictetus

Whoever invented Prince Charming had no idea how far he would go. Romance — the stuff that dreams are made of, and also nightmares. Romance, the incurable disease, the reason for being alive, the reason for wanting to die. Romance, the expectation beyond all hope, yes, it's the romance of your life until it ends!

So what is *this love* that sneaks its way into your dreams and aspirations? Is it your ego tricking you, or a real link to your true self? And when it no longer works, how do you break the ties?

Treating the romantic blues is not that easy. You wish you could pretend that you love butterfly watching, or crystal reading, or celestial navigation more than Prince Charming, but you don't! So what do you do then — find another lover and just go off for a weekend, somewhere in the Caribbean? Well that might be your first reaction, but once you come back, you'll just have to start all over again. So what can you really do?

At first you're too weak from the wounds to feel anything, but then a lot of emotions come to surface. Anger is mixed with pride. Jealousy is mixed with revenge. You'd like to forgive and forget, but all you do is remember. Suddenly you are living with all the clichés of pettiness. They are taking over your life, leaving you totally confused. And figuring it out doesn't help at all, because no matter how much you rationalize, it will never seem fair. So stop torturing yourself! Transitions are hard for everyone.

Sure, once you were used to having two bowls of cereal on your breakfast table, two pillows to sit upon, two robes instead of one hanging in the closet. So now, instead of two of everything, there is suddenly one. One bowl of yogurt, one glass of juice, one pillow, and one you walking around in a space that used to fill two. But, don't worry, you'll get used to it. Just put the other half away, and realize that in doing this, you are going to be fulfilled in a new way. You will be surprised at how soon you will get used to the silence, to the extra space, to that *room of one's own*.

The best cure for treating a broken romance is the realization that you are no longer afraid to be alone, and while you're recuperating, a lot of interesting things can happen. Like you can discover that you are more than just capable of surviving without your partner, you are even better off!

It's always a shock to realize that all along Prince Charming was just a giant roadblock, a detour to your own creative completion and happiness. It was Plato who once said: ''We are trying our whole lives long to find that other half of ourselves.'' And that's okay, if you know where to look!

FRANCES STELOFF

''I choose to be single. I am almost ninety, and I've lived alone on this planet most of those years... I couldn't be complete if I always had to think about another person I was responsible for... Being alone is my greatest need. I think that being alone is not only not selfish, but I believe it's our responsibility — because when you are alone that's the only time you can communicate with the invisible. I know that it's the invisible plane that matters more than this effect plane. *The invisible plane is where all the action is!* Reflection is important. One needs to reflect upon one's experiences in solitude. I don't know how anyone can go on without a nervous breakdown, if they don't have time to be alone. Maybe marriage is okay for others, but for me, being single has been the ultimate path to freedom. Most people who are too busy reaching out never fulfil any promise, because they never follow one thing through... *You need solitude if you are to fulfil your promises.*''

JOAN FONTAINE

''One thing I know now is, that I don't think I could ever again live with anybody. I think that's the trouble with marriage. You live too closely and you never get to be alone. You sleep in the same bed. You probably share the same room anyhow, and if you don't then there's some sort of crisis going on. You never get to be alone...

When I was married, I was never more lonely!''

Chicken Little ... The Sky Isn't Falling In!

Giving your first dinner party for one, is kind of like beginning a love affair with solitude in the kitchen. You have to eat anyway, so you might as well enjoy it. Forget about auditioning for wife and all that. Cooking just for yourself is a great way to forget the blues and to discover a whole new universe, one that lives inside of you, one you never met before, because you were too busy meeting Prince Charming.

Now you can make room for new fantasies and dreams. What's stirring inside your heart can start to stir some place else. It's your turn to stir up a whole new fairy tale. Imagination invents ingredients missing from the refrigerator. Pour Prince Charming out or put him on hold. It's okay as long as you're having fun.

Make Friends With Your Wok

The wok, which originated in the Orient to feed large families, is just as important an invention for the solitary chef. You can throw everything into it, and end up with a feast for ten, and if you're not that hungry, it's perfect for one... The wok itself is a metal pan shaped like a giant bowl. It's the one utensil which lets you create practically anything. Its design is suitable for deep-frying, stir-frying, steaming and sautéing. For stir-frying and sautéing, it has several advantages over a flat-bottomed skillet, since it allows the ingredients to have maximum contact with the bottom of the pan, creating crispy food in minimum time. After trying my first wok experiments, I wondered how I ever lived without it.

Befriend it properly from the beginning by taking good care of it, and the wok will never fail you...*

---

* I recommend using only the classic carbonated steel wok. So-called up-dated versions are teflonized.

Overtone Cooking and Your Wok

Overtone cooking is mixing very subtle ingredients by adding them layer by layer to your wok. It is very much like the Tibetan overtone chanting. They use one note on the scale, like *do* or *re* and out of it they can create hundreds of variations and nuances. Overtone cooking lets you choose a few basic flavors, and then you combine them in interesting ways. You can mix strange and wonderful things like papaya and garlic, or nutmeg and tamari. Sweet and sour, bitter and sweet, you put the unexpected together, and end up with a very refined taste that keeps surprising your taste buds as they detect each one layer by layer.

Overtone cooking allows you to make the most interesting sauces. When stir-frying your vegetables, or chicken, you add these delights one by one until it totally pleases you. If you plan to use onions or garlic remember to chop them in advance. The whole idea of stir frying is to do it fast. It only takes 2 to 3 minutes for some dishes to emerge so have all your herbs and seasonings handy in small bowls ready to add to your creation.

Garlic and Peppermint Sauce

Garlic and fresh peppermint are fantastic together... Add a few cloves of minced garlic, a few fresh peppermint leaves, a bit of tamari sauce, and a bit of tahini-sesame butter, to your bowl. Mix well, and then add some pine nuts... You can mix all of this together in a bowl, or mix it into your wok as you stir fry... Fresh basil, a variety of mint, can also be used instead of the peppermint.

Papaya and Lemon Grass

Papaya mixed with lemon grass makes a wonderful sauce for zucchini or chicken filets... Take the contents of one papaya and mix with one tablespoon coconut, one teaspoon nutmeg, and one tablespoon lemon grass. Hold in reserve bowl. Stir-fry one small chopped zucchini, along with your chicken filets, then add the sauce ingredients for about five minutes and stir for a couple of moments...

And another instant sauce great for eggplant... one apple, ten seedless red grapes, seven walnuts, two cloves garlic, and sage... To eggplant, add apple and grapes, garlic and sage — stir-fry for three minutes then add walnuts and stir another minute.

Treat yourself like company...
Get your wok and cook up some chicken

Chicken is one of the easiest dishes to prepare, and also one of the most sophisticated. All you need is a little imagination, some chicken filets, and your wok does the rest. You can create a gourmet feast for one in less than ten minutes... And when you are in the mood to spend a little more time, you can marinate the filets overnight, so they will be on reserve for when you feel like making a great dish like Chicken Tempura.

Marinating is easy... Just cut up lots of juicy pieces of tender white chicken filets, into perfect bite-size pieces that are easy to pick up with chopsticks or fingers... For two pounds of chicken filets, all you need is half a cup of yogurt, and fresh juice of half a lime... The yogurt should cover the chicken so it looks like there was a light snowfall. A few hours in the refrigerator will do the trick, but marinating overnight is even better.

Chicken Tempura with Fresh Basil

⅓ cup whole wheat flour
1 egg
1 cup of chopped fresh parsley
  and fresh basil

1 small onion, chopped
½ lb marinated chicken filets
a few drops of tamari sauce

Take a large bowl and add ⅓ cup whole wheat flour, and beat one egg into it... Chop up parsley, fresh basil and a small onion. Add some sesame seed oil to the wok, and then sauté the parsley, basil and onion for half a minute. Dip the chicken pieces into the batter until they are covered evenly on both sides. Add them one by one turning them over several times until they become crispy and beautiful like something much better than southern fried chicken or tempura... Then add some tamari sauce, cover the wok, and let this steam for a few moments...

When you are ready to feast upon this incredible chicken, take out your favorite solitude bowl, add some sliced cucumbers and some more fresh basil. Then add the chicken pieces. You can top it with a touch of tahini, or a bit of fresh lime juice... Either way it is great.

He who humbles himself shall be made complete.
He who empties himself shall be made full.

The Simple Way of Lao Tsu

Lemon Grass Chicken

sesame oil	a touch of lemon
½ lb chicken breast filets	1 tspn. cumin seeds, or
7 mushrooms	1 tbspn. pine nuts
6 sprigs fresh parsley	2 tbspns. yogurt
1 tbspn. lemon grass	

Pour enough oil into the wok to just cover the bottom. Slice the filets, the mushrooms, and parsley. Instead of parsley, you can try Chinese parsley, which is fresh coriander, a very sweet tasting variety. Heat the wok for a moment, then add all the ingredients except the yogurt. Stir fry for a few minutes until the chicken turns very white. Then add the yogurt, and more lemon juice. Stir again for a minute, and you have a wok feast for one that takes less than 10 minutes to create...

Let him not be another's who can be his own.

Paracelsus

Sautéed Gingered Chicken

1 medium size red pepper	walnut oil
1 small Bermuda onion	¾ lb filet chicken breasts
3 mushrooms	a few sprigs fresh fennel
a few sprigs fresh parsley	1 tbspn. fresh ginger

Slice the red pepper, the onion, the mushrooms and parsley into tiny pieces. Add oil to wok, let heat for a moment, then add the parsley, let sauté for a second, then add the chicken breasts, let them sauté on a low flame for about 5 to 10 minutes. Then add the red pepper, onion, fennel (the top grassy part), the mushrooms, and finely chopped ginger. Stir them into the oil, and spoon this over the chicken. Then turn the filets over, and let heat on low flame about 5 more minutes, spooning the sauce over it... Wait until chicken turns a crispy brown color, and SERVE...

Cooking is a very relaxing way to spend an evening, and when the inspiration moves you, you can be both imaginative and practical. Baking chicken with vegetables is a good way to prepare leftovers in advance. You can enjoy a meal tonight, with the promise of lots of tasty leftovers for the days to come. The following recipe can serve four hearty meals.

Chicken Marsala and a Pot

2 carrots   ¼ cup butter
4 small potatoes   8 sprigs parsley
4 small onions   lemon grass, a few pinches
5 cloves garlic   1 tspn. basil
2 stalks celery   1 tspn. tarragon
4 large chicken breasts   ½ cup marsala wine
            one earthenware terra-cotta pot

Make sure you soak the terra-cotta pot first, about 15 minutes. This allows it to breathe, and helps to maintain the moisture inside, letting all the natural juices remain in the chicken. While soaking it, preheat the oven to 375°. Then peel all the vegetables and garlic, and slice them. Dry pot, then add the chicken and butter. Set in oven until butter has melted. Then add the vegetables, the herbs, more butter and wine. Let bake for one hour. Turn the chicken over from time to time, spooning marsala sauce over it, making sure it bastes the skin. Take off the cover, and keep off until the potatoes and chicken start to brown, then cover again, and bake another 20–30 minutes. The juices steam the chicken so it is very tender... Let cool, and enjoy!

Chicken with Peach Sauce

1 peach
left-over baked chicken breast*
¼ cup sherry
3 large basil leaves, sliced into tiny pieces

Peel the skin off the peach. Slice it into small pieces. Put the chicken into a small pot, pour the sherry over it, add the peach, and the basil leaves. Put on low flame, cover the pot and let steam for a few minutes. Turn the chicken over once, and stir the peach into the sherry. Make sure there is liquid in the pot, so the chicken doesn't burn. It only takes a few minutes to heat the chicken, and let the peach become a wonderful sauce. It has the same texture as duck with orange sauce, only it tastes more refined in my opinion.

...and a final word for the broken hearted:

When you have lost anything external, have always at hand the consideration of what you got instead of it.

Epictetus

---

* See recipe for Chicken Marsala And A Pot.

What To Do When You Don't Know What To Do!

You're sitting around tonight feeling sorry for yourself, or maybe if you're lucky, you're not feeling anything, and that makes you feel more depressed. Nothing is on television, there is no one to call, you don't feel like finishing the work you brought home from the office, and you still think Prince Charming has the lock and key to your heart, and that you can't get in without him... So what can you do?

Start by doing something right now! Do anything! Start dusting your old records. Start polishing your stainless steel; pretend it's silver. Start cleaning out your refrigerator. When was the last time you defrosted it? Or why not open all your drawers. When was the last time you looked inside? Maybe there's nothing in them, or maybe there is too much. This is the time to clean out, or fill up!

If you don't feel like hanging around, get out of the house! Take a train ride to the end of the line, and come back. Or go to a really wonderful gourmet shop and treat yourself to something you wouldn't normally dare to buy. You deserve it... Why not buy a garlic press, and a garlic braid. They say hanging garlic in your kitchen drives away all the demons and now you can use all the help you can get!

When you get home, take a nice long warm bath. Pour in a small box of baking soda (it's good for your skin). Put on some soothing music and just take it easy. Keep telling yourself you are not the only person in the whole wide world who is feeling so alone, who thinks nobody loves you, who has to go through this process called life... And last but not least, you can start to think about what Frances Steloff once called "planning a couple of miracles."

Be Realistic ... Plan A Miracle

A small piece of paper with a large message was tacked on the wall above Frances Steloff's desk in the Gotham Book Mart. Amidst all her wonderful clutter of books, letters esoteric announcements, and cat food, this sign stood out: it said *"Be realistic, plan a miracle."* It made me laugh, but it's really quite serious. It's all about how you can consciously create your own circumstances. It's how you can transform your thoughts today. And today is when you begin to change tomorrow by letting go of yesterday.

Here is one simple way you can plan a miracle...

In the morning, spend a few minutes thinking about what it is you doubt the most, which is usually everything that is against your miracle. Then write these thoughts down on a piece of paper. It might be something like, "I doubt I'll ever be a parent," or "I'm afraid that I'll never find the right mate," or "I don't think that I'll ever get my promotion at work." Pick the fears that bother you the most. Be very specific at first, but then after writing down the concrete things you doubt, consider the underlying larger reasons behind them.

Once you've made your list, put it away. Forget about it. Then during the day start thinking about where you really want to be, how you want to be, and how you are going to be in all these places at once. Imagine the kind of setting, the atmosphere, the circumstances. See yourself as President, or Queen if that makes you happy. See yourself as having and feeling and touching everything you deserve, even if you don't think you do. Really picture yourself in this new and positive frame.

The whole trick of this exercise is *creative visualization*. It is not enough to just write down your desires, you must constantly hold the image in your mind, as often as you remember. As you know, imagination can be both friend and foe. So feeding your mind with good thoughts is the first step toward performing any outward miracle. And creating confident images in your mind and truly believing in them is a tiny miracle in itself.

Imagination was probably your greatest playmate when you were a child. And then you had to 'grow up'. You forgot how wonderful your imagination could be. You left behind all your childish games, but imagination is just as important for an adult. Only there is a big difference between 'making-believe' and 'making beliefs'. By consciously creating circumstances you are actually making beliefs that really manifest in the real world. And this is all through the route of *images* in your *imagination*.

In order to create the vision you wish to hold, keep drawing yourself the picture of where you want to be. Open your heart to your true desires. Let it come bit by bit, until you have a really clear image. Then keep seeing yourself in this picture. See yourself at the beach, if that is where you'd like to be, see yourself walking on the sand. Keep seeing yourself doing what it is you want to do, and believe in it. And if it's something that is truly possible, it will happen. It's amazing how many people have created the circumstances they love the most, simply by believing in their power of positive thinking.

So, during the day, keep visualizing, and when you come home, write down all your hopes and dreams, no matter how grandiose they seem. Write down the circumstances you want to create for yourself, and then put it away.

Then before going to bed, pick up the list from the morning, and if you still feel like it, look it over. But do so with calm dispassion, telling yourself this list belongs to someone else. It is no longer yours.

When you are ready — right now, tomorrow, or next week, whenever — you will rip it up and throw it out, along with all those doubts in your mind. Read your new list and keep telling yourself. It belongs to me. Keep creating those new images in your mind, affirming your innermost desires, and watch your miracle grow. Someone once said, the three most powerful affirmations in the world are: I AM... I CAN... I WILL... and that takes care of everything. So be realistic... plan a miracle!

The basis of all healing is a change in belief.

Thomas Troward

Laughter Power

To laugh is better than to pray.

Swami Vivekananda

Sometimes when I'm lucky I start laughing for no reason at all. And the more I laugh, the better I feel. Everything I was worried about is suddenly very funny. Losing your ego can be very funny, especially when you really lose it. When you have nothing more to lose, then you know you've won! Swami Vivekananda was right when he said *to laugh is better than to pray.* And you really know that when you feel the power of laughter putting you all together again.

Of course it isn't funny to feel broken-hearted, but taking yourself too seriously can become a real disease. And that's when laughter power really works. It may be the best cure for treating the romantic blues, as well as everything else.

During one of my stormier times, I had a wonderful dream that told me it was time to stop taking it all so seriously... In this dream, everyone dressed like everyone else. Gold and silver stars adorned their heads. Silken robes covered with diamonds and rubies and pearls sparkled in the shadows of the night. And they moved about in their glittery world as if they were choreographed by some strange force that left nothing to chance. They were all wearing the same expression, an expression of no-expression. And attached to the two corners of their mouths were tiny gold rings anchored by a silver post. This gave them room to open their mouth just enough to eat and talk. But if anyone tried to smile, they got an instant shock.

At this point in the dream, I woke up and even though I never found out what happened to those people, I knew it was time for me to remove all my rings once and for all. It was time to laugh, time to truly feel the power of laughter. So if you're feeling sorry for yourself, try it, what can you lose? Start laughing and you'll feel its power. It's like a stream of healing energy circulating within every pore of your body. Laughter is truly the gift of letting go.

Who am I?
Why am I who I am?
When am I why I am who am I?
How am I when I am why I am who I am?
What am I how I am when I am why I am who am I?
Where was I, when who am I asked?

Ways To Avoid Being Alone!

TOM WOLFE

"I used to buy an awful lot of clothes. I used to have a lot of suits made while I was writing, because it was a way of just getting away! Getting a suit made is something that involves about five trips to the tailor. And each one takes about a couple of hours, and you talk about it, and you look at all these different materials, and you feel terrific about yourself as you're getting a suit. After all, food, shelter, and clothing are essential to life. In a way clothes are an antidote to solitude. It makes you think you're not alone. It helps you overcome this sort of loneliness.

Some people sharpen their pencils all day, or they go to the store, and they look around. Everyone has a certain way to avoid being alone. But, one of the great things that now has become a part in people's solitude is desk calculators. It's true for me, and also I bet for a lot of other people, particularly writers... Using a desk calculator is like having a suit made, in that you think you're doing something useful. In fact, the desk calculator is one of the greatest time wasters of all times. You can do all these things with it. It has a memory, and it has square roots in it and everything. You can add up columns of figures, like your bills, and your possible income, particularly if you're a freelance writer. And this gives you something to do.''

Saturday Dinner Solitude

I believe in marriage ... that's why I stay single!

Music: EARL HINES plays DUKE ELLINGTON
The Dinner: *Gingered Salmon*
               Asparagus and Basil
               Watercress and Greek Olive Salad

Gingered Salmon

garlic clove	Greek olives
fresh ginger	a few sprigs of fresh basil
½ lb filet of salmon	lemon juice
asparagus spears	tamari sauce
lemon grass	safflower mayonnaise
8 sprigs of watercress	

Cut the garlic clove and ginger into tiny pieces and tuck these bits into the salmon filet. Use a vegetable steamer to steam the salmon, arranging the filet and asparagus on the steamer. Add a few sprinkles of lemon grass on the salmon. Steam 5 to 10 minutes. Arrange watercress and olives on plate with the salmon and asparagus. Add basil, lemon juice, tamari and mayo to fish, the amount is your choice. It's always your choice... isn't it?

...It's taken me twenty years to learn what to leave out!...

Earl Hines commenting on his piano playing technique

Unplanned Dinners!

What do you do when you've been stood up? Or when some misfortune has befallen your friend, like he or she forgot! Unplanned dinners require certain stand-by ingredients which create nourishing and tasty dinners. The list includes lots of grains, nuts, seeds, fresh vegetables, jars of favorite herbs, lemon, and a few exotic extras like dried chestnuts, and don't forget... humor.

Here is a great stand-by feast:

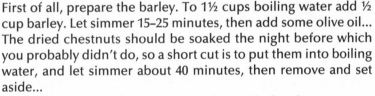

Barley and Chestnuts, Stir-fried Vegetables and Steamed Asparagus

½ cup barley	1 garlic clove
1 tsp. olive oil	7 asparagus stalks
7 dried chestnuts	tamari sauce
1 zucchini	lemon
1 Italian eggplant	sage
4 mushrooms	tarragon
3 fresh okra	fennel seeds

First of all, prepare the barley. To 1½ cups boiling water add ½ cup barley. Let simmer 15–25 minutes, then add some olive oil... The dried chestnuts should be soaked the night before which you probably didn't do, so a short cut is to put them into boiling water, and let simmer about 40 minutes, then remove and set aside...

If you're not in the mood to bother with the chestnuts you can substitute a couple of chopped walnuts instead. Next slice the zucchini, the eggplant (baby eggplant is perfect for one), the mushrooms and the okra. Chop the garlic clove, or cloves if you like it that way. Put asparagus in steamer and put aside. Add olive oil to wok, flame it, and throw in all the vegetables, stir frying a minute or so. Add the garlic, herbs, and tamari to taste. Cover and let simmer... Now turn on asparagus steamer for five to ten minutes. Put the barley into a bowl, add the chestnuts or walnuts, then the vegetables. Arrange asparagus on plate, add lemon. You're now ready for the most wonderful feast for one...

...the return of your absent friend, or some other favorable event raises your spirits, and you think good days are preparing for you. Do not believe it. Nothing can bring you peace but yourself. Nothing can bring you peace but the triumph of principles.

Ralph Waldo Emerson, *Self-Reliance*

Casseroles To Come Home To For Unexpected Company ... Like Yourself!

...A Gallup poll has discovered 30% of the people aren't at home, 50% of them are pretending they aren't home, and 20% of them don't have front doors...

Baked Flounder

2 carrots	3 lbs. flounder filets
3 celery stalks	1 bunch coriander
kelp	sesame seeds
lemon grass	7 whole cloves
basil	2 scallions
sesame seed oil	3 garlic cloves

Dice carrots and celery very fine and place in a large Pyrex baking dish. Add a sprinkle of kelp, enough lemon grass to lightly cover vegetables, a touch of basil and two tablespoons sesame seed oil. Mix well. Bake at 350° for 25 minutes. Remove and add fish filets, chopped coriander, a tablespoon sesame seeds, the cloves, chopped scallions, and garlic. Add a few more drops oil, and then return dish to oven and bake for another 25 minutes...

If you really get stuck, remember what Frances Steloff said, a handful of almonds provides the same amount of protein as a pound of steak... That with a few sprouts might just be it for tonight...

The Sunrise Special

2 oranges	1 or 2 tbspns. sesame seeds
1 lemon (or lime)	honey (as much as you like)
4 strawberries	a few drops 'rescue remedy'
	(Bach Flower Essences)

Squeeze the oranges and lemon, pour the juice into your blender, then add the strawberries, seeds and honey. Put the blender on chop for a few moments, then switch to blend and wait a few more moments until it all turns a creamy pastel color... Then add the flower essence drops; you may need them!

Are you prepared to give up all 'those deep involvements' without commitment?

Don't think about this one now. Drink your *sunrise special*... Wait awhile. Take a walk. Then if you feel like answering to yourself, this is the time.

The comic strip character Charlie Brown goes to his mailbox and it is empty. No Christmas cards yet... "I know that nobody likes me," he says, "but why do we have to have a holiday season to emphasize it." Charlie Brown can get away with making us laugh at this, because he is the hero for all losers, and we love him for this very reason. Of course, for people who aren't single by choice, holidays alone may not be a laughing matter. Single people everywhere are mesmerized by the message that insists it is weird if you are not getting together, be it with family, friends, lovers, or anyone else who needs to get together. "*Tis the season to be merry and not be alone,*" so the musak demands! Even if you want to be alone, there is no escape. There is something about all the fanfare that can overdose you with pressure, if you let it. No wonder a lot of people end up with abnormal cravings for company and SUGAR!

Now, while there is no instant way to create an atmosphere of love, you can concoct a delicious holiday sauce. Maybe once you've doused your heart in this sweet sauce you'll be able to face this holiday on your own terms, without thinking about all the 'good times' you spent with someone else. Stop comparing, judging and deciding which way was better. Remember — this is your moment, and it belongs to you.

Holiday Sweet Sauce ... For Anything!

You can eat this sauce by itself, or put it on ice cream, fruit cake, and anything else you find in your cupboard!

1 pear	1 tbspn. honey
10 almonds (crushed)	1 tspn. nutmeg
2 tbspns. butter	¼ cup milk
2 tbspns. maple syrup	¼ cup raisins

Cut the pear into small slices. Crush the almonds with a garlic press, melt the butter in your pot, then add the pears, the maple syrup, the honey and the nutmeg. Let heat gently for a few minutes. Then add the milk, the raisins, and the almonds. Stir and stir until it all blends nicely together. Then let heat on low flame a minute or so... Make sure the milk doesn't curdle. The whole process takes five to ten minutes. The pears will be covered with nutmeg, resembling something in between a sauce and their original form. Of course you could always just eat the pear, but it isn't as much fun...

A formula is enslavement, a principle freedom.

Mary Crovatt Hambidge,
Apprentice in Creation,
The Way is Beauty

Comforters

There are many comforting ways of being alone that let you forget your loneliness and enhance your sense of solitude. And for the solitary at heart, these comforters are especially important.

How would you like to curl up and be inside your favorite comforter?

Between The Covers
The Personal Diary

You never know who you're going to meet,
You never know who you're going to meet!

Lyrics from an Old English tune

Diary keeping may be one of the most important solitary activities, and for the single person it is an indispensable companion. The diary is a wonderful comforter, and who you meet between the covers is always up to you! It's often fascinating how many strangers are hidden within you, and keeping a diary is a good way of uncovering them.

The journal and the single person enjoy a unique relationship. The single person has the advantage of having more private time. He or she does not have to worry about keeping a lock and key on the pad, nor sneaking in time between other activities. Always present, the diary takes on a special quality as it grows with you.

Many creative people say the diary is their dearest friend. As one single woman said, ''It's my only friend, I wouldn't know how to live without it!'' Of course it's great to be friends with people, but when you live alone it's comforting to know that wherever you are, you can always come home to your diary.

The diary of course, is more than just a friend. It is healer, integrator, mother, father, sister, brother, teacher, analyst, confidant supreme... Very few companions are as understanding as your diary. You can chat with it, cry with it, analyze with it, and sometimes just be with it. You can talk to it after dinner, tell it your dreams in the morning, and it always pays attention.

Sometimes a diary is like a collection of snapshots taken quite spontaneously. Entries are reflections of moods of the moment. Some are serious, some are trivial, some romantic, and sometimes there is

a fine line between what is sentimental and what is sacred. Sometimes it seems the camera has captured the experience of no experience. You wonder if anything really happened that day.

Diaries can also be very embarrassing. There are all those complaints, all that unleashed anger running wild. Emotional drainage, that is what it is, the sort of pages one is tempted to rip up. But they are also you, or were you the moment you wrote them. And when you look back at all these still photos, you appreciate how each and every isolated event fits into the whole pattern, for this is what makes you and your life what it is. The whole process is interwoven stitch by stitch, and you are both the weaver and that which is woven.

In using your diary every day, you will learn to strip down to solitude. Here you can dive deeply into yourself without drowning, for the diary accepts you for who you are. It loves you even when you fail. Remember that this is only for you. It isn't something you'd want to show to even your most intimate friend. So anything goes! Here is the perfect opportunity to stop monitoring yourself, so you really get to meet those strangers in you. Don't be afraid to be honest and blurt out what you mean, without being polite. This is an opportunity to say something for yourself. If you are honest about your feelings and ideas, or even your inability to express yourself, this will all make sense later when you look back.

One of the most rewarding parts of keeping a diary is how it keeps you company later on. It can give you incredible feedback. Gene Roddenberry, the creator of *Star Trek*, once said, ''As a traveler, we are here to experience, not to judge.'' Like a ship's log, your diary keeps track of the journey and can provide you with all the real ingredients of your life. But how you digest them is what makes the difference. Did you learn something from that experience? Are you repeating the same mistakes? Can you detect your own cycles of loneliness, as well as creativity? The feedback of the diary is probably the most honest opinion you will ever get about yourself.

Another benefit of the diary: it is an excellent escape from boredom. Without planning to, I may open an old diary, flip through the pages feeling tired and uninspired, and there it is, right before me — advice on how to concentrate. Or an experience recorded that shows me that I am not as dull as I thought I was. My mood is transformed and I feel a new burst of energy.

I am grateful for all the spiral notebooks that sit silently in their place. When I need to talk to them, they listen. When I need to listen, they talk to me!

FOR STARTERS
Here are a few guidelines for beginning your first journal, as well as some suggestions for expanding as you go along:

WHAT YOU NEED
The old fashioned method for journal keeping requires only a spiral notebook and a pen. Some people prefer pencils, but then make sure to write hard, if you want to see it later on. There is no standard rule of what kind of notebook to use, as long as you like it and feel comfortable about using it. You may prefer a small pocket-size to take around with you, and then you might choose another size and type to record your dreams. I find it useful to stick to the same size and color for different sections. So dreams could be a yellow spiral notebook, your daily journal a grey composition book, and so on...

TAPE RECORDING
Tape recording your diary is another method, or you can do this along with keeping a written record. These tapes are a good way to sort out emotions and thoughts.

I used to call these the 'lonely tapes,' when I began using them. I was half laughing and half crying when I labelled my first tape the lonely tape. That was definitely an emotional drainage session. It was too late to call anyone, too late to go outside, and too early for me to completely crack up, so I just talked into the tape recorder, and told it all my problems. By the time the tape stopped, I almost forgot why I was upset.

Who else but the diary, except for a few saints here and there, or paid professionals, could listen to you like this for hours and hours on end without interruption. These tapes are the perfect place to scream, complain, and just let it all out. Later on, when you've cooled down, you can listen to them and decide if you really need to keep it on record. Nine times out of ten you will not keep it, which is good, because then you can reuse the tape. And if you do decide to keep it, don't forget to record date and time.

EXPANDING YOUR DIARY
Keeping your diary for special purposes such as a meditation log/dream log/or I Ching log can be very helpful. Here are a few tips:

The diary as *Meditation Log*:
This could be a place where you can focus your thoughts, a way to let the affirmations sink into your brain. Here is where you can create your own personal affirmations. *Yes-thoughts* love to live here...

After meditating, you may be inspired to write down your

feelings. Be sure to log the time, date and circumstance of your meditation. For example, maybe you just had a fight, or a loneliness attack, so you sat down to simmer down; include this along with the date. Or maybe after meditating, you don't feel like writing. Fine. Then just don't write, leave the page empty, for that too will tell you something later on.

This is also a good way to transmit healing thoughts to others... If you let your heart guide the pen and truly believe what you write as you're writing it, then you can extend your prayers. This is a wonderful way to radiate your love.

The diary as *Dream Log*:
A place to both record and analyze dreams. Dreams make wonderful material for creative projects. They will remind you to do something you forgot, and help you to forget those things you don't want to remember. They are most important for integrating your life. They are the link between your emotions, imagination and intuition. They keep your right brain busy at night, and they deserve a place in one of your diaries.

The dream log can also be used as feedback later on. You can meditate on the dream, and then analyze from that point. But you also may prefer not to analyze the dream, and that's okay. Just record it and get it out of your system. Just remembering your dreams and writing them down is beneficial in itself. (See Dreams As Healer/ Right Brain Recipes).

The diary as *I Ching Log*:
If you spend time with the I Ching, (See Spend an Evening With The I Ching) then you will definitely need a separate journal for these occasions. I used to keep slips of paper in my I Ching, with all the hexagrams and readings that I got... After a few years my book was like an overstuffed sandwich. So I started to keep a separate notebook for all the future I Ching readings.

Be sure to record the circumstances that lead you to ask the question, as well as the question. You may find yourself writing down several questions before you arrive at the right question, but then you will discover what it is you need to know. After you ask your question and get your hexagram, be sure to record the name of the hexagram and its number. If you get special readings, you may want to write down the highlights of what they said to you as well as your afterthoughts... The I Ching log can give you very wise feedback later on. It has been a valuable resource for me on both the creative and spiritual levels, which ultimately become one.

I just want to tuck myself in, and hold onto all my dreams.

Blessed are your eyes Tea

1 part fennel
1 part eyebright
1 part lavender

One of my favorite bedtime teas is the following concoction: One teaspoon fennel, one teaspoon eyebright and one teaspoon lavender. I add three cups boiling water and let it steep fifteen minutes... The lavender gives this the sweetest aroma. It is lavender after all...

This is a real comforter in every way. It is a nervine herbal preparation, which means it soothes all your tensions. It is great for headaches, and the eyebright is exactly that, great for the eyes... Fennel clears your sight, which means pleasant dreams ahead!

Comfrey is a Real Comforter

1 teaspoon comfrey root
1 cup boiling water
steep for five minutes

Did you know that comfrey means to grow together? That's why its roots make a wonderful tea to help heal internal wounds, colds, and all other respiratory problems. It helps you to breathe better, and calms you down. It's wonderful to sip at night.

Bedside Moods

To your dragons of desire you say...
Get out of the way, get out of the way!
And then the fairy of the dawn appears.

The Violet Fairy Book

Fairy tales reach us in a very special way. Their stories sweep through the corners of our deepest psyche, and suddenly we are aware of feelings that never touched us before... Through these adventures of the spirit we recognize all the characters and forces that live inside of us. And as we go through all the trials and victories of our favorite heroes and heroines, we become the villain, the victim, the saviour. We share all the strengths and weaknesses of each and every character. If they can make it, we know we can make it, for deep within all of us is that stuff of creative courage to transform the worst monster into something good.

There's something about reading a fairy tale that lets us overcome our deepest fears. We laugh as we say, "Get out of the way, get out of the way!" and when the dragons of desire disappear, we truly believe in the power of the fairy of the dawn to appear. All the miracles become our healing.

In fairy tales, transformations are instantaneous, magic moments where out of nothing something incredibly beautiful happens. It is like a fast forwarding film that touches the essence of how life really works on all levels. Out of scattered fragments whole universes appear. A magic ring thrown behind is taken by the western wind and turned into a forest. A little flame from a firefly turns into a galaxy of stars. A whole mountain of troubles becomes a solitary stone, barely perceptible. The child within is overcome with joy and awe. For a precious moment we believe that this is the real way that things happen.

Fairy tales are wonderful healers. They bring us to another level, where we are taken into a newer and fresher sense. Their tales spark the fire of our intuition, embrace our dreams, and truly feed our heart with food from another realm.

Reading one good story before going to bed, can often do more to heal than ten years of analysis. So treat yourself to a good fairy tale. It will give your imagination a lot to dream about... Sleep on it, dream on it, then the next day reflect on it, and see what's inside your heart...*

---

* The entire list of *Dover Fairy Tale Books* is wonderful. I especially recommend the "rainbow" collection edited by Andrew Lang which includes, *The Violet Fairy Book* and *The Lilac Fairy Book*.

SOLITUDE

I have a house where I go.
When there's too many people.
I have a house where I go
Where no one can be;
I have a house where I go,
Where nobody ever says 'NO'
Where no one says anything — so
There is no one but me.

A.A. Milne, *Now We Are Six*,

Solitude Moments

S ome people have the wonderful ability to play alone with the same dedication that they give to their creative work. They know when it's time to take that long-needed pause that allows them to appreciate and enjoy all the little gifts of life. For them the secret of successful solitude is in the tasting. These are the moments that enhance their creative work. These are those moments that are just for them and them alone. It's their way to be spontaneous, to unwind, to be alone for no reason at all. Some prefer to just sit and reflect, some have a secret spot where they enjoy the beauty and challenge of nature, and others do some rather odd things that only they understand.

DIANA VREELAND

"I think that around five in the afternoon, everybody should just stop whatever they are doing and sip some water. We all should have some... You know to be dehydrated is really the trouble with most people. It isn't jet-lag or alcohol. I drink at least eight glasses a day. I think it's absolutely essential. I only use bottled mineral or spring water. I never drink tap water. I don't think it's very delicious. Also I never put ice into it. The reason why most people don't drink water is because it's too cold to get down. Sometimes people ask for water at parties, then they put three cubes of ice into it, and only touch the surface of it. It's just too cold to drink. I like my water at room temperature, nothing too hot, nothing too cold. So I keep all my bottles of mineral water in the living room, instead of in the refrigerator.

I'm very keen on water. I believe it's God's tranquilizer. It soothes me and nourishes me on all levels. To be in water, to watch water, and to drink water are the three most attractive things that you can do. And of course, rain I adore. As I say, it's God's tranquilizer. If you think about it, you will realize it's true. Imagine it: you are in the water or you are drinking it. Think how refreshing it is. Don't forget, we're made of water, eighty per cent, that's extraordinary, that amount. Of course, to be immersed in water is the greatest. To be a great surfer or a great swimmer must be a marvelous experience.

When I go to California, I go out on the beach, and I watch the surfers, and it's literally black when I come in. I mean I can hardly find my way over the dunes to where the car is. I am just as spellbound as they are. I understand the elixir that surfing really is. It's fascinating. I wish that I had been a surfer. The whole universe is together in one rhythm. The sky, the sea and you. It's absolutely ideal.''

Andy Warhol

''I had one dachshund and it got lonely so I got another one as a Christmas present for it, and now they both keep me company. And you know how it is with dogs, you have to walk them all the time. So maybe dogs are the answer... have two dogs and walk them, and you're in solitude.''

Bibi Andersson

''I decorate my house a lot when I'm alone. I love to change things around and play with different kinds of arrangements. I'm not excessive about it, but I do it more than I really need to, because it's a way I can relax and be creative when I'm alone. This is for me and me alone. It's the sort of creative thing I like to do and not even discuss with other people. I don't like to compromise. I really love to do this when I'm alone, whereas cooking is something I do for others. In a way it's like decorating yourself. Some people like clothes. I like aesthetic things, so I dress up my homes.

I never had a home of my own. I went from my mother's house to live with Ingmar Bergman. When we lived together, his tastes took over. Then when I got my first apartment on my own at the age of twenty-four, I had to discover my own tastes. I painted it, and fixed it and decorated it, and it was very girlish, terribly innocent. Since then, decorating has become a way for me to discover my own tastes and likes. And when I discovered myself, I wondered how I could be so innocent and girlish. Sometimes I feel like a little girl with good taste.''

PAOLO SOLERI

''I always have the company of music, and that is a company I like very much. This includes the company of people who have written music too. You can be in the company not only of people who are alive, but you can also be in the company of people who are not living. They are alive through their art. I love all the classical music, and I love Wagner, especially *The Ring*. I used to listen to that over and over again. You could say it was my food for solitude. There is a piece in *De Walküre* that is absolutely superb. It's nice to know that there are people in the universe who can do these things.''

BRITTON CHANCE

''The sea is my food for solitude. There is nothing better than to break away from the land, and go out on the sea with a fair wind and a good sail. I enjoy sailing alone or with my family. It's a marvelous release. I remember one time at Monte Carlo, after a full day of hassle of getting the boat rigged and into the water, it was turning dusk as we sailed out into the sea. And as we tacked through the breakwaters of Monte Carlo, and altered course to a broad reach, it was as if the load of the world had been taken from my mind and spirit... I was alone again! I had found my kind of solitude, an absence of unwanted inputs. There are lots of stimuli that you endure, but don't really want. They are imposed on you. But on the sea, you only have the wind, the waves, the sail and the tiller.

To me, sailing is much more than pleasure. It's a way of life. Being able to sail well, to love it, to understand it, to do it safely and thoughtfully, to be able to go out on the sea when you want to find congeniality with nature, to feel the tide, the wind, the channel. All that is a complex of inputs which is most relaxing. It is my solitude.''

JOSEPH CAMPBELL

''Swimming is a solitary sport for me. It's face down in the water watching the bottom of the pool. I swim forty-four laps in a twenty-five yard pool, eleven hundred yards, about two-thirds of a mile every day. For a young person it wouldn't be anything, but the reason I swim forty-four laps is that there are twenty-two cards in the Tarot pack. And I think about one of them on every two laps.

Tarot cards help me to remember what lap I'm on. When I just concentrated on number one, number two, number three, number four, I found I would miss. I didn't know how many laps I had swum and all that kind of thing. Then I thought: well, there are twenty-two cards in the pack, and I am interested in the Tarot, why not think about them. Then swimming became real fun.

I know each face on every card, so I see the card, and I think what it's all about as I do each lap. I never miss a card because I have to turn around and can't get preoccupied. I guess you could call this a meditation since the Tarot Cards are a spiritual series. I learned a lot from this exercise when I first decided what those cards were about, but now it's just fun. It passes the time, every day twenty-five minutes, while I'm swimming back and forth.''

GREGORY BATESON

''I like to spend my solitude in places where there are a lot of organisms, like beaches or rivers or thick forests. I gently move around in such places using eyes, mainly eyes. For me solitude feeds my visual appetite. It is visually sensual. I'm interested in shapes, forms but not color. You don't see it as well. One of the things you learn as a biologist, is that color is almost invariably insignificant or misleading.

Organisms like the chameleon, hide by hiding their form, and color is the camouflage. It's the paint you put on to break up the form... So you really have to look carefully, beyond the color... I enjoy discovering all sorts of patterns in nature, just looking...''

ROSALYN TURECK

"In order to rekindle my spirit, I always go off by myself into the country. As much as I love cities, I have to get out into the real country. I cannot live without wild natural beauty. I can't think without it. I can't feel without it. It's absolutely essential for me to be close to nature. I love it all. I love the sea, the mountains, as long as it's natural.

I identify with nature and all of life very deeply, so I can just lose myself to the surroundings. Every little insect, and every quiver of a leaf matters to me. At one point in my life, I had a beautiful house in Cambridge with a lake. I sat there one period for three months and just looked. I was able to do that. What I learned from this experience was such an identification with life.

I saw the fish in my lake, but I never caught them. I saw a little insect, not quite the size of a fingernail, with the most gorgeous yellow and black geometric design on his little back. He was walking along as though he owned the universe. You could see he was young, and all life was ahead of him, and he knew everything, and he felt everything. It was perfectly beautiful, I'll never forget him.

Then I saw a Daddy-longlegs, also walking along perfectly happy, and the next afternoon I saw one walking along with a broken leg. I knew the tragedy of that life. I knew how it was suffering and I wasn't anthropomorphizing. I knew what nonsense it is to say certain creatures don't suffer, because they don't have nerves and don't feel. It's absolute nonsense. It's impossible. These are living sentient beings. They are also thinking. There's a level of thinking that goes on, and they are responding to the universe itself. I love to be alone with all these creatures of nature, for they show me how life is so inter-connected."

LEONARD NIMOY

"When I need to be alone, for me it's ten minutes to solitude! I own an airplane and can literally fly away. I can fly away into solitude. At home in California, it's ten minutes from my front door to my airplane, so if I want to fly it's easy. I can be up in the air within ten minutes, flying away to a beach, or a little desert airport somewhere. Then I can really be alone, I am able to hear my thoughts.

Solitude is getting in touch with myself. I settle out. I wash away. I just let the stuff wash away. I like to be alone in a room facing a beach, facing the ocean, which for me symbolizes that washing out of the constant contact realities like conversations, telephone, mail, people. Then if I can tap that residue that is in the center of me, I feel good. I feel solid. I feel complete. I feel in touch. Strangely enough, the more solitude contact I have, that is the more I'm in touch with that center, then the more I feel a sense of well-being about my contact with everything going on around me.

In the character of Spock which I played in *Star Trek*, there is a sense of isolation which is different than solitude. There is a sense of encapsulation, which is the ability to function within an activity, and yet be alone. I do that all the time, but I don't call that solitude. I would have to define that as public solitude... You are actually communicating with people within your own solitude."

GLORIA VANDERBILT

''Early dawn is absolutely the best time for solitude. I like to wake up at five, light the fireplace in my bedroom, put the plug in the electric coffee pot and make myself some instant coffee. Then I open up all the curtains but there is no light in the room except the fireplace.

I can still see the moon from my window. What happens when dawn comes is so extraordinary. Moment by moment the light is changing. It's like going into it, and becoming part of it — in the most extraordinary way — and merging with it in a sense. It's the time when I'm closest to the center of myself. The best ideas come to me then... Everything gets into focus, and into its right place — everything — outer things and inner things. And there's also a wonderful feeling knowing that everybody else in the house is asleep. My children are asleep, and the world is asleep. The light is fascinating then and I really feel like I'm all alone with it...

There's a wonderful Indian poem that says what I'm trying to say... It's called *Salutation to the Dawn* and it's written by the Indian dramatist, Kalidasa:

SALUTATION TO THE DAWN

Look to this day
For it is life, the very life of life
In its brief course
Lie all the verities and realities of your existence:
The bliss of growth
The glory of action
The splendor of beauty
For yesterday is but a dream
And tomorrow is only a vision,
But today well lived
makes every yesterday a dream of happiness
And every tomorrow a vision of hope.
Look well, therefore to this day!
Such is the salutation to the dawn.

Kalidasa

To appreciate the sacredness of solitude, the light and moment, is to be comfortable and accepting of this sacred space... But I haven't always believed that. I didn't always sit with the dawn. It was very difficult for me to really just be, because I had the sense of jam yesterday, jam tomorrow, but never jam today. And therefore, it just took me a long time and really a lot of work to do it.

When I began to sit with the dawn in solitude, I began to really live. It makes one treasure every single moment of life. It's a real search to get to the moment. Getting up with the dawn each morning is my meditation. It's nothing programmed or scheduled in the usual sense, but it really is that for me... Because it is really the deepest kind of communication with oneself... We're all alone, we know that, even with others, forever and ever.''

Sharing Solitude

All things of human wisdom unite.

Emanuel Swedenborg

Love consists in this, that two solitudes
border, protect, and salute each other.

Rainer Maria Rilke

The solitude we share comes from deep within the essence of our center. Some call this our Light, others call it our Spirit, but whatever you call it, it is what connects us to each other. Alone/together, we are interwoven and part of the larger mosaic of life. Sometimes we are strong enough to help a friend, or weak enough to be helped. But who is helping whom isn't as important as the continual chain of giving and caring. In his inspired book, *The Light Within Us*, Albert Schweitzer wrote:

> *I do not believe we can put into anyone ideas which are not in him already. Often too, our own light goes out, and is rekindled by some experience we go through with a fellow man. Thus we have each of us cause to think with deep gratitude of those who have lighted the flames within us.*

From another perspective, perhaps the key to sharing solitude can be found in the two highest commandments given in the Bible, which state: ''First, to love thy God, with all thy heart and all thy might, and all thy soul, and then to love thy neighbor as thyself.'' To share solitude means to be in communion with all of life, but first you must be in communion with yourself. Then you can be in communion with one other person, or even an entire galaxy.

I never asked anyone how they shared solitude. The following responses to this question just flowed naturally during the course of conversation. For ultimately, anyone who has tasted real solitude knows how to share it in his or her own way...

DAVID SPANGLER is one of the few people I've met who can explain how he shares his solitude, because he knows how to be alone with others. He talked about the art of being able to be alone/together. His insights come from the perspective of a mystic, totally grounded in the light, from one who sees God in everyone and everything:

"There is a rhythm to being alone with others, and alone with yourself. Ideally, what I want is the communion that makes both states possible. If I am by myself but I don't have a sense of communion, I am not by myself. My thoughts are reaching out to other people, and solitude becomes something to be endured, rather than enjoyed. That is loneliness.

On the other hand, if I'm with other people and can be with them in their essence, then I am in solitude. So with others I try to move away from their form. It's as if I close my eyes and meditate, so that I'm not distracted by the appearance of things. Then I can get more into the essence. To me the ideal state would be one of inter-communion, where being with people, or being alone are two sides of the same coin.

Solitude is not something I reflect on a lot, yet there are times when I like to be by myself, with only my wife Julie or my Godmother Myrtle around. When I'm alone but with others, it's a withdrawal from extending myself. It's a way to focus inward. People who can share this inward space can be there and be a part of it, without having to be separate from it, or feeling cut off or isolated. The art of sharing solitude is to be able to be in that space of quiet center, without having to shut people off, and saying I want to be alone.

Solitude is definitely a point of replenishment, but if someone is in my environment who can't handle that, and tries to pull me out of it because they can't go into it with me, this creates a difficulty. They feel as though I'm withdrawing from them. They take it personally, and it becomes an awkward situation. This is the kind of person I either need to get away from physically, or I have to explain what's happening and say to them you shouldn't take this personally. It's just what is happening, and you shouldn't be disturbed by it... I try to get them to understand, so that even though they may not be able to fully participate in it with me they can at least understand it and not obstruct the process.

Not everyone knows how to be alone with others, how to share solitude. We have to help each other to understand how to be in our solitude, so that we can relate to each other without grabbing on to each other. We can be interdependent but not dependent. Loneliness is rejected dependency. Solitude is shared interdependency."

GLORIA VANDERBILT

"My friendships are based on sharing solitude. They aren't dependency trips. Once you have somebody you truly care about, you are in their head, and they are in yours. Then you don't need to see them all the time. I have life-long and wonderful friends, who have been very supportive and extraordinary. Years can go by when we don't see each other, because we may be in other parts of the world, but it doesn't matter, because we really have each other. And when we do see each other, we don't have to begin from the beginning."

JERRY BROWN

"I think it's very important to have time by yourself as well as time with others. There needs to be a balance between social activity or activity with others, and just plain contemplation. And I suppose if you think clearly enough, maybe the distinction between 'alone' and 'together' will even fade."

How open is open? Should your soulmate know everything about you? Should you share it all, even your diary? IRA PROGOFF talked about his boundaries of sharing solitude:

"One of the great blessings of my life is that in my workshops and seminars, I feel as though I am teaching out of solitude. I am in a sense able to share my solitude. But this state is what I would call 'active privacy,' because when you are alone with others you must learn to protect your privacy. The question often arises, should you always reveal your soul to loved ones, and if not, how can you share your solitude so that your privacy will not be invaded?

It isn't always desirable to be engaged in an open sharing of personal journals. Being able to share solitude, what I call 'active privacy', means that the individuality, the solitude of a being, moves out of its own nature. But because what this person will have to say or do may be in conflict with what another person wants or needs, even a closest friend, one still requires a space of privacy. The implication of active privacy is to give full value to the privacy and to the solitude of your inner process. In that way, you will be more of a person, and therefore your relation with your loved one will be greater... You have to trust your own solitude!"

DIANA VREELAND

"The person I most like to be with, the one I want to be with, and need to be with, is someone with whom I can lose my own solitude. That is a unique experience, a subtle point, where there are no more distinctions between you and the universe. Then you are no longer conscious of being alone, or not being alone, it just is... That is the moment of perfection. It's very rare. It's called love. And when you are with someone who totally absorbs you like this, then you no longer feel alone.

I feel fortunate that I've experienced these moments in my life, otherwise I wouldn't have grown up... Of course one grows every day of one's life, in one direction or another. It's a continual process. Growing up isn't adjustment to society, it's adjustment to oneself. And unless you are happy with yourself, you can't be happy with someone else."

Actress Bibi Andersson and pianist Rosalyn Tureck talked about performance as a way of sharing solitude:

BIBI ANDERSSON

"Acting is the perfect example of solitude and making contact. There are the other actors plus the audience who are depending on you, and then there is you. You are in the sort of solitude that makes you very responsible for everything you do, and for everything you don't do.

You can feel the presence of the people in the audience as they look at you and just accept whatever choice you make, for this tells them something. And you want to give them your very best. You want to make the right creative choice. As an actress you are always at the edge of responsibility, because you are by yourself, yet at the same time with people. In a certain way we always share our solitude, but on the stage it just seems more dramatic."

ROSALYN TURECK

"To share solitude on the stage is the ultimate joy. This is what performance means to me. People used to say that they would come into the concert hall an hour early, just to get into the mood, and be ready for my first notes.

On stage the communication can be so fantastic, so total. People come backstage afterwards, and I talk to them, and they talk to me. We answer each other and it goes so deep in spirit, that often I walk off the stage in what one might say is almost a state of intoxication. One almost reels with the immensity of it. I feel that in a hall of three thousand people, we are absolutely one. Everybody is there with me, and I'm one with them, we are in the same atmosphere.

Performance for me is sharing solitude on the highest level. It is communion... When I was a young woman I remember thinking very clearly about the nature of performance on that level. This has been my goal all my life. I thought that if, as a result of my playing, one person in the audience walked out of a concert of mine with a new vision of life, then it would have been worth it. Just one person is worth it all, if they receive a vision of life, a new concept, a new revelation of some quality of life.

My idea of performance has always been this. Not even to create a vision, no, not even to create. It was much deeper than that, because already when you say 'to create', it has more of an active western sense in it. Simply, my performance comes out of myself, out of my solitude, and solitude knows how to share itself."

You must let go of yourself
        before
                you can hold someone else...

Sattvically Yours

Of all the restrictive rules, that relating to the taking of sattvic *food in moderate quantities is the best; by observing this rule, the* sattvic *quality of mind will increase, and that will be helpful to Self-inquiry.*

Advice from Ramana Maharshi, *Who Am I?*

Being *sattvic* is the essence of what food for solitude means. It is the interconnection between all diets, between all ingredients that nourish as they heal and bring us ever more into our whole selves. If you truly want the peace of solitude, you have to feed your body, mind and spirit, *sattvic* food. The Hopi Indians have a simple prayer that beautifully illustrates this principle. They say: ''If you want to know who I am, eat my corn.'' For the Hopis, communion with corn is a daily way of life. Planting and harvesting it is a sacred ceremony. Each new seedling is treated like a newborn babe, for they really understand that the earth is our mother. For a Hopi, the *sattvic* seed of love and the kernal of corn are truly one.

The Hopis believe that they come from corn, and to it they shall return. A person's entrance into spiritual life begins with the ceremony of feeding a baby cornmeal. It is a baptism and eucharist that continues the rest of their life. Peace begins in the heart, is extended into the earth, and comes back again and again as the meal is shared. This is *sattvic* food on all levels. Theirs is a deep understanding of many energy links between an inner attitude and the outer environment which are really one and the same.

When the great Hindu sage, Ramana Maharshi, told his disciples about taking *sattvic food*, he was referring to the ancient Hindu system of qualities called *gunas*. This philosophy about the attributes of the universe, can help us decide upon our own particular diet. *Gunas* are the three qualities that describe the inner workings of our mind, and once we understand which quality or qualities we favor, the corresponding ingredients will become clear. These qualities are separated into *sattva, rajas,* and *tamas*.

A *sattvic nature* is clear, light and balanced, it is the ideal state for a person to attain. A *rajasic nature* is active in a fiery passionate way. It is spicy and explosive. A *tamasic nature* is slow, tends to be lazy and leans towards a passivity which is not positive. It is considered darkness, in contrast to sattvic lightness. The nature of our mind and the nature of the universe are so interwoven that these *gunas* or qualities affect everything we do. Sometimes, we tend to be more sattvic, or more rajasic or tamasic. When we are in a quiet listening mood, we are sattvic. When we procrastinate, we are tamasic, and when we are ready to start a good fight, we are rajasic.

But what is sattvic for one person may be rajasic or tamasic for someone else. So, even though a vegetarian way of life is considered sattvic, this may not be the ideal food for you. As noted nutritionist Roger Williams has said; ''Nutritional needs are as unique as fingerprints. What makes a good diet for one person can be seriously deficient for another.'' So how do we decide which diet is best for us, in order to create our own special kind of sattvic food?

Being sattvic is beyond moods. It touches upon the deepest levels of our tastes. Finding the right diet is connected to being in touch with what I call our *spiritual fingerprint*. This is the intuitive voice within each of us that lets us know who we are. It is the small, quiet voice that often makes the largest decisions of our lives. When we learn to trust it, we are on our way to finding out what is best for us and our own nature. It will lead us to tastes on all levels and this includes all kinds of food, from music to the very air we breathe.

The sattvic peace we seek is not only a diet made up of sprouts, seeds, and herbal teas. It's made up of good thoughts and feelings as well. And obviously, it's not enough to just say *yes*, but then eat everything that is *no*. It's being able to co-ordinate our own body/mind/soul dance so we don't end up stepping on ourselves. It's having enough common sense to know what makes us feel energized and up, and what makes us feel depleted and down. It is truly a state of being — a way of living, a way of eating — a way of moving about. It is a way of dedicating our entire life to *peace*.

A Sattvic Diet and Philosophy
Composer JOHN CAGE

When JOHN CAGE talks about sound, he's more of a philosopher than a composer. "My favorite music is no music at all," he says, "and that means the sounds of wherever I happen to be... I think that the sound of solitude is the sound of the environment around us. It's the Taoist oneness. Sound is a multiplicity of centers and each sound is at its own center." Cage's way of life and his philosophy of how to really listen to music reflects his Zen-like attitude. "Keep your head empty, but attentive, so you can enjoy it," he says. "If you keep your head empty, but alert and curious, you can hear music in the subway or anyplace else."

The theories of John Cage about sound revolutionized twentieth century music. He was avant garde before avant garde became the vogue. Logic of the heart *is* the heart of his logic. His love of the I Ching, an age old wisdom based on the laws of change and chance, along with his reliance on 'the gaps of silence', always influenced his creative process. But it wasn't until the age of sixty-five that John Cage turned his whole life around. Long years of consuming alcohol and eating junk food resulted in his close call with death. And that's when he changed and rediscovered a whole new food for solitude, in terms of physical diet. Through the body, he was re-uniting with his spirit again, and now the transformation was on all levels.

John Cage shares his own 'sattvic philosophy.' He talks about his new macrobiotic diet as passionately as he talks about his compositions:

"Don't you think it would be nice for food to be food! People who are concerned about food in relation to such things as health, or the personality, say people are what they eat. I agree. Now I'm really into this macrobiotic diet and I can tell my personality has changed since I met you last time. I've become much calmer. I don't eat red meat anymore. Now I have the feeling I have become the food I eat... But before I changed my diet, my attitude was quite different.

It used to be the Robert Louis Stevenson attitude, which he captured in his fable about the captain and the maid who were conversing on a sinking ship. The captain was smoking a cigar, and the maid questioned if that was wise because the ship was full of ammunition. 'But the ship is already sinking,' the captain said. He didn't think it made much difference, and he threw his cigar into the bin of ammunition, so that the whole thing exploded and sunk more quickly...

That was my former attitude. We should enjoy life, either slowly or speedily, as the case might be, since we're all going to die anyway. We should all go merrily and unthinkingly ahead about health. Eat whatever you want was the idea.

I had several circumstances that changed my thinking and diet. The first one was in Venezuela. The Cunningham Dance Company was performing at Caracas. It was a long plane trip with delays and we finally arrived at 4 am... There was a bus that was to pick us up and take us up the mountain to Caracas, but the dancers were all pooped and asleep, so the driver was the only one who was lifting the suitcases onto the bus. So I got out and helped him. But when I got to the hotel, I couldn't walk. I had ruined my back. I never used to do any exercises.

Anyway, it looked as though I'd never be able to move out of Venezuela. My back was in such a state. But a doctor there gave me some pills that reduced the spasm that had taken place, and he gave me some exercises. It was the first time in my life that I decided to try to do something about my body to keep it going, instead of letting it just sink. It was probably the first time I even realized I had a body. And I began doing the exercises.

Then, one or two years later, I had a very strange pain behind my left eye. It was so annoying, but my doctor couldn't figure it out. All kinds of x-rays were taken and everything was fixed that could be fixed. Then he said in desperation and confusion, that pains come and go, but he couldn't fix it. But I kept complaining to friends and finally Yoko Ono sent me to a macrobiotic Japanese lady who gave Shiatzu massage, and she also changed my diet. And if you please, within a week the pain was gone... Shizuko Yamamoto changed my life.

Shizuko means tranquility, yama means mountains, so her name means tranquility at the base of the mountain. She was the one who helped and guided my through this whole thing. I lost twenty-seven pounds, and now I know I am the food I eat... When you ask me about my food for solitude, it seems to me that it is food. Food is food. Brown rice is brown rice and brown rice has this marvelous effect, even on the personality. It changes people. It changed me...

Change is the nature of the universe, but to consciously transform yourself is not so simple. The music was always changing long ago. But music is a special circumstance, which we do as though we were exercising the mind. Music is like sitting square-legged. It's special. You can do very difficult things in music that you don't yet do in your life.

But when you get involved directly with things like food

changing your personality, you're much closer to daily life. Disciplines in the field of music are simple, but getting them into our daily lives is more difficult. When we're getting into things like food, we're getting into daily life. My music had already changed in the direction that my life now is changing. That's what's so simple, to change music. But to change the life is complex... Perhaps the music led me to the food. But the way I really changed happened more through the pain, and because of it, my contact with the wonderful Japanese lady who changed my diet.

When I first went to Shizuko, she said to me, "Eat when you're hungry, and drink when you're thirsty. Don't drink unless you are thirsty, and don't eat unless you are hungry." I liked what she said, although I didn't fully understand it. I don't think I do yet. It sounded like someone saying, shiver in the winter, perspire in the summer. It sounded straightforward.

But we don't really know when we're hungry. We tend to think that we ought to be hungry in the morning, at noon, and in the evening, but maybe we're not hungry. Maybe we're eating simply out of habit. Maybe we're hungry at some other time. In solitude, we can learn when we are hungry. I'm actually trying to find out when I am alone, whether or not I am hungry or thirsty. I can tell thirst more easily than I can tell hunger, because when you are thirsty your mouth gets dry. But I can't quite tell what hunger is, because I eat too much. Hunger must be an empty stomach, it must slightly hurt. Hunger and emptiness are related. But I'm very apt to eat before I'm hungry, because I still eat according to the hour, rather than what I truly feel. Solitude can teach us when we are hungry on every level. But, I'm perfectly happy to be talking about food.

My personality is changing due to what I am eating. I am calmer all together, perhaps a little bit too calm. And how I'm going to change that, I don't yet know. But I'm pretty sure that it could be changed more effectively through food, than through any other means...

My diet is basically brown rice and some beans, either the black beans, or kidney beans, or garbanzo beans, or lima beans. And it's lots of seeds, like sunflower seeds, sesame seeds and sometimes those pumpkin seeds. Then I love to make the Tibetan barley bread that you can find in *The Tassajara Bread Book*. I enjoy working with it; kneading it is so relaxing. Finally it becomes less gluey and pasty and falling apart, and it becomes itself, it becomes a thing. It can take whatever form you give it. I eat it as a meal, if I am alone, and then there it is for friends who drop by...

Also I like to make both miso pickles, and nuka pickles...
Nuka pickles are in fermented bran, and miso in soybean paste.
I vary the vegetables that I use in miso to make pickles. I've been
experimenting with turnips, carrots, mushrooms, dicon (which is
Chinese radish), cucumbers and whatever else I find... Once you
make the pickles, they say they last forever... Vegetables, pickles
and even beans are seen as a condiment to the basic diet which is
brown rice. Then the brown rice can sometimes be fried with
scallions and celery in a little sesame oil, with some soy sauce, or
with some nuts, cayenne, and sesame seeds.

So, a typical meal alone would be the brown rice, some beans,
and steamed broccoli, with soy sauce and some lemon... I don't
believe in two different diets. I think that the food we eat alone,
and the food we eat with others should be the same. It's like
sharing food for solitude.''

John Cage's Brown Rice

2 cups brown rice
1 tbspn. soy sauce or sea salt
3 cups fresh spring water

I make brown rice in a pressure cooker because it seals in the
nutrients. Covers on most pots are not as tight as the pressure
cooker and keeping the steam in is the secret of getting it right.
This way the steam is locked in, and keeps the precious vitamin
B and all other nutrients in the rice rather than in the air... The
other thing I do is use fresh spring water. I go out to the country
and get it myself... I put the water into those gallon bottles that
you get apple juice in. The spring water usually comes from
Long Island, in Locust Valley, or I get it at Stony Point. I enjoy
making the special trip to go out and get the water. And on the
way I might find some mushrooms, or I might solve a problem
in my work, because my mind would be off my work...

It is easy to make the basic brown rice, and once it's made
you can add herbs and nuts, whatever. It's two cups of rice
which you wash, and put into a pressure cooker. Add a
tablespoon of soy sauce, or you could use the same amount of
sea salt. Then you use three cups of spring water. Put the
pressure cooker over a high flame, and when it comes to its
steaming point, put the heat on low, slip an asbestos pad
underneath it, and simmer for about 40 minutes.

John Cage's Kidney Beans with Herbs

1 cup kidney beans	1 tspn. soy sauce
3 cups water	1 tbspn. cumin seeds

I don't cook the beans in the pressure cooker, just rice... I soak the beans overnight. Then I bring them to a boil for ten minutes, reduce the heat and cook them until they are tender. I try one way or another to get rid of the liquid, to get them near dryness, so that the amount of liquid is like a sauce. I add soy sauce, and in the beginning of cooking might add some herb. This especially enhances the kidney beans. I like to put in cumin seeds which I toast before I use, in a frying pan. The herbs get more fragrance that way. You just throw the seeds into the pan for a few minutes, without using any oil, because the seeds already have oil in them. I never use Teflon pans, they are bad news. I use the heavy French Le Creuset enamel pans...

Brown rice ... and everything nice!

*Let your food be your medicine
let your medicine be your food.*

Hippocrates

Sattvic doesn't mean bland and boring, it means balanced, peaceful, subtle and that can be very exciting! The following recipes are meant to tempt the vegetarian in you, to try a few variations on the same theme, which is always sattvically yours!

Brown rice isn't really brown, it's a lovely creamy color, and when you add some lemon grass with lavender flowers, then you have something really exotic.

Lavender and Lemon Rice with Herbs, Raisins and Cashews

3 cups spring water	1 tbspn. safflower oil
1½ cups brown rice	1 parsnip
1 cup vegetable broth	10 natural cashews
1 tspn. lemon grass	½ cup golden raisins
few pinches fresh rosemary	1 tbspn. sesame seeds
fresh ginger, minced	1 onion, chopped
2 cloves garlic	1 tspn. lavender flowers*

Begin by boiling water, then add rice, broth, and lemon grass. Bring to boil again, and then put on low flame. Add the rosemary, garlic and ginger, reserving lavender flowers for later on. After twenty minutes, add oil, stir and add more water if needed. Then add grated parsnip, cashews, raisins, sesame seeds, onion and lavender flowers. Let this simmer, stirring from time to time. After another fifteen to twenty minutes, it all comes together perfectly... You may want to add a bit more oil, and a few drops of tamari.

This is one of those dishes that tastes better cold the next day... The herbs have a chance to lose some of their potency and blend in beautifully with the rice and other ingredients. The lemon grass has a tendency to take over, so use it sparingly.

The hot rice may taste a bit too 'herbal' for you, but don't worry; the next day their persona leaves and the essence remaining creates a delicious rice dish, cold or warmed again.

* This is dried herb — also used for making lavender tea.

Take a breath of the fresh dawn
for it is as pure as food and drink.

HOPI *saying*

When a chef prepares a stew, and the chef is also a gardener, the process of the tao is fulfilled... When we take responsibility for what we eat, by either growing it, or asking ourselves, would we grow it, then we are participating in the full cycle of *living energy*.

Soybeans have been providing the sustenance of life for millions of people, thousands of years. Yet they are a misunderstood and neglected ingredient for Westerners who are just beginning to discover the joys of tofu... 99 cents can buy a pound of soybeans... This can feed six people and provide as much protein as six sirloin steaks or six fish.

The ingredients in Soybean Stew could all grow in your back yard. These are our gifts from the soil... Simmer them with love, and your stew will surprise you with nourishment on all levels...

Soybean Stew

3 cups soybeans	2 tbspns. olive oil
3 carrots	pinch of thyme
3 celery stalks	1 small onion
1 parsnip	1 bay leaf
1 turnip	½ cup sesame seeds
3 cloves garlic	pinch of kelp or sea salt

Soak the soybeans overnight. Dice carrots, celery, parsnip, turnip, and garlic cloves. Add two tablespoons olive oil to 5-quart casserole dish... add drained soybeans, garlic, thyme and sliced onion. Bake for 1½ hours at 350°. Then add bay leaf, carrots, parsnip, turnip, celery, sesame seeds and kelp, and bake another 1½ hours.

A stew has many variables with one base, a base that gives it a name... Beans provide the perfect foundation. Soybean stew could also be adzuki or kidney stew, just replace the soybeans with adzuki or kidney beans... Experimenting with these basic ingredients, stir up all kinds of stews... You can add sprouts, herbs, nuts and seeds... Select a different spice each time and create unusual broths. Try ginger root, or cloves, or even a bit of licorice root.

Variations: when warming up, add some stir-fried chestnuts with okra... Stir in some cloves and a bit more garlic, a bit of tamari, and something simply sattvic starts to sing!

The Light of The Earth
and Our Spiritual Fingerprint

What man can give an account of or explain how he learned to till the soil, to raise vines, or to make cheese? No one unless he can point to his teacher, and the teacher will in turn point to his teacher, and so on and on, until we come to the first teacher... God had given to each man the light that was his due, so that he need not go astray. Who possesses a truth unless he has received it of a master? No one! We have the truth of the soul from God, otherwise we would not have it. Similarly we have the truths of philosophy from nature, she has taught us without idle talk...

...Just as the herbs in the garden must be sown and planted, and do not grow unless this has been done, whatever we sow is but earth, as it were, that we give to the earth and again extract from it. The same is true of the 'art' that is engraved and planted in us. He who taught it to me received it from the light of nature, and I have received it just as he has; it must be engraved in all of us. Yet it happens that many herbs grow without having been sown, and these are often the best. Such is the power of the earth, and such is the light of nature; they do not rest. Therefore, give heed to your inner garden... and also to yourself that you may learn that which no one can teach you, and which will amaze everyone...

Paracelsus, *Selected Writings*

Starch Snacks

No one *ever* said tempting treats had to be bad for us, or that nutritious ones had to be boring. Without a lot of fanfare we can learn how to truly nourish ourselves so it's not only good for our cravings, but also good for our digestion. And starch snacks are a very easy way to try these healthy treats.

For your pleasure —

Baked Acorn Squash

    1 acorn squash*
    ½ cup water
    kelp
    cloves
    safflower or sesame oil

Preheat oven to 350°. Cut squash in half, remove seeds and wash. Place, cut side down, in ½ cup water in a 1½ quart Pyrex baking dish. Bake 45 minutes. Place 1 tspn. kelp, dash of fresh cloves and 1 tspn. oil in each half and return to oven for 10 minutes.

Squash Sweet and Steamed

Squash can also be steamed. Try Butternut, slice in half, put on low flame and steam 30 minutes. Then add sesame oil, sesame seeds and fresh rosemary.

Autumnal Squash

Sweet & Steamed

1 acorn squash	sesame seeds or cumin seeds
2 spaghetti squash	butter or walnut oil
3 butternut squash	fresh fennel
1 gourd squash** (buttercup squash)	fresh parsley
honey	fresh rosemary

Prepare all the squash using either of the previous two recipes. After either baking or steaming, scoop out all the squash into a large bowl. Add a few tablespoons of honey, enough sesame seeds to lightly cover the top of the squash, half a stick (2 oz.) of

---

* You can eat the entire squash as a lunch in itself, with a small salad; or place the other half in the refrigerator and eat it cold on another occasion... as a snack.
** Buttercup gourd squash resembles a gourd-like pumpkin, except it is the same color as acorn squash, green with white stripes, and it has an acorn shaped top — it looks very strange — but it is one of the sweetest tasting of the entire squash family.

butter or 2 tbspns. walnut oil, as much fresh parsley and fennel as you like (I use a few sprigs of each) and then mix well. This is an excellent snack warm or cold and it remains a perfectly good left-over for about a week in the refrigerator.

Zucchini and Tahini Dip

½ cup sour cream	fresh parsley
zucchini purée (see below)	7 sliced radishes
fresh dill	3 chopped scallions
1 shredded carrot	3 chopped calamato olives
1 sliced cucumber	1 tspn. tahini

Mix ½ cup of sour cream or plain yogurt into 2 cups of zucchini purée. Add other ingredients, mix in well, then add 1 tspn. tahini and mix again. This is a great dip for anything worth dipping, it is a great aside for brown rice, or you could even eat it as a meal in itself.

Zucchini Purée

4 zucchinis	1 tspn. cumin seeds
3 scallions	3 cloves garlic
sesame seed oil	4 sprigs fresh coriander
3 tomatoes	1 tbspn. fresh dill weed
2 sprigs parsley	1 tbspn. sesame seeds
1 tspn. fennel seeds	1 tspn. tamari

Slice vegetables very fine, sauté in sesame seed oil in wok, let simmer in tomatoes, let cool, then add remaining ingredients and purée in blender...

MENUS AND MEDITATIONS 127

Not I but the world says it: All is one

Heracleitos

Eggplant Potpourri with Brown Rice and Pine Nuts

1 small Chinese eggplant
a few slices yellow squash
½ square tofu (4 oz.)
1 stalk celery
a few slices zucchini
few sprigs fresh parsley
5 leaves fresh peppermint

2 cloves fresh garlic
sesame seed oil
a pinch of kelp
1 tbspn. sesame seeds
1 bowl cooked brown rice
a splash of tamari
a handful pine nuts

Slice eggplant, squash, tofu and celery. Place all the vegetables except celery in steamer and steam for ten minutes. Add celery and steam another five minutes. Place in a large bowl and add the fresh parsley, peppermint, finely chopped garlic, oil, kelp and mix well. Then add some toasted sesame seeds. When re-heating brown rice, add tamari and pine nuts with a bit of sesame seed oil.

Be sure to get rid of excess water from steamed veggies before mixing oil and other ingredients.

The roots of a plant fight to support their life.... They seek the source of water 100 feet below the ground, to let one blade of grass bathe in the sun.

Robert Lawlor, *'Lindisfarne Lecture', Sacred Geometry*

Vegetables and Virginity

Keep your attention within yourself, (not in your head) but in your heart.

St Simeon, *The New Theologian*
Philokalia *On Prayer of the Heart*

The following ingredients are strictly sattvic. This is a vegetarian's vegetarian base that keeps for weeks and each time it's warmed over, you add the vegetables and herbs of your choice.

Here is the basic recipe.

Home-made Vegetable Soup ... Broth and Purée

4 quarts water	4 celery stalks with leaves
3 carrots with greens	1 tspn. sea salt
5 potatoes	1 small leek
1 large turnip	½ bunch fresh parsley
1 parsnip	3 cloves garlic
1 small onion	1 tspn. sesame seeds

Into a giant soup pot (6–8 quart), put water, vegetables and sea salt. Bring to a full boil. Then let simmer for one hour on very low flame. Add parsley and garlic, and simmer for another 30 minutes, checking in from time to time with loving stirs... Let cool.

Now you can make two pots of soup — plain broth and purée. Into one set of storage jars, pour your broth pot, which consists of the soup and a few vegetables slightly mashed with a fork. Into another set put your purée, which is the rest of the soup put into a blender along with the sesame seeds. Both pots have a semi-bland flavor, which lets you create all kinds of variations. You can add other vegetables to the broth or the purée: chopped onions, okra, bak choy, tofu, celery... And then there are all your favorite herbs and tamari or sherry, to give it a little zing. When reheating, adding at least one fresh herb like basil or rosemary makes a special difference.

Vegetable purée variation: A favorite variation for me consists of adding: a few sesame seeds, tomatoes, lots of fresh garlic, some soybean sprouts, parsley and lemon grass. Gently warm the purée, stirring occasionally, bring to a fast boil, then simmer a few minutes. Then add a dash of kelp and a bit of yogurt when serving.

Luxurious Necessities: Once you prepare your vegetable purée and broth, you can add all kinds of surprises. Some you keep on hand like a garlic braid, and others you find in corners of your cupboard. Here are a few basics to make your soup a success:

Fresh herbs	Seeds	Spices and Niceties
basil	cumin	whole cloves
rosemary	fennel	cardamom
sage	sesame	thyme
dill weed		oregano
garlic		kelp
coriander		tamari
		lemon grass

Fresh herbs when available add a touch of elegance to everything. But all of these herbs can be dried, and then they last forever.

GARLIC

Garlic and lots of it is not only delicious but one of the 'miracle herbs'. It can cure broken hearts as well as serious medical conditions. I always add a few cloves to all my soups, and if you want to eat it as a preventive medicine, make sure not to boil it. The Hindus say that eating garlic is like having seven mothers and that is all I need to know!

Garlic and Vegetable Soup for One

reserved vegetable broth*	2 sprigs watercress
5 cloves garlic	½ square tofu (4 oz.)
gomashio-sesame seeds	3 sprigs parsley
a pinch oregano	7 okra
1 stalk swiss chard	a splash of sherry

Place vegetable broth into earthenware pot and place on flame tamer over low flame. Add everything except sherry and okra. Heat slowly for ten minutes. Then add more gomashio. While heating broth, place finely cut okra in steamer for ten minutes. Then add to broth with sherry, let simmer and serve!

---

* See recipe page 128.

LENTILS

Lentils go way back to the beginning of culinary civilization. Like millet, it was the main staple in many pre-Old Testament cultures. No longer considered a peasant dish, lentils have been turned into all kinds of interesting dishes, from Indian dal, to lentil soup served all over the world.

Full of protein, it is one of the most versatile of beans. Once you make your basic lentil stock you can add fresh ingredients each time you reheat... Lentils love to take on all kinds of greens like okra, celery, zucchini, string beans. Combine it with a grain like barley or millet, a green vegetable of your choice, and a little tofu, and this is all you need for a healthy and balanced meal.

A hearty bowl of lentil soup is more like a stew. A little side dish of something wonderful like creamy goat yogurt, a bit of great whole grain bread, and who wouldn't want to be a peasant!

This is a basic lentil soup recipe with a few extras that I like to include: You can make a giant pot of this, and it will keep getting better and better, the longer it lives in the fridge, but ten days is about the limit. The cloves and garlic are a natural preservative. Remember to keep in air-tight glass containers.

Basic Lentil Soup Stock

3 large turnips	pinch sage
1 large onion	a few cumin seeds
4 large carrots and greens	7 cloves
6 cloves garlic	5 cardamom
4–5 quarts spring water	pinch peppermint
3 cups lentils	a few fresh parsley sprigs
pinch lemon grass	

Dice turnips, onion and carrots into bite size pieces. Chop garlic cloves, keep some in reserve for later. Add water to a 6-quart pot, heat a few minutes, then add washed lentils. Let boil, then add everything else — vegetables first, then herbs and spices. Stir, simmer a few hours. Check in from time to time, stirring and adding more water if needed. Two hours is a nice stretch for this soup, but use your own discretion. When cool, add to storage jars along with reserved garlic cloves and you will have a base that will give you many small miracles.

Lentil and Lemon Soup

2 cups lentil stock
2 tbspns. spring water
1 tspn. tamari sauce
tofu (finely chopped)
3 cloves garlic

½ scallion (green part)
4 sprigs fresh coriander
1 tbspn. gomashio (ground sesame seed)
1 tbspn. fresh lemon juice
a few bits lemon rind

Add lentil stock, water, tamari sauce, and a few bits of finely chopped tofu to pot. Gently heat for a few minutes. Meanwhile, peel and chop garlic, scallion, and the stems of the coriander. Put into reserve bowl the curly part of the coriander, the garlic and scallion. Add the stems to stock, and sprinkle in the sesame seed salt. Stir a bit, and let heat another minute or so. Slice enough of a small lemon to get about two tablespoons of juice. You may like a bit more, but not too much more. This is enough to add something special to the lentils, and to clarify the soup a bit. Then slice a few bits of the rind, and add it and the juice to stock. Let this heat another minute, then turn off flame. Add the garlic, scallion and coriander. Serve, and add a sprig of coriander to float on top.

Summer Soup Borscht

Russian borscht the way my grandmother used to make it, is one of the best ways to serve a cold soup on a hot summer day. Hot or cold, borscht is beet soup, and the secret is to use only beets in preparing the main stock. Originally a peasant dish, it was served as a main course. Boiled potatoes and cabbage were also added, along with the traditional hard boiled egg, and, if available, it was a luxury to add a generous scoop of sour cream.

7 large beets	2 carrots
3 beet leaves	1 hard boiled egg
3 small cucumbers	3 sprigs fresh dill
8 radishes	a scoop sour cream

Cut the beet leaves from the stems leaving about two inches of stems (save the leaves for salads or for steaming like spinach). Add to a 6-quart pot of boiling water. Let boil, then simmer for one hour. Let cool. Then put in blender for a few seconds until it becomes a purée. Add only the beets and a few stems to the blender, along with liquid. Discard other stems and leaves.

Chop the cucumbers and radishes, and grate carrots. Put the soup into a glass storing jar, and keep the other ingredients separate. When you are ready to use the soup, add the other ingredients: the egg, dill, sour cream, carrots, cucumbers and radishes. You may prefer to add yogurt instead of sour cream, or sliced zucchini instead of cucumbers. A few scallions, and some fresh parsley along with the dill also tastes good. This soup lasts for several days in the refrigerator, and it tastes better and better each day.

Variation: Boil 4 or 5 beet leaves and stems along with a few sprigs of parsley and a few dill weed stems. Let cool. Put liquid through a drainer, discard left-overs. Refrigerate. Add some fresh lime and you have a super-energy, cooling summer drink.

We should become more and more conscious of the fact that all processes connected with nourishment are infinitely delicate. Nutritionists as yet only deal with the coarse exterior of what goes on... And this is why there is no scientific explanation for the survival of Theresa of Konnersreuth for more than thirty years on a daily fraction of the Host and no liquid.

Wilhelm Zur Linden, *A Child is Born*

Seeds

...It is the seed as changed that produces the effect ...
at no two moments is a thing identical.

'Sprouting', The Asian Journal of Thomas Merton

Some seeds grow in our heart and feed us love. They evolve into who we become. And then there are all the wondrous seeds that grow in the earth. What is above is also below. Seeds of the soil and seeds of the soul can both be sattvic. The essence of their energy has a calming effect upon us. And if we find just one of these seeds, we are more than lucky. If we can grow it, cultivate it and care for it, we are more than blessed. Growing means to just be yourself, to be open to the source as it really is...

WINDOWSILL FARMING — SPROUTING

Windowsill farming is one way to grow your own food, and if you live in the city, sprouting alfalfa seeds is ideal for this. Alfalfa sprouts have been called 'the perfect food'. Dr H.E. Kirschner, the author of *Nature's Healing Grasses*, says these sprouts are ''the most 'living food' on earth.'' The alfalfa plant is extremely rich in vitamin K, which is particularly important for vitality and longevity. It is also rich in calcium and contains significant amounts of every vitamin and mineral.

Growing your own alfalfa sprouts is economical, fun and easy to do. All you need for basic ingredients are some alfalfa seeds, a glass jar and some ingenuity. In the beginning of your sprout adventure you will get used to the moods of your seeds, as you watch them grow day by day. Playing nice music for them, and telling them you care helps, but water and sunshine are essential.

HOW DO YOU BEGIN?

Sprouting your own seeds without using a fancy tube sprouter or some gadget you buy in a health food store is easy when you follow the old fashioned way of doing it...

Essentials

1. Glass Jar   With mouth wide enough to get your hand inside to remove sprouts. Peanut butter and mayonnaise jars are ideal.

2. Strainer   To stop seeds from falling out when you rinse them. Handiwipes or paper towels are fine; something to let air seep through.

3. Seeds   Two tablespoons of alfalfa seeds produce a quart of sprouts. You can judge amount by using just enough to cover bottom of jar.

Start by measuring amount of desired seeds, then add 4 parts water to 1 part seeds into jar and soak overnight in cool dark place. Next morning drain water and that afternoon rinse thoroughly. In a few days, the seeds will start sprouting. After three days, if you rinse them two or three times a day, you will see wonderful results... They will grow much faster if you give them more water and attention. The whole idea is to keep rinsing them off. Then, the day before you are ready to eat them (when they've grown into one-inch sprouts), expose them to the sun. Putting them into direct sunlight helps to form their 2% chlorophyll content. You will see whitish yellow buds turn bright green, and this is what provides many of the essential healing nutrients, especially vitamin K. You can put them on your windowsill with the window shut, because indirect sun works just as well. You don't want to expose them too long to the direct sun, just enough to give them a treat.

Sprouts as 'the perfect food' are ideal for all your culinary creations: You can use sprouts in all your salads, or use them instead of lettuce for sandwiches, for omelettes or just eat them alone.

Water is the element which allows the mysterious forces of life to unfold.

Wilhelm Zur Linden, *A Child is Born*

Julie Newmar's Special Seeds for Salads

Actress JULIE NEWMAR shared her special seed secret: I like to crunch down into my tuna or spinach and mushroom salad, especially *after* I put my seeds on it. These health seeds are the very best seeds you can have. You make a combination of four seeds which are *expressly* great for your health. You put them in the freezer and you take a tiny handful of the seeds and throw them on the salad, and this makes the salad *crunchy*.

The Seeds

1. Sunflower Seeds   These are the greatest seeds for your eyes. The Russian soldiers used to put them in their pockets and when they would go to war, this would help them to see.

2. Sesame Seeds   A lovely sweet taste, it makes a great oil that's very good for your reproductive system.

3. Pumpkin Seeds   That's a top quality type of seed, with good protein in them.

4. Toasted Soybean   A wonderful taste and plenty of nutrition.

Make a mixture from the four seeds and freeze in a bowl. This way you maintain all their vitamins, because heat destroys vitamins. They'll keep for 3 months or more. These seeds on salad are better than a main course. I eat salads late at night while I'm working. This gives me enough energy to brush my teeth at night and then go to sleep.

Autumnal Treats — Toast Your Own Seeds

Seeds and weeds are often thrown out because their nutritional value is overlooked. Sattvic seeds from all kinds of squash are rich in nutrients and protein. Pumpkin seeds are traditional and well known for their delicate yet crunchy texture. But their cousins, the acorn and butternut squash, are never considered. So, the next time you prepare autumnal squash, save the seeds instead of throwing them out; they are toasted in the same way as pumpkin seeds.

Toasted Seeds

acorn squash	butter
butternut squash	kelp or sea salt
pumpkin	nutmeg

Preheat oven to 250°. Scoop out all the seeds from the acorn squash, one butternut squash, and one small pumpkin. Separate the seeds from the squashy substance. There is no need to wash them, just place them on a well-buttered flat pan, add a bit of kelp or nutmeg, and let them brown slowly in the oven. Turn them from time to time and add more butter when needed. When they are completely toasted, let them cool, and store them in foil, or else eat them right away.

SUNFLOWER SEEDS

Are you having trouble concentrating? Try the following:

1) get rid of cluttered company
2) eat lots of sunflower seeds.

Did you know that sunflower seeds are good for your memory? They are concentration food. Not only do you concentrate while munching on them, but they contain vitamin B-12, an important source essential for concentrating and mental energy. If you have poor appetite, chronic fatigue and trouble in concentrating, you might have a vitamin B-12 deficiency, plus an overdose of cluttered company. Give yourself a boost with good thoughts and sunflower seeds.

APPLE SEEDS

They say an apple a day keeps the doctor away, but not unless you remember to eat the seeds. Before civilization became civilized, people thrived happily on the seeds of all kinds of fruits. After all, a seed contains the spark of life, it *is* the germ that germinates. What could be a better source of nutrition? Apple seeds, papaya seeds, and cantaloupe seeds are all for the eating, and not for throwing out. Just remember to chew them very carefully, and if you decide to try an apple seed or two, you may be surprised to discover the natural liqueur nature made for us.

GOD NEVER HURRIES:
You want things to happen immediately, but God never hurries.
There is all eternity in which to work and live and be joyful!

White Eagle, *The Quiet Mind*

Sesame Seed Salt

Gomashio

Sesame seeds are part of every Japanese household. Toasting the seeds and then grinding them into a fine powder create a very fine salt ideal for soups, salads, vegetables and grains. You can sprinkle this on practically anything — eggs, tofu, beans, even your fingers.

The traditional way to make gomashio is to use a special serrated earthenware bowl (*suribachi*) and to grind the seeds with a wooden pestle (*surikogi*). You can find both in any Japanese delicacy or hardware store. You can also use any kind of mill, but there is something special about the bowl. Use 1 part sea salt to 7 parts sesame seeds.

Take your seeds and quickly roast them in a wok. This releases a wonderful aromatic flavor. When they pop and turn a dark sandy color, they are ready for you and your bowl. Grind them, and then add sea salt.

CHESTNUTS

There are as many ways to prepare chestnuts as there are gourmet cookbooks. But before you turn them into a wonderful mousse, or use them to stuff mushrooms, you can simply enjoy eating them as a treat. Here are three basic ways to get them in shape for your snack:

Baking

Place ½ lb. shelled chestnuts into a pan and into 400° oven. Heat for 30 minutes, allow to cool. Remove thin inner skin.

Stir Frying

Cut slits into chestnuts. Place some oil in a skillet. Heat for five minutes, stirring the chestnuts. Most recipes say 'shake', but stirring is sufficient. Let cool, then remove shell, making sure to remove inner skin.

In Corsica it's commonplace to cook chestnuts with fennel branches because both are plentiful on the island. The following recipe was shared by a lovely French girl who works in a herb shop.

Chestnuts brewed with Fennel Branches

1 lb. chestnuts
2 fennel branches

One pound of chestnuts gives you about 30 treats. The fennel branches are about 1 foot each, so you might need to break them up. If you can't find the branches in your herb shop, then use a tablespoon of fennel seeds instead. Put the branches and chestnuts together in a big pot, and boil for about twenty minutes. Let cool, peel skin and enjoy.

Thy Faith Made Thee Whole
The Holy Bible scatters this seed of healing in three different gospels:
Mark 5:34... Luke 8:48... Matthew 9:22... Cultivate it with love!

A Vegetarian Way of Life

For me eating alone is a communion with God.

Frances Steloff

FRANCES STELOFF, the legendary Queen Bee who began a little New York bookshop in 1920, never would have imagined then that it would become the great literary landmark it is today. All she ever wanted was a place where rare books and rare people could find a home away from home. In the heart of the busy jewelry district on west forty-seventh street, a small sign stands out. 'WISEMEN FISH HERE', the Gotham Book Mart motto for more than half a century, greeted people like Buckminster Fuller, Gertrude Stein and W.H. Auden as they entered the shop to meet with Frances.

Here was an oasis where they might enjoy a leisurely lunch in the garden, browse through the newest additions, or simply just chat about all that was worth chatting about. Her remarkable energy changed the lives of so many people. Anais Nin, Henry Miller, Tennessee Williams, and Martha Graham are just some of the creative circle of friends who were supported in the initial development of their work, thanks to the persistence, devotion, and kindness of Frances Steloff.

Getting to know Frances was like meeting a little girl who seemed to be growing younger and wiser all the time. She lived alone for most of her 101 years, amidst a collection of books, cats, and mystical thoughts which always kept her good company. I visited her one day at the Gotham Book Mart, and as we were talking, I realized that she appeared more vibrant and much younger than the last time we had met. Her skin had the same quality as a newborn infant, and her eyes sparkled with laughter and clarity. This was most unusual because at 91 she had suffered a minor stroke, and her comeback to life was amazing, even for a younger person. She had been completely healed, and at 93 was busier than ever... We started to talk about age and aging, and she said, ''My dear, I never think about it. If you think about it, it thinks about you!''

Frances was a living testimony of how food for solitude can offer you fulfilment in every way. Solitude was the most important thing in her life. As she said, ''I don't know how people can live without some hours of solitude. I couldn't. I need to be alone, solitude means everything to me. In solitude you learn that every experience has a lesson for you. Being alone is important so you can think about this lesson, otherwise you will have the same experience again and again without understanding its value.''

Her real food for solitude was a total vegetarian diet, and she was as serious about her vegetarianism as she was about her solitude. Whenever you went to meet with Frances Steloff, you knew you could look forward to some good esoteric gossip, as well as one of her great vegetarian meals. She talked about her vegetarian way of life and shared some of her favorite recipes:

''For me, being a vegetarian is a way of life. I couldn't be anything else if I tried. Aside from the question of health, there is a moral aspect. I like to think about the origin of things. When I think of the pain this meat has caused, I can't enjoy my meal. Furthermore, I know that meat is the most unhealthy food that we can eat. I have read and studied all the different aspects and I am satisfied that it is not good food. This is aside from the moral aspects.

When I was younger, I went through a temporary period when I did eat meat. I shared an apartment with a couple of girls. We would take turns cooking and we thought it was quick to cook chops or steak. But I never felt good about it, and during this period I used to have to take aspirin for my migraine headaches. I've never taken an aspirin in the last fifty years, or any other pill. I've never had a headache since then.

I try to select foods that are nourishing without side effects and not just for their taste. You'll find that your palate changes. People think that they have to smoke and they have to eat meat because they have a craving, and that craving comes because there's something missing in the diet. If you have a well-rounded diet, then you don't have any craving for cigarettes or alcohol.

I boiled it all down to a few simple recipes. First I always have the makings of a salad, and a couple of hard boiled eggs. Then if I don't get out, or the weather is very severe, I don't have to worry about eating. There's always something like that in the refrigerator... Then I also make sure I have lots of organic brown rice and millet on hand, plus my favorite herbs and nuts. I keep a big supply of Mountain Valley bottled water, not only to drink, but to cook with as well. I only use the water from the tap to wash my grains, but I would never ever drink it. Breakfast is always a fruit feast. I have four peaches and that's a healthy breakfast for me. I usually have cashews or almonds with the fruit. They say a few almonds is worth a pound of steak, it has the same protein value.''

Frances Steloff's Millet Recipe

"I once read that a Chinese woman was in hiding during the revolution, and all she had was millet. She kept alive for months on this millet. After reading this I always have millet at home. You can eat this for breakfast, lunch or dinner. It tastes wonderful hot or cold. The basic recipe is easy:"

> millet
> Mountain Valley water
> dried vegetables

"Use one cup of millet for four cups of water and cook it for 30 minutes, like rice, or until the water evaporates. Add some carrots or whatever vegetables you have at hand. I like to use a combination of dried vegetables made by a health doctor. I drop a few spoonfuls of these vegetables in the millet and then I have a healthy and delicious meal.

Variation: I can't make a good dish without onions and garlic. I sauté finely diced onions with safflower oil, using a Pyrex-ware or cast iron skillet. Then combine millet, green pepper and tomatoes as in previous recipe."

Salad and Solitude

"I believe that you are fed in solitude, and as they say the truth will set you free. Eating alone is something I enjoy, and even look forward to. For me eating alone is a communion with God. One of my favorite solitary snacks is salad, made with my special dressing. I'm very particular about my dressings. I use a lot of herbs and olive oil, a little bit of vinegar or lemon juice, and lots and lots of garlic and onions.

I take great pains to cut my onions very thin. When you finely dice onions and garlic, you can hardly notice they're there, but you get a fine flavor. I put the herbs and curry into the bowl first, then the oil, the lemon juice, then the finely cut garlic and onions. I stir it all very thoroughly, and to top it off I add some sweet red peppers, which I really love, and eat it sometimes just like I would candy."

Salad:	soybean sprouts	sweet red peppers
	romaine lettuce	shredded carrots
	organic tomato	chopped celery
Dressing:	oregano	onions, finely sliced
	thyme	garlic, finely sliced
	fresh basil	lemon juice
	lemon balm	safflower or olive oil
	curry powder	

Sipping Solitude

...The I CHING Hexagram Hsu/Waiting (Nourishment) No. 5...

──── ────
────────
──── ────　　above K'AN THE ABYSMAL, WATER
────────
────────
────────　　below CH'IEN THE CREATIVE, HEAVEN

All beings have need of nourishment from above. But the gift of food comes in its own time, and for this one must wait. This hexagram shows the clouds in the heavens, giving rain to refresh all that grows and to provide mankind with food and drink. The rain will come in its own time. We cannot make it come; we have to wait for it.

THE JUDGMENT

Waiting. If you are sincere,
You have light and success.
Perseverance brings good fortune.
It furthers one to cross the great water.

Waiting is not mere empty hoping. It has the inner certainty of reaching the goal. Such certainty alone gives that light which leads to success. This leads to the perseverance that brings good fortune and bestows power to cross the great water.

THE IMAGE

Clouds rise up to heaven:
The image of WAITING.
Thus the superior man eats and drinks,
Is joyous and of good cheer.

> *...Setting the mood is like setting the table,*
> *you decide on the ambiance...*

SEAGULLS, SUNSETS AND SPICED TEA

The ambiance of island life is perfect for solitude... There is a whole sensorium of delights. Sea air, clean and invigorating, is an elixir of its own. And then there are sunsets and seashells and endless shores to explore. The mood of a lazy and long afternoon spent strolling on a beach changes with the wind and waves. You can walk along the edge of the sand, following the footsteps of a seagull, completely losing all sense of yourself. And then you make your way home to settle into the pleasures of brewing a pot of spiced tea. The evening is one of quiet contemplation, and as you sip the tea, the calligraphy in the sand created by your friend the seagull is evermore present.

Spiced Tea

2 tbspns. sassafras	star anise (4 stars)
7 cloves	cardamom (3 seeds)
1 cinnamon stick	1 tbspn. pau d'arco

Add to warmed teapot all these gifts of nature, let brew at least twenty minutes to release healing properties. Serve with honey and milk, or lemon. Add another cinnamon stick to cup if so desired...

> *Silence is the first ancestor of sound.*
>
> *an old Taoist saying*

MISO, MUSIC AND A LITTLE INCENSE

Sometimes my favorite food for solitude is soup and silence. The soup is a little easier to make, but the ingredients for silence are always available. Listening to music is one way to simmer into the silence, but not just any music. You need what I call silent music, and Japanese Shakuhachi music is the perfect example. The sound of a solo bamboo flute, filling the entire house, reminds me of being totally immersed in the heart of nature. Wind over waves, and a bell ringing in an empty sky are two images that give you the feeling of how it is to be filled with this music. Of course we each have our own taste when it comes to sipping the sounds of silence. But whatever we choose, be it a solo bamboo flute, or just sitting on a rock overlooking a running stream, we are able to feel the vibrations of healing love. We can truly taste the silence.

In Japan, preparing really good miso soup is considered an art, and the ritual of fixing it with various ingredients is a special ceremony in itself. Add to this a little music and a bit of fragrant incense and you have a meditation to please all your moods.

Traditionally, miso soup is made of a stock which consists solely of chopped kombu — a dried sea vegetable — a little sea salt, and a few slices of carrot. After boiling this and simmering for ten minutes, mild miso paste is stirred in, along with the other niceties. The following recipe is a variation, using an already prepared stock.

Miso Soup

2 stalks bay choy	a few bits chopped tofu
1 clove fresh garlic	1 tbspn. miso paste
½ scallion	3 cups vegetable purée*
1 tiny piece fresh ginger	3 sprigs fresh coriander

Miso paste, bak choy/Chinese celery, and fresh coriander/ Chinese parsley, are always available at any decent Oriental vegetable market, and sometimes you can find this at your local health food store and supermarket. Bak choy is the same green used to make the leafy part of won ton soup, and you can prepare it like that. Or else chop it the way you would dice celery for a tuna fish salad. Dice the garlic, scallion, ginger and tofu, put in reserve bowl. Then add the miso to purée stock and let slowly heat. Make sure to stir the miso paste thoroughly into the stock, so no lumps remain. When you get the right consistency, add the garlic, ginger, bak choy and tofu. Heat gently for a few minutes, stirring as you please. Pour into bowl, and add more tofu, the coriander and chopped scallion. It looks like lilies floating on a pond.

* See recipe for vegetable purée page 128.

Sometimes solitude is like sipping the universe through a straw and you don't have to try very hard. So let go... And when you decide that slowing down is really good for you, you will discover a whole new world of brews and beverages, the kind that truly give you the tranquility and peace you deserve.

BREWS AND BEVERAGES

Brews and beverages that are as good for tummy as they are for your cravings.

If you are interested, here are a few coffee substitutes: hot carob with cashew milk; ginseng; dandelion root; blackstrap molasses; lots of good humor and patience.

Peppermint and Rosehip Tea

Peppermint tea is a stimulant like caffeine, without the negative side-effects. It's useful for circulation, headaches, stomach cramps, and it tastes good too. Rose hips, the fruit of the wild rose flower, not only adds an extra natural sweetness, but is an excellent source of vitamin C. It aids in digestion, and combined with peppermint, it will give you a feeling of up energy, without shocking you into it like coffee or caffeine loaded tea.

ACORNS FOR BREAKFAST

In his book, *Eat The Weeds*, Ben Charles Harris writes: "Acorns have always been esteemed as a wholesome, nourishing and strengthening nutriment... They have been found to remove nervous complaints when other medicines failed and that by roasting they lose their astringent quality." Acorn shells, along with "barley, bedstraw, chickory root, groundnut, oats, peanut shells, Mexican (chick) pea, rye and soya bean", are all perfect coffee substitutes.

There are some excellent Swiss Instant Beverages that you can easily find at your health food store; *Bambu* made with chicory, figs, wheat, barley and acorns, is my favorite. You just stir in a tablespoonful to each cup of boiled water, and add a little milk. It even looks like coffee, only tastes better.

Actress Bibi Andersson loves to drink potato broth. She says it's the Swedish remedy for colds:

Bibi's Broth

One thing that I was weaned on living in Sweden is a simple potato broth. I love potatoes and I eat them raw just like carrots. But what I do is peel them, and let them soak overnight in some water. Then the next morning I sip the broth which is very nutritious, and then the raw potato is less raw. This drink gives me a lot of energy and I really enjoy it.

Actress Julie Newmar has another remedy for practically anything. She drinks this all the time. It gives her that extra boost of energy that helps, especially when working:

Julie's Juice

It's very boring when you have to clean out your vegetable juicer, but I love fresh vegetable juice so it's worth it. I get together all my stuff, and then into the juicer go — 3 fresh carrots, 1 fresh papaya, 10 strawberries, juice of half a lime, some plain yogurt — that's good for your digestion — ice, and a tablespoon of sesame oil. That will really juice you up for the day!

The Peach Drink

Perfect for breakfast, when you feel like sweet beginnings and no caffeine.

Peel 2 large peaches, and slice into a bowl. This makes about 3 cups depending on the size of your peaches. To the blender add 1 cup grapefruit juice, 6 or 7 fresh peppermint leaves, 2 tablespoons sesame seeds and 1 package of instant ginseng. Depending on your taste, add as much honey as you like, or simply omit. I like 1 tablespoonful, which is just enough to give it that extra sweetness. Blend for a minute or so. Loaded with energy, this is a great way to begin your day.

Peach Soup

Follow the same instructions as above, except omit the ginseng, and add more peaches. You may want to experiment to see how thick you want the soup. Adding another cup of peaches turns the drink into a wonderful cool summer soup. Garnish with more peppermint leaves.

....Honey........the dew distilled from the stars and the Rainbow ....ARISTOTLE ...

Lionel Stebbing, *Honey as Healer*

Sweeping Up Your Karma

*We shall invite Beauty to come as a guest into our homes. We shall
sweep away the dust and the spider-webs, not only from the corners
of our houses, but also from our relationships, words, thoughts — in
order that our spirits may breathe easily.*

Nicholas Roerich *Realm of Light*

Someone who was in Zen practice for twelve years, went to the
teacher and complained. "Look," he said, "I've been sitting for
twelve years, and my mind still goes crazy! What use is *zazen*, if those
wild monkeys still trample all over my mind? Why should I go on? It
all seems useless!" The teacher just smiled, and for a long time said
nothing. Then he said: "Twelve years! How many lifetimes do you
think Buddha lived before he became the Buddha? How many
centuries passed before the Christ Consciousness chose Jesus to be in
charge... Who do you think you are? Yes, now you have only one life
to live, but can't you be just a little bit patient? Can't you just do the
work?"

Sweeping visions are always nice, but we also need a broom.
According to ancient doctrines of karma, one of the reasons we are
still here, is because we have a lot of cleaning up to do. Like it or not,
that is how it is. So, can we change our past? Can it all be swept away?

It takes a long time to collect all the mental dust, all the hidden
feelings and thoughts pushed into cluttered closets, swept under
tired old rugs, and you know the rest... Nine times out of ten, most
of us don't even know that our house is long overdue for a super
spring cleaning. But when the cobwebs start to fall into our soup, and
anger starts to break out all over — we know! It's too bad that so many
of us wait until these feelings come to surface. Maybe it's in the form
of a migraine, maybe it's lower back pain, maybe it's something more
dramatic. But then the cliché is right: no pain, no gain. As
Ramakrishna, the great Hindu saint, once said: "You have to be sick
of being sick, tired of being tired, before you will change!"

"*I am guilty of guilt!*" — so says an Ingmar Bergman character in
one of his films. It's both funny and tragic to recognize the assortment
of *cluttered company* we entertain, but why do we keep them around?
Is it just the basic fear of being alone, or what we imagine it's like to
be alone? (Silence *is not* golden.) Is it because we're afraid to be
without company, and if it's pain, guilt and despair, then we assume
that's the way it has to be. At least it's company.

It requires discipline plus humor to change, and of course *patience*.
It takes courage to cultivate the positive side of yourself, rather than

giving in to the negative. But this is what the whole business of *transformation* means. Transformation isn't just some new buzz word flying around the holistic movement. It isn't just a poem about caterpillars turning into butterflies. It isn't just some elite esoteric hard-to-live notion.

Transformation begins with cleaning up all your *cluttered company*. It is wringing out that enemy in you, so you can really treat yourself like company. It is befriending your thoughts, being kind to your mind. It is changing your whole attitude about who you are.

The Ladder of Forgiveness

A solitude game to release resentment

We all need to climb the ladder of forgiveness, which is also the ladder of love and light. We go up with all our burdens to ask for forgiveness, and in ascending we become humble. It is said that *healing is a release from the past.* A past that hasn't yet been resolved often follows us about, like a shadow we can't shake off. Whatever it is that bothered us — or perhaps we bothered it — whatever it WAS, becomes an IS and WILL BE... It lives inside us, cramping our present. It lives in our present, like it or not. It makes us feel helpless and when we feel that we can't change what happened, we never hear the end of it. "What if I did this or that, what if this or that happened instead? WHAT IF!" That's why healing IS a release from the past. That's why we need to forgive our pasts totally, to forgive our futures in advance, and most of all to forgive ourselves.

But how do we go about forgiving? Saying it is one thing — meaning it is something else, and practicing it every day as routine, is again very different. When the chips are down, when others hurt us, or we hurt them, do we truly forgive, or ask to be forgiven? Most likely we don't. It's easier to resent than to forgive — or so it seems. It's easier to suppress feelings than to confront them. So we keep them on hold, give them their own room, their own bed, even a few good books to read, and we throw away the key. Until one day, all the occupants begin to protest. Resentment becomes part of the woodwork. We carry these feelings around and pay for the extra baggage. We carry these resentments around and don't even realize it. Until one day...!

Of course when we are truly in pain, when we feel like powerless victims of circumstances, it's hard to believe there is a way out. It's hard to believe that we can do anything to change our past karma, or even control what will happen. But that's why I believe we all need to ascend the ladder of forgiveness. *The pure power to forgive* IS the transforming thought that takes resentment and turns it into love. The *choice* to forgive gives you the power of love.

The whole idea of this exercise is to become aware of all your hidden resentment, and then and only then will you be able to discard it, and transform it:

PICTURE A SPIRAL STAIRCASE... your ladder of forgiveness. Decide upon its setting. I imagine it in an old beach house leading up to the top of the roof, where you can see the entire ocean. Or you can see it in itself — surrounded by a lovely, amorphous aura of light. At the bottom of the staircase is this giant bag full of resentment. Pick it up and feel its load. Heavy isn't it? Now I want you to consciously carry your resentment bag all the way up. As you ascend the first flight, think about what's inside your bag. What bothers you the most, what do you really need to throw out? Keep ascending and keep reflecting until you decide what you want to give up. What would you truly like to forgive NOW?

See the original circumstances that made you angry or hurt. See the person or people involved. Then with all your heart say: I AM READY TO RELEASE MY PAST. Take it out of your bag, and see it in the LIGHT. Hold it there. Then release it! Forgive yourself and everyone else involved. Then move up to a new level. Keep going up and up like this, reflecting, releasing, and forgiving until you decide you've reached the top. Now you are ready to totally forgive. Now it's time to throw out the BAG itself. Watch it fall to the bottom of the stairs. Then see it transmuted by the most beautiful aura of light.

THE LADDER OF FORGIVENESS will always be here for us to climb as often as we need it. Obviously in one exercise we may not get rid of everything, but at least our load gets lighter. For today, let go of what you can. The more we stop stuffing stuff into the bag, the easier it all becomes. Then there is nothing left to forgive and everything to PRAISE!

Perfect love casteth out all fear!

YES!

How to Spend a YES-DAY With Yourself

What could be a better affirmation than YES! Here is a great recipe for positive thinking... It is the *transforming thought* supreme... For solitaire you need cards and a place to sit quietly by yourself. But there is a way you can play solitude all day. I call it spending a YES-DAY with yourself. Its motto is easy to remember: REMOVE DISTRESS — SAY YES! Its equation is simple: YES = NO STRESS.

One of the rules of courtesy is to *think before you speak*. Well, when you start enjoying a YES-DAY, you will not only watch what you say to others, but what you say to yourself. You will learn to *think before you think!* You will start to think about what you are thinking. The following solitude game is a step-by-step process to help you to transform your thinking.

Yes-day Steps

1. *Resolve*
2. *Watch*
2. *Ask*
4. *Let go*
5. *Replace*

1. *Resolve*:   Begin your day with the resolution — I WILL SPEND A YES-DAY. Keep telling yourself: Today I will accept a yes-day... Hold on to the thought. Convince yourself that no matter what happens during the day, you will stick to your decision. See the ''yes'' in others rather than the ''no''. If you can't see the good, then move on... Try as hard as you can to be YES, to breathe YES, to walk in YES, to think YES, to treat others in a yes-way.

2. *Watch*:   Okay, you are resolved to spending a yes-day. But how do you begin to do this? You begin the process by WATCHING. Watching your thoughts during the day is the crucial first step to living a YES-DAY. When you begin to watch, you will be

surprised how often the same negative broken record repeats itself. All the hidden *cluttered company* comes to surface, because now you make the effort to pay attention. By watching without judgment, you can discern which thoughts are part of the YES-DAY, and which patterns persist in saying no... This kind of awareness is like *babysitting for your thoughts*. Watch and observe during the day, doing your normal activities. You don't want to make an entire project out of paying attention to every cry, otherwise you would never get your work done. The way to watch is the way you would watch children playing in a playground. Let them do their thing, but keep one eye open in case they get in trouble.

3. *Ask*:

Once you begin to recognize the patterns of your thinking, you are ready to clean up all the *cluttered company*... You are ready to move into step three of this process, the step that lets you ASK. Ask yourself: Are my thoughts giving me energy, or are they taking away my valuable time and energy? ASK: Are these thoughts robbing me of my peace? DO I WANT YOU HANGING AROUND IN MY BRAIN? If you ever have a conflict about whether a thought is a YES-THOUGHT or a NO-THOUGHT, just check into your feelings. Ask yourself honestly: How do I feel right this moment about this person, or thing, or situation and my connection to it? It is positive or destructive? For example, maybe the name of someone you once loved crops up, or a past experience flashes by, that was once supportive and nourishing. BUT are they important now? ASK: Are my thoughts feeding me more food for solitude,or are they eating me up? Are they making me feel good, or are they stirring up separation and loneliness? Are my thoughts cultivating love, or just aggravating me? ASK: Do I want to FIGHT with my PAST and WORRY about the FUTURE... OR FORGIVE the PAST and have FAITH in the FUTURE?

> *Leave this place and do no harm!*
>
> Supergirl commanding the destructive force

4. *Letting go*:   It's hard to let go of attachments of the past, but if they are no longer working for you, and with you, the time has come to say good-bye. Sentimentality never helped anyone. If you want to experience real love, then your mind must be clear. It must be open and ready for new thoughts. It's always shocking to give up that which has worked for you before, be it mantra or Prince Charming. But if it is no longer a loving connection it must be transformed. After you ASK about the nature of your thoughts, you have the option to practice the next step; LETTING GO. When you decide to let go of the negative thought, it will go away by itself. Here you choose to lose! But sometimes you need a gentle push to make it work.

Try this simple exercise: The moment you recognize a NO-THOUGHT, get rid of it by saying out-loud. I _____ am willing to let go of this disruptive thought disturbing my solitude and peace. If the negative thought comes back, keep repeating this affirmation, until the bad vibes get the message and willingly go away. Remember — they cannot refuse to leave, unless you let them stay.

The key to letting go is being aware of the pattern. You have already resolved yourself to *yes*, you have put out an alert to watch, and you have questioned whether this is good or bad for you. Now all you need to do, is *willingly* let go. And if you can't — don't worry about worrying. It will happen.

5. *Replacement*:   After letting go of the draining thought, you are ready to replace it with a supportive thought... Cultivating and growing YES-THOUGHTS is what you are doing when you spend a yes-day with yourself. And this is the way you start creating your positive self. Replacement is the step that plants the seed. To replace the old thought with a new thought can be done in many ways.

You can either use an affirmation, or practice complete silence.

You can actually feed yourself a new source of energy by thinking loving thoughts. You can replace the bad news with an immediate broadcast of good news. You can make up your own affirmation, repeat a nourishing line of confidence, and keep feeding it to yourself.Something like: I _____ am willing to accept all the love and healing I require right now. Or, if you prefer, you don't need to think in words. You could visualize a beautiful scene, see someone you love, or recall a pleasant sensation, something you like to taste or smell.

The other method of replacement, which is much harder to practice is the method of SILENCE. You don't replace the old thought with a new thought immediately. You wait. You trust the space of silence. You let the thought empty out, you let this process flow. You just keep waiting in silence, and then you begin to enjoy the space. You feel the anxiety pouring out of your brain, and it is like a real sensation. And when those old negative thoughts disappear, you know you have won. You have won the privilege of spending a YES-DAY WITH YOURSELF.

495. At times people are ready to admit the power of thought, but they do not apply this admission to themselves. They dream of great thoughts but will not discipline the small ones. They will ask how to transmute thought into action. One must begin by disciplining the smallest thoughts and then, only, create a thought that moves mountains.

Helena Roerich, *from the Agni Yoga book, Heart*

Zen And The Art Of Cleaning Up!

Yesterday I swept a lot... Today I sweep again,
and tomorrow... let the broom decide!

Zen teaches us how to let go, to empty, to get rid of unwanted thoughts. It is truly the art of cleaning up our 'cluttered company'. It is a continual process of letting go in order to receive. The Zen master would probably say, letting go just to let go. You receive because you receive; you just let go because you can... and you clean up because that is what you are doing!

The image that stands out for me is one of emptiness. But this isn't a cold clearing out or a sudden stripping away of things and thoughts dear to us. It is a way of cultivating a new space, an expanded consciousness. It is emptiness, yet abundance. It is a still, quiet place; it is going into the silence, uncluttering, serene.

It is what I think of as *embracing emptiness*, and *supporting the silence*. Embrace the emptiness, support the silence. HOLD THE IMAGE...

When you forget the *art* and do the work,
then cleaning up becomes zen...
If you forget the *zen* and do the work...
then cleaning up becomes an art!

We may say that for the mind there is a single avenue to essence, namely attention. Awaken attention, intensify it, purify it into white flame, and the actual and unsubstantial object of intuition will stand before you in all its living immediacy and innocent nakedness....

George Santayana, *The Realms of Being*

The foundation of faith is concentration.

Anonymous, *The Silent Voice*

The going beyond, the 'non-activity', are the means for us to attain mental freedom. In truth we have nothing to do. It is a question of 'undoing,' of clearing the ground of our mind, of making it, as much as possible, clean, void. The Void is, here, for us always a synonym of liberation.

Alexandra David-Neel* and Lama Yongden,
The Secret Oral Teachings in Tibetan Buddhist Sects

---

* See: *If You Want To Be A Hermit*, pp. 214–15, for more on Alexandra David-Neel.

...Alice thought to herself, "Then there's no use in speaking." The voices didn't join in this time, as she hadn't spoken, but to her great surprise they all thought in chorus (I hope you understand what thinking in chorus means... for I confess that I don't), "Better say nothing at all. Language is worth a thousand pounds a word!"...

Lewis Carrol, *Alice in Wonderland*

... The worst times of all have been when I've wanted to be just one. Try walking out on the ocean beach at night, looking at stars, thinking, Be one, be one. Doesn't work, ever. Just when you feel ascension, turning, wheeling, and that whirring sound like a mantel clock getting ready to strike, the other selves begin talking.... The only way to quiet them down, get them to stop, is to play music. That does it. Bach stops them every time, in their tracks, almost as though that's what they've been waiting for....

Lewis Thomas,
The Medusa and the Snail: More Notes of a Biology Watcher

In a monastery in medieval Japan was an elder monk of whom the young novices stood in much awe — not because he was severe with them but because nothing ever seemed to ruffle or upset him. So they found him uncanny and were frightened of him. Eventually they felt they could not bear it any longer, and decided to put him to the test. One dark winter morning when it was the elder's office to carry votive tea to the Founder's Hall, the novices ganged up and hid in a corner of the long and winding corridor leading to it. Just as the elder passed, they rushed out yelling like a horde of fiends. Without faltering one step, the elder walked on quietly, carefully carrying the tea. At the next bend of the corridor stood, as he knew, a little table. He made for it in the dark, laid the tea bowl down on it, covered it so that no dust could fall into it, but then supported himself against the wall and cried out with shock: "Oh-oh-oh!" A Zen Master telling this story commented on it: "So you see, there is nothing wrong with the emotions. Only, one must not let them carry one away, or interfere with what one is doing."

Irmgard Schloegl,
The Wisdom of the Zen Masters: Stories and Sayings, II

Recognition and liberation are simultaneous.

The Tibetan Book of the Dead

The Great Liberation Through Hearing in the Bardo is the Tibetan road map to salvation, grace, peace of mind and heart. This extremely detailed esoteric guide to the inner planes of being is another version of the Book of Revelation. All the paths to healing, to light and love, ultimately lead us to our stillpoint of rest and repose.
I love that statement:
recognition and liberation are simultaneous.

> *Persevere in gentleness*
>   *and it will lead to resolution.*
> *Persevere in weakness*
>   *and it will lead to strength.*

Huai-Nan-Tsze,
The History of the Great Light: Original Instructions in Tao

WU-WEI

I am being breathed.... life is doing it for me.

Nancy Wilson Ross

Nancy Wilson Ross is explaining the Taoist principle of *wu-wei*: "The secret of Zen is letting go, the secret of Zen is being yourself." She is giving a talk at the New York Theosophical Society, and her subject is the influence of Taoism on Zen. She is showing the interconnections between the two great movements, and she uses all her disciplines to make a point. At a given moment she will pause, and start to tell a story about her childhood. That is Nancy Wilson Ross the novelist. Then she takes out two poems — one by T.S. Eliot, and the other by Basho, a Haiku poet — to show the contrast between Eastern and Western perception. She covers great spans of history, and manages to tell little stories in between. That is Nancy Wilson Ross the Zen scholar and social historian. But no matter how scholarly the sources, Nancy Wilson Ross, the very personal person, stands out.

Putting it mildly, she is a character. She appears more like a little girl dressing up, than this brilliant and elegant woman who has shaped the course of spiritual/cultural history. I listen to her talk with great interest, and flashes of our meeting in her Old Westbury home three years before weave in and out of what is happening now. She is into 'finery,' I think, noting her creamy silk blouse, strand of pearls, and scent of expensive perfume. But then look at her hands, look at her face: they belong to a woman of great character, someone who is a worker… You can be a grand lady, but still get your hands into the ground.

The principles of the Tao are very much like Zen, and often it's difficult to distinguish between the two. ''The great quality of the Tao is *wu-wei*.'' Nancy Wilson Ross is explaining the essence of Zen, and even though I have been a long-time student, I understand it for the first time.

She continues to speak about *wu-wei*: ''It is not inaction in a normal sense, it is inaction in the sense of letting go, of giving up ego demands.'' She tells a story about when she was a child, when she heard a story in which the last line was: ''He ceased to breathe and he died.'' So she got very nervous about her breathing, and began to run around the house, asking, am I breathing, are you breathing? Her mother reassured her that she had nothing to worry about. She said, ''The great thing about your breath is that you don't have to do anything about it… You don't have to worry about it, it just goes on…''

That childhood experience made a very vivid impression on her, and as she relives the moments with you, you slowly capture the essence of the meaning of Zen. ''Everything is breathing,'' she says, ''the grass, the trees. This is *wu-wei*.''

''I am being breathed… Life is doing it for me. I am being breathed… I do not need to run it.'' She talks about the special way Zen art presents the harmony of life. ''Harmony is one, not two.'' In the great Zen paintings, ''Man is there, he is at one with the rocks and trees and streams. He is a part of the great totality of life. If he is really enlightened he wishes to be like the clouds which just float, or the bird who flies and leaves no tracks.''

After the talk, I go up to greet her, and it seems as though I had just been sitting in her living room moments before. A lot has happened in three years, but the moment is still the same. I begin to breathe.

The Rainbow Recipe

Stained glass windows of the sky
you the angels who pass by...

When I sat down and thought to myself what rainbows mean to me, I realized how words couldn't possibly describe something so miraculous as a rainbow. The rainbow is an image that speaks for itself. You simply have to see it for yourself. And each time, of course, the experience is different. Different for you, different for me, yet the same.

In truth, the rainbow is a *surrendering of our sight*. Our eyes surrender to it, our hearts are filled with it and on all levels our eyes are truly opened. To be with it, absorb it, let it absorb us — this is another level of seeing. "I'm going through the looking glass," said Alice, through it, not at it, now that's a way of looking. Alice never met Paracelsus in Wonderland, but if they did meet, it probably would have been under a rainbow. A little girl and a wise, elderly alchemist both knew about the inner and outer nature of life. Paracelsus was fond of contemplating the "two lights of man". In his selected writings he gives us an entire chapter about these two incredible lights. The heavenly lights from above influence the earth; that we all know. Just like we know that the rainbow is a few zillion drops of refracted light that decided to get together. But most important is who arranged that? Do we know that? Are we close to the one who created all the metaphors and realities of rainbows and all that is truly beautiful?

The rainbow is not only that incredible archway in the sky, but it is our inner truth, an inner form of who we were before and who we will be after we spend our time here on earth. It is a way to healing through the etheric body, an image that truly holds our heart.

Some pigments are just for seeing, others find their way into flowers and butterflies and stained glass windows and all kinds of sacred art. Auras everywhere paint up entire realms.

Pastel Protein And Your Blender

We have no art... we just do everything as well as we can.

An old Balinese saying

There are recipes just for cooking and recipes just for looking. You can spend an entire evening watching the sky change, as well as whipping up some sunsets in your blender. I like to think of these treats as pastel protein and the blender. The artist in you gets the chance to create all kinds of combinations, mixing not only high class nourishment but making a personal statement. This is your visual feast. Drinks so beautiful to see that the color alone feeds you plenty. I've always wanted to thread a rainbow — and this is definitely one way to do it!

Imagine northern lights, a still point in the sky that somehow swirls and moves within itself; this is the great blendings and bendings event. Sip it while you can, for tomorrow it will be gone. Think of early dawns and dusks and dreams of spectrums from afar. And then get your palette ready, take out your blender, and begin. The basic ingredient for your creation to come is *grapefruit juice*. This is a lactose-free shake with a wonderful rich creamy texture.

The essential ingredients for these fruit shakes are: grapefruit juice, fresh strawberries, sesame seeds, and honey. Once you combine these basics, you can add all kinds of little surprises — like fresh peppermint or spearmint leaves and fresh shredded coconut. If you want an extra dose of energy, a great pick-me-up drink in the afternoon could include a package or two of instant ginseng. Or you can also add to the strawberries, half a papaya, ten pitted cherries, and lo and behold you've just made a lovely cold soup. Any way you fix these drinks is always a beautiful way to give you that special boost without ever shocking your system.

Here is one variation: Imagine pink poppies and the texture of crushed velvet. This drink and some fresh fruit could be dinner on a hot languid day:

Strawberry Cooler

8 fresh ripe strawberries
2 cups grapefruit juice
4 tbspns. fresh lemon or lime juice
1 tbspn. honey or maple syrup

4 fresh peppermint leaves
½ cup organic sesame seeds*
6 sliced and pitted cherries (optional)

Blend for 2 minutes. Serve.

This recipe gives you about 3½ cups of shake. If you want to make a quart at a time just add 3 cups juice. After blending it, you can enjoy a glass or two, then refrigerate the rest. The next day blend it again, and add more fruit, a bit of shredded coconut, and more peppermint leaves. And if you really feel adventurous you can add a few *lemon ice cubes*:

Lemon Ice Cubes

Take 4 lemons and squeeze all the juice into a bowl. Add enough pure (not tap) water to fill ice-cube tray. Pour juice mixture into the tray and freeze. Substitute oranges, grapefruits or limes and go for it!

Use a cloud as a tablecloth...

In the book called *The History of Great Light*, Book 1, Original Instructions In Tao, by Huai-Nan-Tsze, the eighth Taoist Immortal is described:

8. Ho Hsien-Ku. Called the Immortal Maiden. In a vision she was instructed that if she ate mother-of-pearl she would gradually become immortal. She lived in the mountains and became more and more ethereal, floating from peak to peak. At last, dispensing with earthly food, she attained her quest. Her symbol is the lotus, the flower of open heartedness.

---

* There are 42 grams protein in every cup sesame seeds.

Pigments Of My Imagination

Once I made a soup that was so beautiful, I didn't want to eat it. I thought, how can I just sit here and eat this painting? I wish I could share it with someone else. I sat around waiting for the soup to cool, wondering, is it selfish to serve myself such beautiful auras? *Spectrum soup* — the mood of the moment gave me the name. Sentimental perhaps, but really this was something truly sacred. The beauty, the texture, the soup itself, ethereal yet grounded. It had a creamy miso base, an ocher base like a sandy shore. Then there were bits of fresh coriander, the same color green as young scallions, which in Japanese tradition is the perfect shade for the kind of Kiminos worn way back when the *Tale Of Genji* was written. *Asagi* is what it was called. Then bits of bright red cherry tomatoes floated about, along with tender pale green cabbage leaves, and orange carrots, and pearl colored potatoes and bits of brownish chopped kombu. Those were the apparant shades, the rest of it was an amorphous subtle variation.

There are many ways to sip auras like a lady, many pigments of the imagination — some that live forever in the *brainbows*, some that end up in the sky, some that swim and float in the soup. Yes, pigments, protein, pastel blendings. All of it is a visual feast, a food for the heart as well as sight. For presentation is so very important. How you present it to yourself is how you will then offer it to others. Living in these rainbow realms isn't just for company: it's for you — you alone but not alone. And even if you wonder if it's selfish to serve such spectrums, you still deserve it…

Spectrum Soup

1 tsp. sea salt	7 leaves cabbage
11 pieces chopped kombu	2 tbspns. mild miso paste
4 carrots	7 cloves garlic
4 red skinned potatoes	3 cherry tomatoes
1 large onion	2 sprigs coriander

Into a giant stainless steel pot (6 quart) add enough pure water to ¾ fill pot. Add sea salt, chopped kombu and carrots, peeled and chopped. Let heat until it comes to a boil. Then add peeled and cubed potatoes, peeled and chopped onion, and shredded cabbage leaves. Cover pot, and let simmer for about an hour, bring to boil, and let simmer again another hour. Also, remember to check in a few times with lots of loving stirs. Now, add a little more water, and let simmer a few minutes. Then add the miso paste, making sure to really blend it in. At this point the soup becomes clarified, and the cabbage leaves are barely perceptible. Allow this to simmer another ten minutes or so. Then let cool.

For storing your spectrums, two large 2-quart glass jars are very handy. What I usually do is chop the garlic cloves into tiny pieces, and then put equal amounts into the two jars. This is a natural preservative, as well as an enhancer for the flavor. Then I add the cooled soup, and refrigerate. You can keep it there for about two weeks, and each day the soup gets better and better. You may end up with another quart or so, and I usually have some of that right away, but of course you can store that too.

To serve, just reheat gently, add the chopped cherry tomatoes, and sprigs of coriander. On other occasions I've tried fresh spinach, which really loves to be with the miso base. Greens like okra, bak choy, parsley, or scallions, also blend in nicely. However, with this particular soup, mushrooms have a hard time. So stick to the tomatoes, and another addition of a green, and perhaps a touch more of miso.

ENJOY!

Stargazing

The friends I seek are seeking me.

John Burroughs, *Waiting*

Stargazing into the night, into our hearts, piercing into the center beyond the center, imagine all those mandalas, all those centers of consciousness. And all we have to do is look up! ''Look up!'' said Jesus to the man born blind, ''Look up and receive thy sight!'' Yes, all we need to do is look up — and the whole spirit of simply being there, of having the whole sky to ourselves, for a moment, for an evening, for eternity — now this is fabulous food for solitude.

The sheer beauty of the stars is something that one can appreciate without effort. Then there is the sense of awe and wonder about it all. Stargazing from earliest times has been a source of inspiration to scientists, poets and children of all ages. Meeting stars, the kind in the sky, is just like meeting friends, only more reliable. They can always be depended upon, once you get to know their habits. They are the one thing in the cosmic sky show that never changes, and if you show up, they will be there too.

In the beginning of your stargazing, forget about all the *why's*, just concentrate on where and when, you don't need to know why,

not yet. Just enjoy the fun of seeing all the star-pictures and you and your favorite constellations will grow accustomed to each other.

But you know how it is, you like to know why. You can get very involved with wanting to know why they are there, why you can see them, and why they don't fall on top of you, and by the time you ask all these questions, it's morning, and you've missed the whole trip. So let go, remember *Stargazing* is for fun. It's not for celestial navigation, or astronomy class. Just go up to your roof, onto your meadow or mountain top, make yourself comfortable and start to GAZE.

If you plan to do some stargazing tonight, you might feel like you need a guide. Alice-In-Auraland would be the perfect choice to hold your hand, as well as make all kinds of clever remarks, but most likely she will not be available. So, I would like to recommend a wonderful book instead. It's a classic, known to star-lovers of all ages.

Appropriately enough, it is called *The Stars, A New Way To See Them*. Published by Houghton Mifflin Company, it's available in paperback. It is the beginner's guide to starwatching, and as the author H.A. Rey states: "This book is meant for people who want to know just enough about the stars to be able to go out at night and find the major constellations, for the mere pleasure of it." Rey has created a new way to see the stars. Now the constellation of LEO the Lion, looks like a lion, rather than a scientific geometric diagram.

It also has maps of all the seasons, so you can see the stars as they change positions throughout the year. It has basic information that lets you easily locate all the stars, and it also answers all the questions that might have prevented you from going out in the first place. It shows you how, where, and when, and then tells you why the stars are stars.

After you have had some fun gazing at the stars and learning to locate their positions, you might become interested in how other people first saw the universe. Have you ever wondered how the stars, our luminous friends of the night, just hang there without falling on our heads? In a wonderful source called, *The Gradual Acceptance of the Copernican Theory of the Universe*, by Dorothy Stimson, we find many amusing anecdotes about our friends of the night:

> *According to Plutarch, though Thales (640?–546? BC) and later the Stoics believed the earth to be spherical in form, Anaximander (610–546? BC) thought it to be like a 'smooth stony pillar.' Anaximenes (sixth cent.) like a table.*

Aristotle claimed it was the fixed and immovable center around which swung the spherical universe with its heaven of fixed stars and its seven concentric circles of the planets kept in the places by their transparent crystalline spheres.

The stars were an even greater problem. *Anaximenes thought they were 'fastened like nails' in crystalline firmament, and others thought them to be 'fiery plates of gold resembling pictures'. But if the heavens were solid, how could the brief presence of a comet be explained? (p. 10)*

Dorothy Stimson,
The Gradual Acceptance of the Copernican Theory of the Universe

All greatest things have a humble beginning. The divine is nearer and more common than we are apt to think. The earth itself is a star, in the sky, little as we may suspect it.

John Burroughs, *The Light Of Day*

*Blessed are your eyes, for they see
with the sight of God.*

*When ye pray, remember, ye receive.
Return not then to doubts and questionings.
The price of answered prayer is this:
    BELIEVE;
    And then thank God, and give
    your soul its wings.
Only believe, have faith and do not doubt.
Then, like the giant lens that pierces space,
Glimpsing far worlds, oh, turn your soul about
And let the stars illumine your face.*

Bessie Beihl, *Blessed Are Your Eyes*

The Rainbow Body

I want to tell you how the name *rainbow body* came to be. One night, in early autumn, a Tibetan Buddhist Rinpoche was reciting mantras to prepare for his death. The entire family surrounded his bedside, and prayed silently with him. At the appointed moment, he passed from here to the other side, and as this happened a triple rainbow covered him from head to foot. Its mist-like splendor kept weaving round and round him, until at the final moment it changed into one luminous white light, went out the top of his head and slowly rose above all the disciples in the room. From then on, these auras were referred to as the rainbow body. And that was thousands of years ago.

There are many wondrous tales of similar experiences, rooted in religious tradition, that convey the same idea. The Upanishads from India, Chinese Taoist writings, and the Hermetic Teachings of the Egyptians are well known examples of this esoteric knowledge. Each one in their own way knew about the power of the rainbow body as a key to healing and to spiritual growth. And out of this wisdom came very sophisticated technique/ways to be in and of the light. An awareness of the correlation between sounds and colors, between inner and outer spectrums as one organic whole, became metaphor as well as the reality of being in the rainbow body.

Later on, the early Christians also understood these relationships. When Paul said to his disciples, ''Until Christ be formed in you,'' he was speaking about the light within. Most of the Revelation of St John centers around the number seven, the number of all the colors of the rainbow. Here we have one of the most profound and detailed descriptions of our inner spectrum. Chapter four and chapter eight, particularly, give important clues concerning the correspondences between our seven chakra or energy centres. The irresistible imagery of suns and moons and stars wrapping themselves round people on thrones, the sea of glass like crystal, the seven angels and seven trumpets, create a scenario one will never forget. But the drama of it all can't fool the sincere student who is ready for the journey within.

The rainbow image, as a truth within itself, has always played an important part in spiritual development. On one level, getting into the realm of auras and healing may seem contrived or new-age chic to some. On another level that doesn't matter because for those who believe in it, there is a foundation of ancient sacramental practice to rest upon, as well as the direct experience itself. It's one thing to talk about the light within, that divine spark that lives within each of us. But it's something else again to truly feel its presence, a magnificent energy that constantly calls upon us to receive love and healing. In this inner spectrum, images weave in and out of our deepest psyche. Auric realms come and go. It is up to each of us to make something of it. And this is what it means to raise our rainbow body.

Growing our colors — that is the image that is most outstanding for me. This thought came to me thanks to Priscilla, a misty morning, and an island tucked away at Lake George. It was off-season, so the whole place was isolated except for the sweetest mallard duckling I ever saw. There she was, Priscilla my rainbow friend, wobbling to and fro on the dock next to the spot where the boat was moored. I wish you could have been there to see her flapping about, showing off her newly grown rainbow wings. She kept trying to fly up and into the boat, but she couldn't make it, not yet, for she was just beginning to grow her colors. I began to feel sorry for all her effort, but then I realized that this little creature would never give up. One day all her colors would be grown, and fly she would, as high as the sky and probably beyond that.

We are, of course, just like Priscilla in trying to grow our colors. The difference, however, between Priscilla and us, is that, no matter what, she will receive her rainbow body. With you and me that is an option for us to decide. We can choose to try or not try — to fly or not fly. We can choose to consciously cultivate and raise this precious child within. And then, like the Tibetan Rinpoche, we too shall receive our rainbow body.

How to get in touch with your own inner spectrum is a part of the rainbow recipe from me to you. But, whether or not you have a natural ability, or even the desire for that matter to explore auric realms, isn't as important as realizing, REAL EYES-ing, that no matter which route you take, the HOLY LIGHT, the light of God, of true spirituality — *is within you*. In fact all of these ingredients are just a way of preparing the palette to get you into the mood, to simply cultivate peace of mind, purity of heart, and to evermore *remember* — that our real Rainbow Body is the Holy Light itself.

Mother Serena on the Inner Rainbow

If you find the world of auras and healing intriguing, I suggest you read what MOTHER SERENA has to say about our rainbow body, and then experiment for yourself. Mother Serena has a way of describing the inner planes of being that takes us on a journey into a whole beautiful realm of colors and vibrations. At first, it may seem like she's addressing a kindergarden child, but that's because she truly believed we are all 'children of the light.' She seldom talked about the nitty gritty details of healing through auras, because she was more concerned with our faith to simply trust in the light of God.

In a rare moment, MOTHER SERENA offered the following insights, her special recipe for feeling and seeing the Holy Light within:

''For me, the *Inner Rainbow* contains the secret of all healing. So consequently, when you learn to tap into this incredible source of color, it's amazing what happens. Every living soul on earth has a spark of God in them — and that spark, when it is allowed to express itself, can produce very beautiful vibrations, and as a result, very beautiful colors. When those color/vibrations go out into eternity, they leave in a wave, in a great huge circle, which is like the waves in the ocean. Only this is forming the sea of light. And these waves can help people who might not even know you exist, because they respond to it on a subconscious level. Some of them will say, 'Oh, it's funny, a few minutes ago I felt terrible, and now I feel wonderful.' And this is because of that vibration you emanated. You sent it directly to them, it has touched them and obviously affected them for the better.

We sometimes forget that vibrations cause a stirring in all the different elements we are exposed to. And if we keep this in mind, we would be more careful of what we think, and how we affect ourselves and others... These vibrations affect our bodies on all levels. We have our physical body, our etheric body and our astral body. But, in terms of human evolution, we are just beginning to form our mental body, which is like a mental sheath, a cloth-like substance. When the day comes that it's fully developed, we will no longer need airplanes to go overseas. We will travel by air with our thought. If we wanted to be in Sweden or Italy, or anyplace else, the moment we would think of the place we would be there. Now, wouldn't that be wonderful!

Of course this is all related to our inner rainbow. But what is it, and how does it work? First of all we must remember that we aren't just one body, in the sense of just being a physical flesh and bone form. And once we truly realize this, we can begin to understand the nature of our rainbow body, and how it is able to send forth light. Stating it simply, the inner rainbow is the color that our various bodies emanate, when we are active in that plane of consciousness.

For example, when we are busy on the etheric plane, the etheric body is then very active and so it vibrates and then radiates light. When we are on the astral/emotional plane, which means we are being stirred emotionally, we are going ahead and also radiating color. The distinctions between these various bodies are subtle, and the higher you get to the spiritual plane — the more refined and invisible it is.

The distinction between the *etheric* and *astral body* is that the *etheric* takes care of all physical activities, whereas the astral takes care of all emotional activities. The astral is more related to our fleeting moods, which are more psychological in nature. The etheric plane is closer to the earth. It is what gives us our vital forces. It generates health/vitality. Our etheric body gives us our physical well-being, but this is not seen by ordinary conscious-ness. It works on the invisible plane.

Most of the time we do not realize how many vibrations we emanate. However, we do know this: when a person enters a room, and their vibrations are, shall we say, of a negative type, that they are all disturbed, we feel something. We don't know what it is, but if we could see with our spiritual vision, we would then notice that this inner rainbow would be in a very disturbed state. It wouldn't be harmonious, instead it would be full of darts and fragments. It would be a broken aura and you could see the areas where it was disconnected from the circle. And so, when we think we're imagining the idea of 'bad vibes', we really are seeing the truth on another level.

Everything in the universe vibrates, and color is vibration. Even the so-called dead matter that we believe is life-less, vibrates. And the moment in which that article ceases to vibrate, it disintegrates, and the same thing pertains to ourselves. Everything that we do, we think, we feel, emanates a vibration. We may not realize it, but it all vibrates in its own way. When our vibrations are harmonious and we are at peace within ourselves, that vibration then produces very beautiful colors. We each have the solar spectrum, and each person has their own special shade which makes their inner rainbow unique.

Have you ever seen the color screen of the solar spectrum? It begins with a very sharp red and then it gradually merges into a pink, until it finally ends up on the violet blue side. Now, all these colors are within us, and when they mingle with each other, they produce new shades and colorings. But how they mingle depends on us. That's why we can't say that everybody has the same shade, because they don't all have the same thoughts and emanations. *What we think is what we produce in our inner rainbow.*

Even though there are universal meanings for specific colors, each person has their own basic interpretation. For instance, some colors are attributed to great activity, and others are more tranquil. Blue, for example, is attributed more to peace. Have you ever noticed that when the sky is very blue you feel very peaceful. So, when you emanate this color, it has a peaceful effect on someone else. Or if you see a golden color, you could be in

ecstasy just because you saw this color. There are numerous examples like this, and eventually we learn which shades we respond to the best. And when you get all the colors together, they become white. That's why to me, white means unity.

During the time of our healing prayers, I ask everyone to try to envision a light that covers the person they are praying for, from head to foot. And this light must emanate from the heart of the person sending it, so it radiates real love. I usually try to envision a very soft shade of gold and a little mixture of pink and white. It's a difficult thing to describe, but it's there. Also I might envision a very soft shade of violet. The softer the shades you envision, the higher you will be on the *celestial spectrum — inner rainbow*. And this is the key to healing. The darker and stronger shades are closer to the physical realm. But they too have their benefits.

Red, for instance, is ruled by Mars, and Mars is the energizer. So, if one is exhausted, a good dose of red could energize them, give them a new burst of energy. But when we go into the realm of spirit, we go into all the shades that soothe us, and so we then speak of all the delicate shades. We raise ourselves to that rate of vibration and to that realm.

During our healing service, sometimes I see auras, and other times I don't. But I do not go into the idea of phenomena in any way. I am more interested in the idea of sending out/radiating something. Then when I want to know if the person is actually responding, I'm apt to then see their aura, to see how they're responding. The aura shows me the vibration level that individual is emanating. As I said before, we are always in a constant state of emanating something. That's why I feel it's so important to broadcast good thoughts, and I always remind people to remember that. For even though we may not yet realize it, *thoughts are things*. So when we think and we think vigorously, we're sending out a wave of vibration that could go to the end of the world!

People often ask me, 'How can I really get in touch with my own source of color and harmony?' What I suggest is, first of all, really relax. I tell them to relax as much as they can, especially their hands. The hands should not be in a clenched position, but rather they should be extended, opened, so that they are completely relaxed. Or else, one can gently have them sitting on the lap. Either way, palms opened, or on the lap, it's okay as long as you know they are relaxed. Then feel your toes and feet relaxing, and then your back too must be relaxed. Don't force anything, just feel relaxation. Of course this in itself is an exercise.

Many people spend their entire lives trying to relax and they find it a very difficult thing to do. But if they succeed in doing that, they will find a new world opening before them. If you're very tense, you will not be able to do anything. But if you imagine the *light* with all your heart, that will ease you up. *The idea of relaxing is really to let the light work through you*, to let it flow, to let it circulate, so in a sense *you are not doing anything*. For some people, the harder they try to relax, the less they relax. So not trying in that sense is a way to just be.

Sometimes soft and soothing music can help to heal and relax. And naturally the right colors are very relaxing and peaceful. I have a tendency to like very soft shades of green. You notice that nature in all her glory displays a green lawn, and green trees. And in the lawn and trees are different shades of green. Also, if you look at a bud, you'll see all kinds of green nuances, then later, strangely enough, other colors come into that bud. And have you ever noticed the velvety texture of a red rose. Take out a petal and the part closest to the stem has very soft shades of gold and sometimes pink. Right in the mandala/center of the rose, you have the faintest nuances of coloring. Then you look at the outside of that rose, and see the beauty of that velvety textured red red rose and wonder, where does it all come from? And that's the amazing thing! Who created color? Who created vibration? And for me, there's only one answer — GOD. For God is everywhere. God is vibration too. This is what we mean by the emanations of God, for God is Light. And out of this light, He created everything through vibration. Vibration is a living thing; if we could only realize it. It's a spiritual emanation that's coming out of everything and everyone. Remember this always, and you will get to know your rainbow body, in a way you haven't yet imagined.''

The following — a Christian orthodox mantra — was Mother Serena's favorite prayer for evoking and calling upon the light:

Oh Heavenly Father, the Paraclete of all Wisdom and Spirit of Truth. Thou who art in all places and who fillest all things. Treasury of Inspiration and Giver of Life. Come and take up thine abode in us, and cleanse us from every stain and save our Soul. O Holy One. (Holy God. Holy and Mighty. Holy and Immortal One. Have mercy on Us.) — thrice.

Imagine Windows in your Toes

But there is also an inner form which is not a shape but a shaper.

St Augustine

The subtle body, sometimes referred to as the *Rainbow Body*, as Mother Serena said, is the key to restoring vital energies. So in a literal sense, it is what keeps us *all together*. Since the word AURA comes from a Greek root which means breeze, it all connects to the idea that aura therapy is a direct way to circulate healing energies. Weaving your own tapestry of light is a way to circulate these auras to literally encircle yourself with a sheath of healing light. For we are made not only of flesh and blood, but of LIGHT, of rainbows and spectrums of delight. IMAGING allows us to work with this, play with it, shape it, just BE WITH IT and IN IT...

The following meditation is a step by step guided exercise that lets you step into your auric body. Visualizing your rainbow body, is a creative way to raise that wonderful Rainbow Child within you...

So...
Imagine Windows In Your Toes
Imagine Brainbows!

Visualizing your rainbow body...

BEGIN by getting comfortable... Lying down on your back is most effective with your feet propped up on a pillow. Also playing the meditation music of your choice can be very helpful, but so is sheer silence.

Seven Steps:

1 — Starting from the top of your head and flowing down. Imagine a rainbow covering you from EAR to EAR.

Hold the image

2 — Extend this from SHOULDER to SHOULDER.

Hold the image

3 — Extend this from HIP to HIP

Hold the image

4 — KNEE to KNEE

Hold the image

5 — ANKLE to ANKLE

Hold the image

6 — IMAGINE WINDOWS IN YOUR TOES... Let the rainbows flow out of your toes and direct this energy upwards to encircle your entire body. Keep going until this comes up and over your head.

Hold the image

7 — Weave the aura now covering you from head to foot to head, so it returns to your feet. Reverse the entire process. Now begin with your feet. Imagine windows in your toes and let the energy move upwards.

A few images and tips

These steps are an ongoing flowing movement, circulating around and around you. Just feel these energies breathing over you. SPRINGS — SHOWERS — CIRCULATE. Those are important images to remember. Imagine floating in a bath of light. Feel it supporting you, surrounding you with its warmth and lovely sensations — tingly vibrations — massaging you all over,. Imagine a WARM BREEZE. Imagine a COCOON OF LIGHT weaving and spinning round and round you. Whatever you imagine, remember DON'T FORCE, just let it happen. You may discover a particular hue or shade that appeals to you, be it a pastel lavender or a golden light. Work with the colors/rainbows that please you. Don't worry if you can't call upon a specific shade for a specific chakra. In the end, the rainbow knows what you need. The more you practice, the easier it will be to call upon your rainbows to heal you and to surround you with their lovely spirit.

Flames Of Reference

Harness thy fiery energies to the service of the Light.

Jacob Boehme

How mysterious is the light? The glorious light that feeds the plants and our souls as one. As Teilhard De Chardin said, "Someday after we have mastered the winds, the waves, the tides and gravity, we shall harness for God the energies of love. Then for the second time in the history of the world, man will have discovered fire." A flame needs oxygen to burn. Did you know that the word inspire literally means to breathe into? Without the breath of God there would be no light. Without breath there would be no thing — nothing! And so we have our trinity of FIRE — DESIRE — INSPIRE.

I hope the following sparks from science, mysticism, and plain ordinary feelings bring you evermore into that wonderful realm which is so mysterious yet so apparent — OUR LIGHT.

THE RAINBOW DANCE

You have your eyes, you have your ears: look with your eyes on the things of Nature, hear with your ears what goes on in Nature; the spiritual reveals itself through color and through tone, and as you look and listen, you cannot help feeling how it reveals itself in these...

People gaze open-eyed at the rainbow. But if you look at the rainbow with a little imagination, you may see there elemental Beings. These elemental Beings are full of activity and demonstrate it in a very remarkable manner. Here (at yellow) you see some of them streaming forth from the rainbow, continually coming away out of it. They move across and the moment they reach the lower end of the green they are drawn to it again. To one who views it with imagination, the whole rainbow manifests a streaming out of spirit and a disappearing of it again within. It is like a spiritual dance, in very deed a spiritual waltz, wonderful to behold...

Now picture to yourselves: There before me is no mere rainbow! Beings are coming out of it and disappearing into it — here anxiety and fear, there courage... And now, here the rainbow receives a certain thickness and you will be able to imagine how this gives rise to the element of Water. In this watery element spiritual Beings live, Beings that are actually a kind of copy of the Third Hierarchy.

Rudolf Steiner

At a time when composers and intellectuals in general were closet mystics, Johannes Brahms had the courage to reveal his homage to Christ. For Brahms, ''Jesus was the world's supreme spiritual genius... He was conscious of appropriating the only true source of power as no one else ever was.'' In a rare interview we learn how Brahms received cosmic vibrations of eternal truths. And here he could very well be talking about the subtleties of our rainbow body, as he elaborates on how he channels the Holy Spirit during the course of his creative process. Brahms talks about the inner realms of his soul, his sense of surrender, and how he worked through and for God. In the following passage he responds to the question: 'How do you contact Omnipotence?'

That is the great question. It cannot be done merely by will-power working through the conscious mind, which is an evolutionary product of the physical realm and perishes with the body. It can only be accomplished by the soul-powers within — the real ego that survives bodily death. Those powers are quiescent to the conscious mind unless illumined by Spirit. Now Jesus taught us that God is Spirit, and he also said, 'I and my Father are one.' (John 10:30)

To realize that we are one with the Creator, as Beethoven did, is a wonderful and awe-inspiring experience. Very few human beings ever come into that realization and that is why there are so few great composers or creative geniuses in any line of human endeavor. I always contemplate all this before commencing to compose. This is the first step.

When I feel the urge I begin by appealing directly to my Maker and I first ask Him the three most important questions pertaining to our life here in this world — whence, wherefore, whither, (woher, warum, wohin).

I immediately feel vibrations that thrill my whole being. These are the Spirit illuminating the soul-power within, and in this exalted state, I see clearly what is obscure in my ordinary moods; then I feel capable of drawing inspiration from above, as Beethoven did. Above all, I realize at such moments the tremendous significance of Jesus' supreme revelation, 'I and my Father are one.' Those vibrations assume the forms of distinct mental images, after I have formulated my desire and resolve in regard to what I want — namely, to be inspired so that I can compose something that will uplift and benefit humanity — something of permanent value.

Straightaway the ideas flow in upon me, directly from God, and not only do I see distinct themes in my mind's eye, but they are clothed in the right forms, harmonies, and orchestration. Measure by measure, the finished product is revealed to me when I am in those rare, inspired moods... I have to be in a semi-trance condition to get such results — a condition when the conscious mind is in temporary abeyance and the subconscious mind is in control, for it is through the subconscious mind, which is a part of Omnipotence, that the inspiration comes.

Spirit is the light of the soul. Spirit is universal. Spirit is the creative energy of the Cosmos. The soul of man is not conscious of its powers until it is enlightened by Spirit. Therefore, to evolve and grow, man must learn how to use and develop his own soul forces. All great creative geniuses do this, although some of them do not seem to be as conscious of the process as others.

'Not I, but the Father that dwelleth within me, He doeth the works.' Jesus proclaimed a great truth when He said that, and when I am at my best while composing, I too feel that a higher power is working through me... Jesus also said, 'The works that I do shall ye do also, and greater works than these.'... The same power that enabled Jesus to work His miracles, we call it God, Omnipotence, Divinity, the Creator, etc. Schubert called it 'die Allmacht' but 'what's in a name?' as Shakespeare so aptly questions.

It is the power that created our earth and the whole universe, including you and me, and that great God-intoxicated Nazarene taught us that we can appropriate it for our own upbuilding right here and now and also earn Eternal Life.

Johannes Brahms, from *Talks With Great Composers*

THE ASSERTION OF THE I
All that ye need is near ye
God is complete supply
Trust, have faith, then hear ye
Dare to assert the I.

Power is within and about ye
Keep toward the light thine eye.
Naught can come near to route ye
Who have dared to assert the I.

Origin unknown
Arthur M. Abell, *Talks With Great Composers*

Where there is power, there some result or other is produced. No ray of sunlight is ever lost, but the green which it wakes into existence needs time to sprout, and it is not always granted to the sower to live to see the harvest. All work that is worth anything is done in faith.

Albert Schweitzer, *The Light Within Us*

A few sparks from The Realm of Light by Nicholas Roerich

ANGEL — The Blessed Silence!
Where is the limit of Radiance? Where is the measure of might? Light itself reaches the invisible and sound immerses... No glimmer stirs; not even the fragrance of prana. This is the highest tension. Only the heart knows that silence is calling and that the chalice is brimming.

With the eyes of the heart we can see Be-ness.

You see how important it is to create your essential energy. You will hear about scientific energy, occult energy — these are all symbols for the same thing — creative energy... You know how electricity is created by the crossing of two energies. That is a beautiful moment when two immeasurable energies create something physical and measurable...
We are speaking about the Beautiful because when you realize this scientific energy — the greatest power which is in each of you — then you shall release this energy, and energy will grow. *

Nicholas Roerich, *The Realm of Light*

When we talked, GOPI KRISHNA** shared his insight on what I call 'brainbows':

"According to Indian tradition, THOUGHT ENERGY is prana. In the use of spiritual awakening, this prana energy actually changes like an electric current. Because of the kundalini experience I had, a very powerful current of prana permeated my brain. My whole brain is now flooded with another energy than that which floods yours or others. This energy is so remote and so extraordinary, from that which science now defines as energy. Our brain is normally held by light — by cerebral spinal fluid and by psychic energy. Normally, biologists are not able to define

* See the Rainbow Body p. 166
** For more on Gopi Krishna see The Mystical Experience p. 231

what energy supplies our brain, our neurons, and there is a difference of opinion between them. Some believe it is a chemical energy, but they aren't able to determine its character. However, many biologists, like Wilder Penfield, the neuro-surgeon who experimented very successfully in the States, and others believe that THOUGHT ENERGY is totally different from all the other known energies — like the energy of gravity, electro-magnetic and chemical energy.

When the kundalini makes his home in the brain, then the reproductive system is working totally in the upper direction. So, from a physiological/psychological/mental point of view, I am not considered normal, because my brain is flooded with this light. Yet, this doesn't mean I could be fed by light alone. I believe that's because my body was regulated by one form of energy for thirty-four years. So, when in the thirty-fourth year another energy suddenly entered my body, then all my nerves, all my brain cells, all my organs had to get accustomed to this new energy. And it took me twelve years to do that.

Even now, the force is so powerful, that I cannot allow my stomach to remain empty for long periods. Because in that case the strain on the organs would be too much. So now this energy takes whatever I eat, and I eat a healthy normal diet. Yet, I refuse to take in any poisons. For me there is absolutely no alcohol whatsoever, or smoking. And I must have regular hours for my sleep and for my work.

As far as my daily practice, for me now nothing is necessary. I don't feel the need to be alone, or to meditate formally. I now live in the state of light. It is my natural state of consciousness.''

I asked historian BILL THOMPSON what he thought the food of the future would be? And without any hesitation he smiled and said LIGHT! And then I said, do you really believe that? And he said:

''Yes... and it will be direct! We'll become plants again, photosynthesis. There are saints in the past who have not had food. You know in the *Autobiography of a Yogi**, he talks about the saint who would not eat any food. She would not eat any food

---

* The Yogi, of course, is Swami Paramahansa Yogananda, the saint is Therese of Konnersreuth, who deeply impressed him enough to write an entire chapter about her.

except Holy Communion. She just fed on the light. I think she took the energy to the prana, directly from the biosphere.

Of course, whether or not this is true is debatable. As a myth it sounds interesting, it could even be feasible. According to the book, many people would come to see her, and verified this fact. And there have also been saints chronicled in India who would not eat food. And it's certainly true that when your energy is high, and when you're in a place of intense concentration, or intense yoga, you eat less and you sleep less.''

'Therese Neumann the Catholic Stigmatist', is the name of the chapter about this incredible saint who dined solely on the light. In the following passage, from *Autobiography of a Yogi*, we find a conversation between her and Yogananda, who traveled all the way from New York to the small Bavarian village of Konnersreuth, just to meet this remarkable woman. He, like others, was curious to find out if it was really true, that 'this healthy, well-formed, rosy-cheeked and cheerful' being never ate anything:

'Don't you eat anything?' I wanted to hear the answer from her own lips. 'No, except a Host (a Eucharistic flour wafer) at six o'clock each morning.'

'How large is the Host?'

'It is paper-thin, the size of a small coin.' She added, 'I take it for sacramental reasons; if it is unconsecrated, I am unable to swallow it.'

'Certainly you could not have lived on that, for twelve whole years?'

'I live by God's light.'

How simple her reply, how Einsteinian!

'I see you realize that energy flows to your body from the ether, sun, and air.' A swift smile broke over her face.

'I am so happy to know you understand how I live.'

'Your sacred life is a daily demonstration of the truth uttered by Christ: Man shall not live by bread alone, but by every word that proceedeth out of the mouth of God.

Again she showed joy at my explanation.

'It is indeed so. One of the reasons I am here on earth today is to prove that man can live by God's invisible light, and not by food only.'

'Can you teach others how to live without food?' She appeared a trifle shocked.

'I cannot do that; God does not wish it.'

Paramahansa Yogananda, Autobiography of a Yogi

May I know all the sounds as my own sound
May I know all the lights as my own light
May I know all the rays as my own ray,
May I spontaneously know the bardo as myself.

        Inspiration Prayer, from The Tibetan Book Of The Dead

    Color is the sufferings of the Light.
        Goethe

The sun (the highest of the devatās, or, as some writers transpose, the angels) is to be meditated on as honey; it is made from the karmas enjoined in the four vedas and the secret doctrines; it is carried by the sun's rays and is lodged in cells on the four sides and on the top of the orb; the honeycomb is the intermediate world hanging from the cross-beam of heaven. The group of devas known as vasus live on the honey on the east, and the four other groups live on honey on the other four sides and on the top. By this vidyā a person gets into one of these groups, enjoys its honey and has the supremacy in the group, and his will is never frustrated. Here, in addition to meditation on the sun and on the five-fold honey, one has to meditate also on the vasus enjoying the honey; for he has to become a vasu himself, and the rule is — what one meditates on, that he becomes.

    Rāmānuja, *from John C. Plott, A Philosophy of Devotion*

    Release is in the eye.

Yin Fu King, *Chinese Book Of the Secret Correspondences**

---

* The above quote comes from Paul Brunton's chapter 'The Mystery of the Eye,' p. 226. I recommend reading the entire book *The Quest Of The Overself*, published by E.P. Dutton & Co., N.Y.

I began to think of the soul as if it were a castle made of a single diamond or of very clear crystal, in which there are many mansions. Let us now imagine... some above, others below, others at each side; and in the center and midst of them all is the chiefest mansion where the most secret things pass between God and the soul....

Now if this castle is the soul, there can clearly be no question of our entering it. For we ourselves are the castle: and it would be absurd to tell someone to enter a room when he was in it already! But you must understand that there are many ways of 'being' in a place...

In speaking of the soul, we must always think of it as spacious, ample and lofty, and this can be done without the least exaggeration, for the soul's capacity is much greater than we realize, and this Sun, which is in the palace, reaches every part of it.

St Teresa of Avila, *Interior Castle*

A History Of Luminescence

The subject of light, especially luminescent light, aroused the curiosity of everyone throughout all times. Primitive stories that emerged out of superstition are just as fascinating as how the great minds of the universe questioned the mystery of nature. In *A History Of Luminescence* by E. Newton Harvey*, you not only learn about the process of ideas and thinking, but you are also taken back into antiquity through a multitude of creation myths from all cultures. Light, literally and metaphorically, becomes the star in all these captivating tales. Here we have a book that is full of continuous inspiration, as well as being an in-depth scholarly work. It is probably one of the best books about natural phenomena ever written. It is *the* Source/Bible on luminescence.

Luminescence is that wondrous light sometimes called 'cold light' because it emits its energy without heat. We find its phenomena working in the likes of such examples as the glow of phosphorus, the aurora borealis, the light of the sea, and the firefly as well as glow-worm. Of course, as Harvey points out, "One of the problems of the historian of luminescence is to sift the true from the false report. Stories of luminous jewels and luminous stones have been handed down from earliest times, but in most cases the light has been due to reflection rather than light emission. The instances of luminous human beings are fascinating to read of, but it is quite certain that man has never acquired the ability to produce a light like a firefly."

E. Newton Harvey, scientist and historian, has left us an enormous gift with this volume on luminescence. Each and every page is written in such a way that it will touch the mystic, the philosopher, and the scientist, as well as the curious person who cares about the mystery and wonder of light. Even though it is primarily concerned with questions of natural phenomena, this book is spiritual in its way and draws you into it with a magical energy. Because of its density, it's not the sort of book you expect to read from beginning to end, unless of course you so desire. For me, it's more like the experience of using the I Ching. You open it up, flip through it, and no matter where you land, you're in for a real inspiration. You can spend an entire lifetime with a book like this!

My favorite parts are everywhere. I especially like all the sections about fireflies, who I consider to be my friendly mystical insects. They

---

* *A History Of Luminescence (from the Earliest Times until 1900)* by E. Newton Harvey, published by The American Philosophical Society, Philadelphia, 1957. This hardcover book is Volume 44 of the Memoirs of the American Philosophical Society. It is available in libraries and through the Society. (692 pages)

always carry their own light around, and as Harvey pointed out, modern day engineers can't even begin to reproduce their structure. Then there is a choice piece on Paracelsus, another one of my mystical friends. Our father of modern medicine, and the sixteenth century's most famous alchemist, apparently anticipated the discovery of phosphorus one hundred years before the preparation of its sample became 'official'. You can read about *ignis lamben*, the silent electrical charge in the air, one of the phenomena reported to be truly luminescent. I could go on and on about lots of curious facts, but then I would never be able to do the whole work justice.

You simply have to read it for yourself to discover all the ingredients which will nourish and delight you. But just to whet your appetite, here are a few passages. To begin, let's start at the beginning:

Mythology

Light has always occupied an important place in superstition among all peoples. The contrast of light and darkness is so striking that many races have adopted some story of the origin of light in the history of creation...

Among some cultures, living beings came before daylight in the sequence of events and it is interesting to note that they were thought of as luminous. The Altaic race of Siberia believed that before the sun and moon appeared, 'people who then flew in the air gave out light and warmed their surroundings themselves, so they did not even miss the heat of the sun.' Light and heat are almost universally associated in the minds of all peoples. (pp. 11, 12)

The appearance of light without fire or without heat is immediately imbued with a supernatural significance. Since the start of the Christian era, many miracles have involved a light shining under mysterious circumstances or a luminous region of the human body, the hand or the face of a saint. The folklore and superstition of every people, especially those from mountainous regions, is full of mysterious lights, ignes fatui, corposants, feux follets, *corpse candles, glowing hands, glowing tree trunks, and shining animals, many of which undoubtedly had their origin in observation of true luminescences, electrical discharges or phosphorescent wood...*

The word 'light' has often been used figuratively, as in Scandinavian mythology. Balder, the second son of Odin, was said to be a very fine and good man, and so beautiful and fair that light shines from him. The New Testament statement that, when Jesus was transfigured, 'His face did shine as the sun and his raiment was

white as the light,' is clearly a figure of speech.* The student of luminescence is too frequently confronted with the many meanings of the word 'light.' (p. 13)

Whether they knew it or not, some of the greatest minds in the field of science were mystics. Anyone who had a lifelong relationship with *light* must have been a closet mystic. In some cases, the quest for the understanding for luminescence might have been strictly science, in others, it was a spiritual avenue to pursue. In his chapter on the seventeenth century, Harvey devotes several pages to Thomas Bartholin, a Danish physician born in Copenhagen. Bartholin wrote the outstanding book of luminescence of the seventeenth century called *De Luce Animalium*. In it, as Harvey states: "It is not surprising to find that Bartholin's treatment of the *light of men* in Book I is full of mysticism. There are many references to the Bible and to writers of antiquity... Bartholin wrote about the shining face of Moses and the light of the human soul." He also wrote about sparks of light he witnessed as coming from all parts of the human body. He saw this as electrical phenomena, and what he was reporting is the now verifiable phenomena known as human auras, proven to be real due to the new technology of kirlian photography.

There are times one feels that Harvey is apologizing for his little references to 'spirituality', and that's okay. The scientist/historian in him must keep it all in perspective. But because of his scholarship, we are turned on to such incredible creative spirits as Thomas Bartholin, who had no taboos regarding his esoteric wisdom.

Through his great work *De Luce Animalium*, Bartholin has given us a seventeenth century recipe for LIGHT, that covers all spectrums.

The third book of De Luce Animalium *deals with the cause of the light of living things... the final cause is the purpose of the light... Under final cause, it is not surprising to find the statement that (Book III, Chap.9):*

'Light has been created by God for the perfection of the universe with such beauty and form emulating divinity as he deemed necessary for a perfect example of his glory amidst the mortal and frail... In his primary intention he looked toward its usefulness for man.' (p. 113)

---

* And the student of 'spiritual light' is also confronted with the literal meanings of light... So one could easily ask, how does he know this was a figure of speech, was he there? But let's not get into mystical mischief, at least not yet!

Right Brain Recipes

Solitude Games and other Ingredients
to awaken intuition

He gave them a heart to think with.
Ecclesiasticus 17:6

The experience of seeing is as personal as the experience of being. Powers of perception are given to each of us, but how we channel these energies is up to us. *'Right brain thinking'* has become a new-age cliché, but a cliché with a soul. To me, it conjures up a whole realm of IMAGES – images that heal, images that inspire. It brings us into the realm of imagination, the realm where images are born, live and die. It is here that intuition – the silent voice – gets to speak. It is here that we get to play with our insight, our dreams, and other ways of seeing.

The great gift of the right brain is its ability to visualize images of wholeness for us. And through these impressions we are transformed. If anyone was a 'right brain person' as the lingo goes, then Jesus was certainly that person. He understood the power of images to heal. When Christ said, ''*Now* is the acceptable time for healing,'' very few people realized how simple it was and *is* to activate this principle. All that is needed is the desire to be whole, and the willingness to *begin*.

Seeing is believing, as we say, but real faith is believing without seeing, which gets us into imaging the invisible. Here our heart is opened, and then we truly SEE. So, was Descartes right? ''I *think* – therefore I am.'' Or do Scriptures really say it all: ''He gave them a heart to think with.'' I *am* – therefore I think!

A Way To Listen

A special solitude game

The following solitude game is a special way to let you listen... to use your eyes as EARS.

...and then there was silence in Heaven for about a half an hour.

Revelation

Revelation's thirty minutes is a lot of silence, maybe more than any of us can hope for in a lifetime. But by playing this game, you might receive a few seconds of real silence, and this can change your whole day. To listen with your eyes means to receive forms *without interpreting* their message. You just accept them as they are. This is pure SEEING.

How long can you listen with your eyes without thinking anything? TRY THIS SIMPLE EXPERIMENT:

1. *Choose something that is visually pleasing to you..*
   Sky-watching is great for this experiment, especially when there are a lot of clouds or stars you can see. Sunrises and sunsets are ideal for watching the changing light, but if you can't meet them, use any desirable subject of your choice.

2. *Let your eyes focus in at the subject, aim directly at a center point.*
   You are kissing the form.

3. *Let the form come to you. Let this center point enter your visual field.*
   Let the form kiss you...

4. *Let these signals penetrate your vision – be impressed by it, and let its impression enter your mind.* You know the expression, we are going to *take in* the sights. Well, that's exactly what it means. Here you are taking in your visual feast; in a sense it's like swallowing it.

5. *At this point, there should be no separation between your eyes and the form. There should be no awareness of* distance *between you and the cloud, or you and the stream flowing in the valley below. No matter how far away or how close your subject is, there should be no space between you and it.* Like a kiss, it becomes a movement of stillness. You kiss it, and it kisses you, and then you are both one together.

6. *See how long you can listen without talking... How long can you play this game without thinking anything?* When someone is kissing you, you don't want to talk, do you? Give the centerpoint within the form a chance to enter your eyes, then see the whole form. Let it talk to you, listen to what it is saying by simply seeing it.

This experiment may seem obvious, and very easy to do. But you will be surprised at how hard it is to stop your flow of thoughts and simply *see*. In the psychological way we view time, Steps 1 through 5 appear to occur in a matter of seconds. But biologically, this visual experience happens in a matter of milliseconds. You get a visual imprint before a cognition.

The perceptual system of the brain photographs the image, and stores it in its perception bank faster than the cerebral cortex makes an opinion about it. By the time you think *blue*, the blue sky has already been digested by your visual center. One would expect that all you need is the experience of seeing, and not all the thoughts, since the speed of seeing is faster than the speed of thinking. But the thought process peculiar to human beings has a way of compensating for its otherwise limited senses. It has to interpret all the data, and make some sort of new pattern out of it. We refuse to solely trust our instincts by letting them do their own thing. And wisely so, for this is what separates us from the animals. Our thoughts allow us to do, not to be. But, there is a time for left-brain thinking, and a time for *right-brain-being*. And then there is something we can learn from both the animals and angels.

For this exercise, the way to respond is to be silently receptive. It's important not only to watch the sky, but to watch all your inner dialogue. It's important to let go of the flow of thoughts, so you may savor the object of your choice. For example, if you are watching a sunrise, you may follow the changing light through the passing clouds. Suddenly you start thinking and interpreting. You start to connect *these clouds* to old ideas you had about clouds. It's like a flashing signal that says, ''Oh I recognize these clouds, they remind me of the clouds I saw while sailing on that island.'' Or, you may think, ''Oh *now* I finally understand what that book *The Cloud of Unknowing* means!''

Of course it's inspiring to make associations, but then you are talking to and about the clouds, rather than listening to what they want to say to you right this moment. Remember – this is your visual feast, so take the time to be with the clouds and see them NOW as they are. Be with them, by giving them your *undivided* attention. Let them nourish you now! Later on there is plenty of time to reflect. Then you can make all sorts of new connections, based on how *these clouds* fed you, rather than holding onto old ideas of *other clouds*. Later, while you are reflecting, you will be able to feed the clouds, with your own process of feedback. Then you can talk to them, and your response will be based on the moment of beauty you let them share with you.

Reflection means to bring back the original image or circumstance. But first you must meet with the original. As I hope you have discovered in trying this exercise, by meeting I mean truly being with it, experiencing it, and allowing it to be absorbed. As an old Buddhist verse called *FAITH IN MIND* says:

> *The more words, the more reflection*
> *The less you understand the Way,*
> *Cut off words, cut off reflection*
> *And you penetrate everywhere.*

BROTHER DAVID STEINDL-RAST

''Food for solitude, expressing it in my tradition and in my vocabulary – as monastic, as Christian, and as catholic, in the sense of all embracing catholic – is living by the WORD of God....

Everything is the word of God. EVERYTHING. Every person, every situation, is a word through which God speaks to you.... To attune yourself to that, is how you live by it. You're nourished by it....

For example, if a glass fell on the table right now, that could be considered a word. In this sense, a word is a sign that embodies significance and that has all the meaning within itself. It does not point like an exit sign points toward the door, and if you want to get out, you have to leave the sign behind. If you really want to get into the sound of the glass, or if you want to see the glass, you do not leave it behind. If you give me the significance, you can have the sign.... But you look at it, and you open yourself to it, and you listen to it, and you savor it....

Solitude is a time in which you hear less. Because you have more of an opportunity in silence to attune yourself to it, then hopefully when you come back, you will be sufficiently attuned so that in the midst of the noise of everything else, *you can also hear that silent voice of God.... or the deep meaning behind all things....''*

DIANA VREELAND

''The brain and thoughts are an elaborate mechanism – I believe we are an elaborate mechanism, and we should keep that mechanism in very good shape. *How you think is how you will find your life.* Everything I see is beautiful, because I am only looking for that which is good. If you see the beauty in life, and if you appreciate the harmony of the universe, it will all come back to you. I am a great believer in the imagination. Yes, my imagination is really where I am most of the time. But, my eyes are not closed, they are opened.

Imagination *is* food for solitude. It rests one. It focuses on things that are important. It's rather like putting things in order. Your imagination comes forward, and you're dealing with that. You're not dealing with other people's thoughts and imagination entirely. You're dealing with your own, which is good. After all, only what I think about, is what I think. For example, someone is standing here. You love him, and he's standing there, but I don't. Therefore where is the love? It's in your imagination. The man is the same. It's only the imagination that sees, and it sees what it wants to see. There are different aspects to the truth, and different ways to feed your solitude...''

Imaging the Invisible

The following solitude games are what I like to think of as *See-in Sessions*. Looking inside, befriending your inner life, as well as training your inner eye to hold images – all of this gently awakens insight. In *Imaging the Invisible*, you can hold the thought, play with the image, visualize to your heart's content. Solitude games are a wonderful way to link all the energies within, a way to get all your centers together. And most of all they are a lot of fun. So what they do, or don't do, is not that important. Analyzing is not the way to begin. Just trust the process, trust the ability of your images to heal, to make you happy, to open up a few new vistas of possibility. It's really very relaxing to think in this way. *To think without words.* Imagine that!

For these sessions, except for the open eye exercise, keep your eyes gently closed and take the time you need to relax. Also, when you play these games, you may or may not see your *'third eye'* in between your eyebrows. For some this comes easily, for others it never shows up. Whatever – don't strain it, don't worry about it, and if it comes naturally, just relax into it.

Develop New Ways of Seeing...

GAME 1: To SEE is to BE!
* Imagine that you are imagining.
  What room of your mind's house are you in?
* Are there windows?
  If so, open the windows in your room.
    What do you see?
* Are you willing to see where your mind's eye wants to take you? Are you happy here?

GAME 2: Color as SOUND. Sound as COLOR

Normally we *see* pink but we don't *hear* pink, because we're not used to responding to it like that. But when we truly relax and get into a deeper state, a more holistic state – all these distinctions between sight and sound begin to disintegrate. The perceptions of seeing and hearing actually integrate, blending into an amorphous state. In this state, we can easily cross between the realms of color and music to balance our energies, as well as spirit.

Playing the following game will help you to experience this healing process. Rainbow realms will come together and ''those who have eyes will see, those who have ears will hear.''

Before you begin ... a REMINDER
The musical octave and color spectrum share the same wavelength. The scale of *do-re-mi-fa-so-la-te-do* has the corresponding colors of red, orange, yellow, green, blue, indigo and violet. And then on *do* we start with red again.

> * *Listen to music: What color are the vibrations?*

Choose the music you like, then settle into yourself. Concentrate on the space between your eyebrows, keeping eyes gently closed. Place your fingertips lightly over your eyelids or try palming (putting palms over eyes). Envision a circle – a moving circle that comes close to your forehead and then goes back and forth deeply into your head. Do you see this circle filled with one color or shade? Is it changing colors? Watch the colors as they change. LISTEN to the music as it changes. Can you pinpoint the corresponding color and sound? Try changing the radio station to test how the colors change according to vibrations.

> * *Look at the colors of food you prepare. Look at the colors in your environment. Can you hear their sounds?*

To get started, you may like to sit in a garden of beautiful flowers. Or you can look at an orange, lemon or lime. Choose the color or colors you like and work with that. Let it happen. A lavender field may remind you of a violin concerto, an orange may make you start whistling a certain tune. Pinpointing the note or tone isn't as important as getting an over-all feeling. Sometimes you might hear the sound inside your head, sometimes you may receive a gentle hum in your ears, sometimes just a silent suggestion passes through. If you can see the red in the rose, and really hear how it sounds, that is wonderful. If you can't, that's okay too. The whole idea of these two variations – sound/color, color/sound – is to help you to develop your natural gifts.

Some people see the color in the sound, some hear the sound in the color. And some can do both easily. They can easily translate one wavelength into the other. They can be in all realms at one time. But, what about you? After playing and experimenting at your own level, you will discover which variation is simplest for you. Here, I don't want you to force what doesn't work. If you really can't respond to either exercise, after many sessions, it's alright. Remember this is just a solitude game, not a mission. Onward to GAME 3...

Change the patterns and order of learned processes...

GAME 3: *(Memory Muscle Stretcher) open eye exercise*

LIBERATE YOURSELF by reading backwards for a change! READ the words from right to left – READ them vertically – but whatever you do, do not READ them the way you usually do.

HERE are two short passages for you to play with NOW:

	TRUTH			TRUTH
A –	IMAGINE WHO YOU FEEL AND TOUCH NOW AND ALWAYS	or	B –	IMAGINE WHO YOU KNOW AND RESPECT NOW AND ALWAYS

1. Read both A and B the correct way as a passage with the title. Read them as separate passages.
2. Then, start from the last line and read it from right to left... from the bottom line read until the top line, ending at the title TRUTH...
3. Try reading it from the top line from right to left, and then go down to the next line. Include title at end.

Sometimes these passages make absolute sense in both directions, and then sometimes they are totally irrational. That's good for you. It gives your left brain a rest, and lets your right brain STRETCH itself. Try making up your own passages that make sense both ways. Experiment with these reversable thoughts. SEE what happens.

GAME 4: THE MIRROR REVERSING GAME
The reflection sees you!

Stand before a mirror. Look inside. Imagine the REFLECTION SEEING YOU. Try to see the mirror as it sees you.

Instead of standing before a mirror, stand in front of a blank wall. Imagine what the wall sees as it looks at you...

You can play this game wherever you go. You can imagine what the tree sees as it sees you. Imagine what the plate of food sees as it sees you. IMAGINE... whatever you please. See yourself in this new light.

GAME 5: PAINTINGS THAT THINK
Thoughts That Paint

This game is especially for you, if you have trouble visualizing. It will help you to see whole pictures, and come up with specific images on cue. You will learn to frame the image, and imagine the frame. You will discover your own personal images of healing, your own personal symbol of solitude.

There are images to hold, and images to release. Paintings that think, thoughts that paint, animate. Inside our psyche, living energies are constantly changing forms. We can create new forms, new ideas, and truly transform old forms, old patterns – all those painful memories of the past.

You know the expression – to build our dreams and aspirations. ''You shall dwell in the house of the Lord.'' And so we end up living in the house we create. Thought-forms are the building blocks of who we become. Think of where you want to be. Hold the images – set them free!

DAYDREAMING is something most of us do at some point or another, sometimes consciously, sometimes not. When we are aware of these playful moments, we are already on the way to participating in this exercise.

I want you to consciously DAYDREAM. To close your eyes and paint the picture you want to see. But if you can't visualize anything specific, if you really don't know what image you want to paint, don't worry.

Just take a leisurely WALK WITH your EYE. Let it stroll around, let it wander where it will. You don't have to have any particular place or image in mind.

It's like going for a Sunday walk in the country. Just go out for a walk, see where the road takes you. There will be lots of turns, and new spots. Lots of hills and trees, and ponds, and beautiful sights all around. Let your thoughts paint the scene you like the most, and once you settle into where you want to be, frame it – hold the image. Then go on to something new.

The perfect function of spirit is pure intuition… By intuition I mean direct and obvious possession of the apparent, without commitments of any sort about its truth, significance, or material existence. The deliverance of intuition is… pure essence…

We may say that for the mind there is a single avenue to essence, namely, attention. Awaken attention, intensify it, purify it into white flame, and the actual and unsubstantial object of intuition will stand before you in all its living immediacy and innocent nakedness…

George Santayana, *Realms of Being**

---

* *Realms of Being* by George Santayana, Charles Scribner's & Sons, N.Y. 1942, Chapter VI 'The Realm Of Spirit/Intuition' – p. 646, and Chapter I 'The Realm Of Essence' – p. 15.

Ask And You Will Receive
Dreams as Healer

...Why does the eye see a thing more clearly in dreams than the imagination when awake?...

The Notebooks of Leonardo da Vinci

I am continually fascinated and amazed at the ability of my dream life to sort out so much information, and then to make something creative and beautiful out of it. I never think of dreams as something only to interpret and analyze. I like to believe in them for what they are, something like a gift I am about to receive. For me, dreams are wondrous reflections from another world. Why call it the unconscious, or subconscious, as if it were beneath everything else? Maybe it's above. Maybe it's just our friends of the night who come to pay us a visit while we're asleep. Because when we're awake — if that's what you want to call it — we are too busy to notice them, or let them in. So, they come to help us, when they know we can't get in their way. Dreams come in many forms. And like all pure and potent images, they have the power, beauty, and immediacy to heal.

Dreams often tell us what we *need* to know, not necessarily what we *want* to know. They can advise us, amuse us, comfort us, open us to new horizons, and yes, sometimes they can scare us as well. But as someone very wise once said, it all comes to surface because it wants to be healed. In dreams, we receive the greatest stories ever told, the most beautiful images and landscapes ever seen, the most bizarre, the most profound, the most original presentation of things known and unknown.

ARE YOU READY TO RECEIVE YOUR DREAMS? Are you ready to receive? Are you open to your own healing? Are you open to what is ahead, no matter what it may be? Then ask and you will receive. Sometimes you know what you really need, but then again you may not know at all. So start by asking your dreams to tell you what you need to know.

There is a special delight in preparing to go to sleep, when you know that your dreams ahead are truly healing dreams. I have always admired how the Spanish people say *Pleasant Dreams: "Que suenos con los angelitos!"* The literal translation is: May you dream with the angels!

FOR YOUR RECEPTIONS AHEAD ... There are many ways to prepare for your visions of the night. Here are a few tips:

1. Empty your tummy and empty your thoughts.
    Some people avoid watching TV or movies, or reading news-papers, because they believe it will interfere with the purity and originality of their dream images to come. Other people prefer to soak in a long and leisurely warm herbal bath. This helps to release and relax thoughts. Concerning diet: You don't want to sleep on a full tummy, but a cup of camomile tea, or any sattvic drink, is beneficial.
2. Meditate in your way, or say your evening prayers.
    Reciting mantras or prayers is a longstanding tradition in the art of creative dreaming.
3. State your purpose.
    Some people ask for specific healings for themselves or others. Some people ask to go into auric realms and just be comforted... They ask to receive the HOLY SPIRIT. Some ask for solutions to creative problems. Some ask how to overcome obstacles in their life. Or you can ask to actually see something you can't yet imagine... Like your ideal mate, your dream house, or whatever.

I personally believe that all you need to do is truly ask from your heart, and then let your dream world do the rest. Give it the credit it deserves to do its thing, and it will eventually reveal everything you need to know. Just having dreams is healing in itself.

> *One night, I dreamed I was a butterfly, fluttering here and there, content with my lot. Suddenly I awoke and I was Chuang-tsu again. Who am I in reality? A butterfly dreaming that I am Chuang-tsu, or Chuang-tsu dreaming he was a butterfly?...*
>
> Chuang-Tsu, *(Taoist Philosopher, fourth century* BC)

Remembering Your Dreams

Keeping Tract of The Journey

The ritual of preparing to receive visions and insights is just the beginning of your creative dreaming journey. But unless you remember your dreams, all of these remarkable ingredients are lost – evaporated into dream heaven! To dream and forget, what a loss. How many times do you remember having an incredible dream, but you can't remember anything about it! So if you want to hold onto and savor your dreams, *write them down*. Keep a dream log by your bedside. Then you can continue to use the feast of the night for creative life to come.

The most important thing you want to do is capture the immediacy of the experience. So the moment you wake up, get it all down on paper. Don't wait. In writing down your dream, write down whatever comes to you immediately. Write down the highlights. Forget about the logical order, unless the sequential events come to you naturally as you remember them. For example, the first thing you may remember is a color, a feeling, a sentence someone says, something you say, a voice you hear talking, or anything else. No matter how irrational it seems, get this down on paper, before it disappears! Later on you can try to sort it out, if you need to.

Practice recording your dreams as an EYEWITNESS. This is an eyewitness report, and not an interpretation of what you are seeing. All the analysis can come later. A big problem a lot of people face when recording the material, is that they do not like what they see. So they either consciously or unconsciously edit it all out! But those scenes often tell the truth. So, be honest, be non-judgmental. Be like an objective camera – catch the whole picture. Remember, that like all true healers, dreams come to purify our lives, to help with the clutter. Dreaming is spring cleaning, and we can actively participate.

Another helpful tip – in your dream log, leave a few spaces on the top of the page, to fill in the time and date of the dream later on. That time and energy spent thinking about this, and then writing it down, can be those few crucial moments when you lose the whole dream. Also, keep a few blank pages, or another section, for later reflections and meditations...

Dreams, like our waking reality, have to evolve. They too, will mature, develop and grow. The more we receive and remember our dreams, the more conscious we will become. There gets to be a point along the river of our dreams, that the two streams converge. To dream at all is a rare gift, to remember them is to be blessed twice!

In the sixteenth century, the great alchemist Paracelsus gave advice about the intricacies of the dream world. Like everything else he wrote about, this was rooted in the purest understanding of 'inner life.'

The interpretation of dreams is a great art. Dreams are not without meaning wherever they may come from – from fantasy, from the elements, or from another inspiration. Often, one can find something supernatural in them. For the spirit is never idle. If the earth gives us an inspiration – one of her gifts – and she confers it upon us through her spirit, then the vision has a meaning.

Anyone who wants to take his dream seriously, interpret it, and be guided by it, must be endowed with 'sidereal knowledge' and the light of nature, and must not engage in absurd fantasies, nor look upon his dreams from the heights of his arrogance; for in this way nothing can be done with them. Dreams must be heeded and accepted. For a great many of them come true.

For the most part presentiments appear to man in so unimpressive a form that they are ignored. And yet Joseph discovered in his sleep who Mary was and by whom she was with child. And because dreams are not sufficiently heeded, no faith is put in their revelations, although they are nothing other than prophecies…. The wise man must not neglect them, but recall that Christ too appeared in invisible form and was ridiculed. If he understands that inconspicuous things must not be ridiculed but judged with wisdom, he will also know Christ.

The dreams which reveal the supernatural are promises and messages that God sends us directly; they are nothing but His angels, His ministering spirits, who usually appear to us when we are in a great predicament…. Of such apparitions we must know how they take place and how they come to us; when we are in great need, we can obtain from them God's kindness if our prayer pours in true faith from a truthful mouth and heart. Then God sends us such a messenger who appears to us in spirit, warns us, consoles us, teaches us, and brings us His good tidings.

From time immemorial artistic insights have been revealed to artists in their sleep and in dreams, so that at all times they ardently desired them. Then their imagination could work wonders upon wonders and invoke the shades of the philosophers, who would instruct them in their art. Today this still happens again and again, but most of what transpires is forgotten. How often does a man say as he wakes in the morning, 'I had a wonderful dream last night,' and relate how Mercury or this or that philosopher appeared to him in person and taught him this or that art. But then the dream escapes him and he cannot remember it. However, anyone to whom this happens should not leave his room upon awakening, should speak to no one, but remain alone and sober until everything comes back to him, and he recalls his dream.

PARACELSUS, *Selected Writings*

Getting It Together

Remember the philosopher's saying that:
No one is nearer to me, than me myself.

Epictetus

Right Brain Recipes has its own special ceremony alone. This is the ceremony of Holy Matrimony… and it all begins inside YOU! Truly creative people perform this ritual all the time. They know that the secret of success is to marry the two parts of their brain. They let right-brain intuition and left-brain reason work together to solve creative problems. The concept of our divided yet harmonious brain begins to make sense, only when we put it all together. Instead of separating the powers of our mind, we can learn how to fruitfully integrate all these energies so they work together:

Ceremony of Marriage
Between Right and Left Brain

The whole idea is to make peace with yourself. YES … PEACE OF MIND. So first of all, be in a comfortable position. You may or may not decide to make up some verbal vows for your left and right brain; if so, then let them take their vows, but then I want you to get into the best part of this ritual, which is to do what your right brain does best, and that is IMAGING.…

To get yourself into the mood of this ceremony, join the palms of your hands. The simple gesture of joining two hands in prayer says more than you think. So begin with your hands. If it's easy for you, continue with the soles of your feet, but most important, join all the thoughts inside your brain. Let them be silent. The whole point here is imagery, imagining, visualization, symbols, forms, shapes, colors, pictures, anything that is not verbal/wordy/chatty.

You are going to imagine a blending of energies, between your right and left brain. So, choose two separate images. Give your right brain an image and left brain an image. Then watch them blend/unite/come together.

For example: it could be two colors like blue and yellow becoming green. Or a circle joining with a triangle, or the roots of a tree becoming one with the light of a cloud. Your ceremony could be as simple as imagining a circle of light, being filled with the shape of a heart. Whatever you choose, get it together, until it becomes one image form. If you can't receive any particular impression, don't

worry, don't force it, just let it happen. The images will show up, in the way they are needed, and if not they aren't needed. Quiet surrender, emptiness, may be what your union requires. Remember this is your ceremony, your marriage, your peace of mind.

(22) When you make the two one, and when you make the inner as the outer and the outer as the inner and the above as the below, and when you make the male and the female into a single one, so that the male will not be male, and the female not be female... then shall you enter (the Kingdom).

Unknown Sayings of Jesus Christ
from the Gnostic Gospels of Saint Thomas

Solitude Nuances

Routes and Roots

There are two ways of getting home;
and one of them is to stay there.

G.K. Chesterton

If You Want to Be A Hermit

Hermit time is a very special kind of solitude. It could mean taking a long journey to the other side of the earth, or just turning off your phone for the week and treating yourself to a monastic experience. This is a time to let go and just be. A quiet moment is extended into a few days, a few weeks, a few months and for some even longer. It is a moment of solitude stretched long enough for you to know it made a difference.

Of course there are many kinds of retreats and each person has their own particular purpose in mind for picking up and just getting away. But basically there's a difference between retreating and spending time in creative solitude. Everyone I talked with agreed that the main reason they needed to hermitize was to simply just be and do nothing without any expectations of creative results.

As Brother David Steindl-Rast said, ''Being empty and doing nothing is the whole spirit of hermitizing.'' And the story he tells about Taoist poet Han Shan gives us a wonderful image of this kind of emptying: A hermit sits along the river all day and writes poetry on rocks and then throws them into the river. Where they flow makes no difference to him. Later on others find them and maybe make a book out of it. But for our Taoist friend, being with the river — just being empty — is enough.

Obviously, not everyone has this talent for 'doing nothing.' Some of us find it very easy and others constantly work at it. Sometimes the ceremonies suggest themselves, especially when we leave ourselves alone. Little rituals like walking along the same soothing stream, or making a fire, or listening to the leaves drop, and if we're lucky listening to our ego drop with it — all of this helps. It helps us to assume a new rhythm that allows us to be in tune with ourselves and at home in the universe. This is a delicate process of slowing down. It is coming back to the source of our innermost spirit, a secret and silent place that demands nothing of us except to be there.

If we are willing, the retreat teaches this way of emptying. It allows us to just be, to trust. And when the noise inside the head stops, the heart begins to listen.

A Conversation with Brother David Steindl-Rast

BROTHER DAVID STEINDL-RAST is no ordinary monk. His perceptions about solitude come from the insight and practice of a true hermit who has spent years 'listening to the word of God.' He is as much at home in his Benedictine monastery, as he is meditating with Zen Buddhists. Like Thomas Merton whom he knew, Brother David studied Zen, and truly cares about the contemplative aspects of all religions. And unlike other recluses who prefer to shut themselves off from people, Brother David willingly comes out into the world to share his solitude.

Brother David truly understands and loves people, and wherever he goes he has a way of opening the hearts of everyone present. As you listen to him speak, you can't help but feel his passion and concern for planetary peace and universal love. His sense of spiritual/ecology crosses the borders between all religions, and no matter who he is addressing, the message always gets across.

Imagine meeting an Austrian accent with a California spirit wearing proper monastic attire. Imagine meeting beautiful eyes that hug you with just one glance! It's difficult to ascribe labels to Brother David because he is so complex, yet so simple. A catholic/zen/mystic, some would say, and I would just say that he emanates loving understanding. He is above all a compassionate holy man with a strong sense of solitude as well as a wonderful sense of humor.

He has the sort of intellect that probes beyond the chit-chat of normal academic thinking. His distinctions make us really stop to think and feel, and to laugh at ourselves, if we have the courage to do so. His insights will not let us get away with our ego and all its mischief... And that's exactly what we need.

Once when I shared a rare visit with him, he said something that will stay in my heart forever. He said, "There is a difference between self-surrender and self-abandonment. Self-surrender is done with dignity. You give up what you really have or what really belongs to you... Self-abandonment is when you give up that which really doesn't belong to you. You think you are giving up something, but you are not. It's giving up that which is lost... Self-surrender is giving up that which is found and that is how God comes to you." Need I say more!

Hermitizing with Brother David is like being part of a Zen story. For him the joy of being alone also has to do with the struggle. In the true Christian/Taoist spirit of being one with nature, we are brought into his personal experience of spending nine months on Bear Island...

In the following highlights from our conversation, Brother David speaks to the hermit in all of us. Here is our permission to be alone for all the right reasons. Here is a rare interview that could help you decide if you want to be a hermit!*

"The experience of hermitizing is often misunderstood. Why to do it, how to do it, where to do it and so on. First of all, let me say that a hermit must have a deep experience of communion with humanity. Without this, you cannot be a hermit, because you would only be lonely. You would not be really solitary. To be alone and be cut off from others would make you very unhappy, but to be alone, and to be deeply united with others, in deep communion, that is a possibility for which many people long. That is what I call solitude — over and against loneliness.

The human community always has two dimensions. There is a pull towards being together that everybody experiences in various degrees and the pull to be alone which everybody also experiences; some people more and some people less. Unless these two pulls are holding us in balance, nothing is possible, not even the human community.

Now each of us has to find where we fit in. If you have the particular psychological bent that makes you desire solitude at a specific time in your life, then that is what you are called for. You could say a person has an extraordinary need to be alone or you could say a person has an extraordinary talent to be alone. Somebody else who doesn't have this need, can't experience this. They don't need it, but they also can't do it. They get fidgety and nervous and could even have a nervous breakdown. Of course, the capacity for being alone to a certain extent is necessary for our psychological and spiritual well being.

But it means different things to different people. For some it may mean an hour, a day or less. For others it means many weeks or a year. I wouldn't want to streamline or idolize this need. It's just according to our particular nature and talents.

There is also the matter of the difference between spending time as a hermit and spending time in creative solitude. One can't make water-tight compartments out of the two, but one can distinguish between them, and then connect them. Although the

---

* Brother David besides being a great person, holds all kinds of academic degrees, including a PhD from the University of Vienna, where he studied child psychology. This, along with being a true child of solitude, has gone into the making of several books on the contemplative life. For your retreat I highly recommend these two: *A Listening Heart* (Crossroad) and *Gratefulness, The Heart Of Prayer* (Paulist Press).

two can coincide, a hermit's life is simply free space and not necessarily creative in the sense of producing something. While I may need some time for creative solitude, I first of all need that empty space... There is too much accumulating in me. I have a very rich imagination and very rich and full experiences. I meet thousands of people, and have thousands of experiences. I just need empty space for this to settle. As Lao Tzu says, leave muddy water alone and it will eventually settle and purify. This is primarily what I mean about spending time in the hermitage.

The whole idea of doing and being has a very old and venerable tradition. In the Chinese and Taoist tradition, Han-Shan, the so called author of the Cold Mountain Poems, writes about this union between doing and being. These poems are a good example of what it means to hermitize. The essence of it is to do nothing. The poet writes his poems on the rocks and lets them float away in the river. To me that expresses perfectly my idea of being a hermit, of empty space. It's such a beautiful metaphor. A person writes poems on rocks, not in books, and he lets them float down the river. Only later do others gather them and perhaps make a book of them.

By definition, one is a hermit if one lives alone. That makes me a part-time hermit. I spend as much time as I can being alone. For instance, I spent one whole winter from September until May on Bear Island in Maine where there was practically no one except myself. We were two brothers. He respected my silence and vice versa. No one else was there then, except a Coast Guard post of one man.

I guess one ought to be able to empty one's thoughts as C.S. Lewis suggests, into that 'abyss of great silence when you can no longer hear the echo,' no matter where you are, but the environment helps. It should be possible to be silent anywhere, but for me it's easier in a setting like Bear Island. Some people might feel trapped being alone on an island, and others would feel trapped not being there. I really love big empty spaces, with lots of sky or desert. I'm not very happy in a hermitage in the woods, yet this is considered one of the classical places for retreating. Again, it is just a matter of tastes and psychological bent.

There are, however, three things that are fairly constant in the process of retreating. The first is that when you finally get to a place where you have no immediate obligations, you just rest. And sometimes it can take a long time to rest, so you just sleep a lot. Monks who follow traditional practices say that it's okay to sleep all the time you're on retreat. If that is what you need, that's it! It's part of the unwinding. You let your body do what it needs to do, and it knows what is best. Of course sleeping all the time is not ideal because you ought to be there long enough to do something after that. Still, if that is what you need, then you've done something.

After resting, there are two other things for me. I may do some writing or research as I did on Bear Island. In fact, the main thing that I wrote there was the entry on the 'Monastic Life' for the *Encyclopedia Americana*. But the third aspect of retreating, and most important for me, is the real hermit time. It's just walking in the woods, and listening to the woodpeckers and watching the sunset and watching the seals. It is listening to the wind and the sound of the surf and being out on the ocean. The setting on this little island of just a few acres and lots of ocean all around it, suggests this idea of open space and the free space with nothing in particular to do. For me this is ideal.

When it comes to the process of retreating, I don't believe there are neat stages that you should follow. Some of the great spiritual experiences that you expect to happen at the end of your fifty or sixty years in a monastery happen during the first three months, and nothing ever again for the rest of your life. The same thing is true when you go to an island knowing you can spend nine months there in solitude. The first two days you may not be sleeping. You're not resting at all. But you have the greatest experience of open space, of solitude, of a hermit's life. Then you get tired and you sleep, and then somewhere in between you wake up and do some creative work, and you fall asleep again. It doesn't go in stages. In my observation I would only say that those three elements are usually there — the open space, the resting and the creative solitude.

Some people may feel guilty about giving themselves permission to just be alone and 'do nothing,' but I don't feel that way... In fact, for me personally I feel that I deserve permission to have a lot more solitude than I get, so I never have any bad feelings at all. I only have a little self-pity that I don't get more... Of course I'm half joking, but I'm trying to ascertain for myself, what is God's will for me. If you think that this is what God wants for you, in other words if this is what you need (that's how you know what God's will is), then you try to get it.

One of the great insights that stands behind the whole concept of being a hermit comes from John Cage, and is expressed in this poem: ''If you let it, it supports itself. You don't have to. Each something is the celebration of the nothing that supports it. If you remove the world from your shoulders you notice that it doesn't drop. Where is the responsibility?'' Now that's a real monk's poem. It's even a hermit's poem! This has been very important to me and other monks as well. In fact, a Buddhist monk once told me that this was one of his favorite passages. ''Where is the responsibility?'' It doesn't by any means say you have no responsibility, but it places the responsibility in the right place. And you remove it from your shoulders because the world does not collapse.

Hermitizing truly enhances my spirituality. That's why I need to retreat. After a while I feel more truly alive. I have more zest for living, more joy in living. Of course one can't really distinguish between being half dead and being a little more alive and aware and joyful in life. That runs down after a while when you're not doing what your particular make-up calls for. If you were geared towards social interaction and you were too much alone, you would lose your zest for life. In my case it's the opposite. If I'm too much with people, I lose my zest for life. I'm only half alive. I need solitude to revive myself. I've been very lucky in the kind of hermitages I found, very blessed. You choose it of course, and you look around for it. You could say that solitude chooses you rather than you choosing it. It all goes together.

If you really want to go deep while hermitizing, then the best and the worst will coincide. They are the kind of experiences that you can't really talk about. T.S. Eliot in the *Four Quartets* says we can only say there we have been, but we cannot say where, for that would place it in time. What happens in solitude is that you can't re-experience it. You can't even fully remember it because it is the opposite side of the kind of experience that we have now. To say there is a merging of loneliness into solitude or the dark into the light, is still only conceptual. What really happens is that somehow you flip over like a bug and you're lying on your back and all you see are little legs that are trying to grab for something that isn't there.

You watch these beautiful little bugs on the roses and the peonies. They're just like little jewels. But all of a sudden they fall down and lie on their back, and all you see are those little legs that move like French locomotives that have all their moving parts on the outside. Everything is turned upside down and everything becomes frightening and terrible. You can't even re-experience it. It's the opposite side of the weaving that we normally experience. That is both the most horrible and on the other hand, the best, because you expose yourself to that. *You have no alibi when you are in a hermitage!* You have no scapegoat either, you can't blame anybody else, it's just you...

A HERMIT'S SCHEDULE

One of the most appealing things for me about being on Bear Island was the opportunity to be able to make my own schedule. I could follow the schedule given by nature... The time before sunrise is most important. So typically, I would go down to the ocean before sunrise, see the sun rising, and wash myself in the ocean, even if it was very cold. You just do a little bit of it to be in touch with the water. Living with nature like this is wonderful. When it was night, I knew it was night. There were no electric lights to flip on. I had to live with the rhythm of nature and that's a beautiful way to be. And I had to fend a little bit for myself. I had to carry the water and get it out of the well, and pull it up in a bucket and break the ice. Sometimes it took a long time. I had to shovel myself out when it snowed. I had to sometimes go a long way to gather firewood to keep myself warm. That sort of thing was very enjoyable to me. All this is my food for solitude.

You watch the animals and you watch the birds, and you're just in touch with things that you're normally shielded from when you are in the city or other environments. Even the struggle is part of it. Once, the ocean was very wild and we couldn't get ashore. We had to wait many weeks before supplies arrived. We weren't even sure that we could get ashore with the coast guard boat. All these kind of experiences make it more interesting. They make you feel more alive. Struggle and all of it makes you really want to be there and away from the world. This is a very special sort of solitude. You feel like you've really earned your peace.

Of course living in touch with nature while you are on a retreat doesn't mean you become a sort of noble savage. There is always a sense of ceremony and meals are a part of that. Whether you eat once a day or twice a day or three times, it is always desirable to set the table. This is part of an ancient monastic tradition that goes back more than a thousand years in written tradition. Hermits ought to sit down, have a tablecloth, a candle and maybe a flower. They should not nibble as they go along. (This is always a danger.) The ritual of eating alone is just as important as waking up to the dawn.''

The Hermit's Diet

If you want to be a hermit even for a week, then I'm sure you'll appreciate the following diet developed by Brother David and some of his Brother Benedictine Monks. They created it so they could 'go off and be really alone.' Brother David said that once you decide upon the basic ingredients you like, you can create something new each time with just a few essentials and lots of imagination. As he says:

"This diet allows you to be very well fed and active. It gives you all the nourishment you need so you can do active physical work. Yet this diet does not need cooking and does not need refrigeration. It is one you can buy in bulk, so it's quite inexpensive. You can store it for many months. This allows the hermits to be alone without having to worry about going out for shopping. Its main staples are granola and peanut butter loaf which is made by mixing peanut butter with dry milk and honey. Then the nutritious values are brought out."

Here are some highlights from the original hermit diet, exactly as Brother David sent it from the Benedictine Monastery:

STAPLES
(can be mail-ordered wholesale through healthfood outlets or co-ops)

- Peanut Butter (*recommended brands: Deafsmith or Walnut Acres*)
- Granola (*some basic kind; you can spruce it up by your own additions*)
- Brewer's Yeast (*the open kind, that comes in bulk, is tastiest and least expensive*)
- Tamari soy sauce
- Raisins (*make sure your brand is not boycotted by the United Farm Workers Union*)
- Sunflower seed (*shelled*)
- Seeds for sprouting: alfalfa seed, lentils, mung beans, green peas, et al.
- Herb teas (*in most places you will be able to collect and dry your own*)
- Almonds (*we provide 3 almonds a day per person for good health*)
- Honey (*can be bought in bulk from bee keepers directly*) ⎫ no need
- Instant nonfat dry milk ("Carnation" comes in 50qt. boxes) ⎬ to buy these 3 items in a special
- Blackstrap molasses (*Barbados molasses tastier, but more expensive*) ⎭ health food store

RECIPES

- **Peanut Butter Loaf**: Mix peanut butter with dry milk and add honey according to taste. Knead until it no longer sticks to your hands. Form into loaves.

- **Soup**: One large mug of hot water. Add 4 teaspoons of brewer's yeast and 2 teaspoons of tamari soy sauce. Stir well. Add salt to taste.
- **Hot drink**: One large mug of hot water. Add 3 heaping teaspoons of instant dried milk, one teaspoon of molasses, and honey to taste. Stir well.
- **Cold drink**: Add five teaspoons of honey to a quart of cold water (this gives quick energy). When left standing in a warm place for 2 or 3 days, this "mead" gets a kick, which some people like.

COMPOSING MENUS

A box with all staple items is placed in each cell and replenished according to individual needs. It turns out that one person often uses a great deal more of one item than another person does. Different people make different selections and create different menus. The range of possible diversities is surprising.

The secret lies in what painters call 'setting the palette.' If you use all your colors in every picture, or a little of everything on the list of staples in every meal, the result will be sheer monotony. But by adding raisins to your granola at one meal, sunflower seed at another, and eating it as it comes out of the box at a third meal, you can create variety. Similarly, you may add to your sprouts, honey, yogurt, raisins, sunflower seed or tamari sauce at different meals. By adding a greater variety of nuts and dried fruit to the list of staples, the possibilities for changing the menu from meal to meal could be greatly increased without basically changing the diet. Both short- and long-term residents at the Benedictine Grange have, however, found the list given above ample to provide the spice of life.

Raising our own food was not part of the original experiment but given the right setting, one could surely improve this diet by planting a small garden or by collecting wild-growing fruits and plants.

In a space ship you adjust your eating habits to your task. A hermit's task is to explore inner space. Yet there is more of a temptation in a hermitage than in a space ship to start 'playing house'.

A safe rule of thumb is this: if you can do without it, do without it! — Always keeping in mind that some of the most superfluous things are the ones we can least dispense with and remain human, e.g. putting a flower even on a hermit's table.

A REQUEST

Please do not ask for further information. (Too many people keep bombarding hermits with mail.) When in doubt try different possibilities. Basically, it is all a matter of making up your mind. If you like, add your favorite vitamins. (Some of us at the grange do.) If you distrust even the best diet, you'll get sick. Yet, the margin within which a diet will keep you healthy, as long as you think it's good for you, is broader than one might assume. Go ahead and experiment.

... So far we've gotten to nine months with Brother David's retreat, but what about nine years!...

If you were an anchorite in ancient times, then spending nine years in solitude would be nothing (just a drop in the ocean). There are famous tales about anchoresses in India who lived in caves, or on mountain tops in order to keep silence. They literally anchored themselves there for years and years, grounded in the devotion of their faith. Long, long journeys were made by many a pilgrim, who would travel endlessly, just to spend even a day in the presence of these special souls. These are the great mystic saints who by the very nature of sheer contemplation changed the consciousness of the world at large, by simply sitting still.

In *The Way of the White Clouds* by Lama Anagarika Govinda, we learn a great deal about pilgrim life in Tibet. One gets an excellent idea of what it means to become the type of devoted hermit called the *lung-gom-pa*, who might very well seem like a mythological character created especially to demonstrate super powers of endurance and solitude. In his tale about the hermit Abbot of Lachen, Govinda describes this extraordinary practice:

> *... After completion of his nine years' practice in uninterrupted seclusion and perfect silence, [the lung-gom-pa is allowed to go to his pilgrimage to] all the main shrines and sanctuaries of Central Tibet... After having performed this pilgrimage the* lung-gom-pa *finds a suitable retreat or hermitage of his own, where he spends the rest of his life, preaching, teaching, meditating, and pursuing his various religious duties. He will bless and inspire all those who come to him, heal the sick, and console those who are in distress. Healing is mainly done through the power of the spirit.* (p. 91)

Lama Govinda then tells about the hermit Abbot of Lachen, who preferred to stay in his cave rather than go out into the world to preach as other spiritual leaders did, after all their solitary initiations:

> *One day a Western Scholar approached his cave and asked to be admitted as a* chela *(disciple). The hermit pointed to another cave in the vicinity and answered: 'Only if you will stay in that cave for three years without a break.'*
>
> *The* chela *was none other than the famous French Orientalist and explorer Alexandra David-Neel, whose books on Tibet were so outstanding they were translated into all the major languages of the world. One of the main gains of her life in the solitude of those years*

has been expressed by her in the following significant words: 'Mind and senses develop their sensibility in this contemplative life made up of continual observations and reflections. [Does one become a visionary or, rather, is it not that one has been blind until then?']
(p. 100)

Hermitizing

Never am I less alone than when I am by myself: never am I more active than when I am doing nothing.

Cato

You may not want to be a hermit all the time, or even be called a hermit... Hermitizing sounds so much nicer. Just say, I'm hermitizing for the weekend... And if someone asks you what's that, just say, I'm taking a romantic holiday for one!

Hermitizing is for the hermit hiding in all of us...

The following people share their insights on how to be a contemplative in the midst of a very active life.

For historian, WILLIAM IRWIN THOMPSON, hermitizing is getting back to basics, being with as little as possible. As he says,

> "In a city you're feeding yourself all the time, and having to go to lunches, and having to go to dinners, and sometimes even having to go to breakfasts! You want to get away from all of that. So, if you go into solitude, you take less, not more... It's a getting away from being stuffed with food, so you can taste food for solitude."

His Zen-like one bowl/one meal a day creates a lean atmosphere where everything is simple. Only bare necessities are taken, and a few spiritual books to encourage the energies of solitude. This is a time to let go, and just like for Ira Progoff and Brother David Steindl-Rast, a time to be empty...

Here he talks about hermitizing on the island of Iona:

> "I was once alone in Iona for a week living in a house by myself. It was a retreat of getting away — getting away from a lot of cooking and food, getting away from listening to music and just being absolutely silent, not talking to anyone, not writing, not taking any work with me, not doing any work.
>
> All I took as companions for the retreat were *The Cloud of Unknowing** and *The Dark Night of The Soul* by St John Of The Cross. Both are, in a sense, road maps of people who have gone on ahead. The books themselves helped reinforce a quality of

---

* Is it a food for solitude coincidence that the version of *The Cloud of Unknowing* Bill Thompson brought with him on this retreat happened to be the translation with comments by Ira Progoff? Perhaps not, for all hermits eventually meet in one way or another.

solitude and meditation... *The Cloud of Unknowing* deals very much with solitude and the process of the soul's relationship with God. It's a lovely book because it asserts the non-technique approach. In retreat there's no technology that one can use. One has to be innocent of all those additives.

Because part of solitude is slowing down the body, the metabolism and the steady stream of thoughts, I went back to absolutely the purest, most simple kinds of food for this retreat. I can't imagine trying to cook Coquille St Jacques in a hermitage! I ate just one meal a day. It was the same meal with variations... All I needed was one small bowl of oatmeal, with milk and honey, and hazelnuts and apricots. Sometimes I'd add dates or raisins. This actually had all the nutritional stuff I needed. It has all the protein... Oatmeal is my favorite for retreats, just like the Tibetans eat just barley or millet...

I also ate at the same time every day — at noon. That made it better for meditation. When you get up in the morning you have an empty stomach, and your meditations are quieter. If you have one meal in the middle of the day, then sometimes you can take a nap afterwards, get up and have a sunset meditation. Then you can read, and have a late evening meditation, say from nine to eleven o'clock or from eleven to one a.m. I meditated a lot in Iona, five or six hours a day.

When it comes to hermitizing and creative solitude, I really agree with old patterns like those of the Plains Indians. You withdraw, and you have your power vision when you're a teenager. You're alone in absolute solitude, and the vision of your life is given to you. Then you return to society, and spend the next sixty years of your life working it out. There's a good description of that process in *Black Elk Speaks*, in which he has a power vision. Yeats talks about this too, how you're given it in your teens and the rest of your life is just working out what you've been given. I feel fortunate that my visions came in my teens, and so I follow this Indian pattern...

If you look at the historical pattern of discovery there is a definite link between hermitizing and creative solitude... There are all those great visionaries who had to leave the cities, go on retreat and then come back... Look at Moses, he runs away from Egypt, and then out in the desert is where he experiences the burning bush... We think of Muhammad's vision in the cave, or Gauguin who leaves the stockbroking company to paint in Tahiti.

One of the most interesting solitary figures would be Descartes. He had this compulsion to go into his room and then he had very profound dreams. He heard thunderclaps and saw visions on the ceiling... That's how he got the whole vision for remaking western philosophy and creating the new mathematics. Even though he's always used as the archetype in modern Cartesian rationale, the process by which he created analytical geometry and the foundations of his new philosophy, were totally irrational. They were most visionary, and explosions of the unconscious. And they came out of profound solitude, of just going into retreat, into his room..."

Not everyone craves to be alone, but for some people like psychologist IRA PROGOFF, there is an essential craving for long stretches of solitude. Ira, who many see as a spiritual social catalyst, is a hermit underneath it all... In fact, he admits,

> "And now I will tell you the conflict in my life. I got myself involved in an artwork that has a social task. And I became captive of the Intensive Journal Method, that I had created. When I did it for myself, it was a tool to help me hermitize and be creative. It helped me to be creatively alone. I still have it, but so do all the other people who I feel responsible toward."

Being director of Dialogue House, the process he created to help others with their creative solitude, has its ups and downs for Ira, who truly craves to spend long durations of time alone so he can think, write, and just be. But he manages to work out shuttling between sharing solitude, in his workshops, and sipping it all by himself.

Here he talks about the essence of retreating, and how hermitizing can sometimes lead to creative solitude:

> "For me, the most important reason for being alone is to do nothing. That's why I like the phrase of Lao Tzu which says, 'muddy water let stand becomes clear'... All those times of feeling muddy is a quality or condition in ourselves. To use this image, in the modern world we often have the sense that if we're muddy then we have to analyze the nature of the mud and interpret it. But then, this may even stir it up more and spread it. The idea I am talking about is a very systematic process of doing nothing — to do it in a way that allows the material (the mud) to shape itself.
>
> If I'm going away with a particular piece of work to do, even if nobody else is there, that's not really being alone. If I go on retreat and take notes with me, which I have done, then each morning and night my mind is on what I have to do. That's not a bona fide retreat, because there is no time for nothing! In essence, being alone is doing nothing, but not many people experience that. Based on all the people I've met as a psychologist, I think that to be *alone/alone* may not be desirable for everyone. You may go on vacation, but then you end up doing a lot of things all the time. I think you just have to know how to do nothing, and ultimately that's a quality of oneself... So, whenever I have hermitized I have always tried to empty out all preconceived ideas, so I could just be. I try not to put anything into where I was, but rather to let it all out, and let whatever happens just happen.

There is no set way on how to be alone, but there is a balancing principle within oneself. It is a sensitivity to one's own inner process and the need of establishing an awareness of that process. Then one learns how to balance or center oneself. When muddy you become quiet, you let the muddiness settle. This means realizing too, that sometimes there is nothing, and that is time for activity. Being quiet is not good at the wrong time, nor is being active at the wrong time. But each has a way of balancing.

Hermitizing as doing nothing can lead to creativity. That's how my meditation book *The Well and the Cathedral* happened. I was on a retreat. I was being onto myself, and becoming quiet, and I became conscious of a stream of imagery and language that I felt I wanted to write. So I wrote it. It kept on building after that. I think that's how a lot of what would be called poetry gets written... A person is 'doing nothing' or being empty, or being unfocused without an object. There is no goal. Then something begins to move of itself.

The monk in *The Cloud of Unknowing* says something is stirring. It stirs of itself. When something stirs of itself, one follows it. But if you have a goal with it and you try to control it, that changes it and the way you are because then you are focused. You have to trust and accept it for what it is. If you can just remain a channel for it, be just a recorder of it in a detached way, then it may become something... You let the cosmos stir you, also knowing that sometimes what stirs will have no way that you can use it in a particular form. You let ir stir knowing nothing is ever wasted whether it has a particular use or not...

The heart of the experience of being alone then is to follow this balancing principle. The most important part of the retreat for me is to clear up that mud. If I feel muddy, I have to become quiet, until there is a feeling of clarity. And how I end up doing nothing, being empty, doesn't matter... I might be walking, I might be sitting, I might be watching the ocean. It doesn't matter as long as I am becoming quiet... Then if something emerges out of this, it's a gift, but one I do not expect...

It seems to me that the capacity to be alone is something which develops in a person. The capacity to be alone builds a little bit each time. It's like being an athlete. Each time you do a little bit of an exercise your muscles get stronger. So you're building up solitude strength. To be alone for four months right at the start would not make sense for someone. It could even be dangerous. So the secret of hermitizing is to start in small doses.

What holds me up, what supports my retreat is the experience of many little bits of aloneness... As a teenager I would hermitize a little at a time… I remember walking out early on a Saturday and I would come back when it became dark, and I'd go out on Sunday again. These walks along the beach were my first tastes of solitude…

I would walk along Plum Beach all alone. I knew I could find a log that had washed in and I could sit on the log. I also knew that nobody else but me would want to be there, for these were off-limited and banned beaches. I always thought it was very spiritual to be able to find these secluded beaches, beaches that no one could swim in, to be alone amidst the danger, to be where no one else wanted to be… I used to think that it was an instance of basic truth; that the stone that the builders rejected becomes the cornerstone. I felt that things that were overlooked by the world, were then free to be used in creative ways, and to serve a creative function. These abandoned beaches became my spot for solitary walks. They became my private beach and private island.

In these early years, I didn't plan what I had to do when I was alone. It was sheer freedom. But the more my life has proceeded, the more developments, patterns, and pathways there are, the less possibilities of freedom I feel. As the specifics of a life take shape, the less chance there is for exploring. Maybe that's why I sometimes feel trapped. I don't have as much opportunity as before to just be alone and do nothing. To have that sort of freedom is special, even though there is another kind of freedom in limitation and set boundaries…

Retreating is wonderful if you're prepared for it, and if you really feel the need for it. Today I crave for longer stretches of solitude, because then there is a chance for more to happen. Having the luxury of say four months, allows an accumulative experience. More happens for me then, that would likely drive somebody else crazy, or at another time in my life would have driven me crazy…"

Today when Ira feels the need to retreat, he hermitizes in a secluded beach house. This is his secret solitude spot, known only to him and a few friendly seagulls. Here is where he spent four months totally alone one summer. And like Brother David and Bill Thompson, he had his own kind of hermit diet:

"When I was putting together *At a Journal Workshop*, I gave myself four months to be really alone. I was out on the island in my little shack near a beach. Since I didn't see anyone I had to create my own kind of diet, one that really fed me food for solitude. Eating alone and preparing the food became a sort of relaxing ritual. It got my mind off the writing, and I really enjoyed trying new things, like making cole slaw. For me this was haute cuisine. Knowing that grated cabbage is good for you, also had its appeal.

It seems to me that the idea of grating cabbage on an old-fashioned grater doesn't call for scrupulous instructions. I can say without any equivocation that the success of my recipe for making cole slaw was immeasurably improved when one of the salad dressing companies brought out a dressing that plainly said, cole slaw on the label... And even though I didn't make my own dressing, I would always grate the cabbage and even parts of my fingertips. If you are being a hermit, cole slaw is a great thing to make.

But, I didn't live on just cabbage for four months. I had lots of salad. I'd make up a big bowl of all kinds of mixed salad, and keep it on the table, so that throughout the day I could come and take a little bit, and then take a walk and keep going... Into that big bowl, I would put any fresh vegetables that were available, like lettuce, tomatoes, cucumbers, radishes, cauliflower pieces, broccoli spears, all finger food...

My diet when I spend a lot of time alone is different than when I am in the city, and tend to go to restaurants a lot. On the island I am almost a vegetarian, even though I don't plan it that way... For breakfast, I eat a lot of fruit, like apples and oranges, and sometimes some whole grain dried cereal. But it's mostly fruit which gives me a lot of energy to start the day..."

JOAN FONTAINE

"At heart I am a gregarious hermit. I simply must have time to be alone. In solitude there is a battery recharge, that's what solitude is for me. It's like the tree in winter. It's the sap going down, and the roots are waiting for spring. There are many things you could say were my sap when I am alone, but most of all it's the precious solitude itself.

If you want to be a hermit, then there are lots of ways you can feed yourself solitude. Often I've arranged to have a place which is my private retreat. No one but me knows where it is, and I'll go there and stay alone for a month. This is a place where I can sit by the fire and have absolutely nobody. I can recharge and start a new project. I really need to get away. I really need a solitude retreat, if I'm going to work creatively.

I have to get rid of all the noise. I have to get into the position of needing. Usually the creative part of me is thoroughly filled by all the people I know. It's too active. It's too much. It's like being on a 'coffee-jag' all the time.

I need to get down to deprivation to light the fire that creates. It won't be created, unless I do that. I want to give myself creative expression. To do so, I have to start way down there, in a kind of cold basement, and let it begin to grow, like a tree in the snow. Then it will work.

If I were married, if I had people around, it would never get a chance to develop. I would be too busy waiting on them, or cooking their dinner. I can't help it. I'm a Japanese wife underneath it all... That's why I need to have physical retreats. It's the only way to protect my creativity.

You can spill over your creativity on other people and lose it. And it's lost. It's like oil on the water. You can just spill it around taking care of everybody. But then you stop existing. Or, you can harbor it, protect it, and make something of it. It is your choice. My choice is to make something of it.''

Retreating Into The Silence Of Sacred Space

Why are some people so attracted to the environment of sacred space? A room, a cave, a cathedral, a quiet hill known only to the clouds above it, even a closet can become sacred space. Monasteries tucked away in solitude spots of nature all have a certain aura about them. But why? What makes them so special and nourishing? How does sacred space really support the inner solitude journey, the journey that lets us become one with ourselves?

Awesome physical beauty may be one reason why people choose a certain place for retreats. But beyond the visual feast there is another aspect that can easily be called the gift of silence. Sacred space, unlike ordinary space, enhances sacred sound. It is through this atmosphere of silence that being all one becomes possible. In the pulsating presence of sacred space there is a dancing energy and yet a stillness. When you enter such a space, an all-embracing feeling takes you over. It is as though silence lives in the space and totally inhabits it. Have you ever been hugged by silence?

Indeed, sacred space is holy space, and holy means it is alive, animated with the spirit... The angels always live there. In the words of Britton Chance: "In a quiet way in his own personal solitude, a true scientist can listen to nature, because the sounds of nature are louder than his own sounds. His own sounds can be muted."

And so we experience the sacred architecture of nature, as well as the nature of sacred architecture. But most important of all is the sacred space within our hearts. And as the silence deepens we retreat into our true solitude where inner and outer environmental energies become one.

In an essay called 'Geometry At The Service Of Prayer', Robert Lawlor writes about how sacred architecture enhances this 'gift of silence'... Here he describes a famous twelfth century Cistercian Abbey near the southern French village of Le Thoronet:

> The architecture of sacred geometry offers direct physical support for meditational practices, giving the two most cherished environments of spiritual life: that of intensified exposure to universal or divine harmonies, and the gift of silence. No outside sound of man or nature could penetrate the thick stone walls, and here the mind wrapped in silence was able to follow the ear to a confrontation with the eternal.
>
> In the work of the Swiss physicist Hans Jenny, we sense the all-pervading importance of vibration and rhythmic periodicity in the physical world from galaxies down to nuclear structures and meson clouds. Because the tissues and cells of our bodies are almost entirely made up of plasma (that is, liquid particle suspensions), living tissue is particularly responsive to the organizing power of sound. 'The universe is only God repeating His own name to Himself,' said Ramakrishna...
>
> At Le Thoronet, the celibate monks worked together, growing wheat and olives, maintaining a totally self sufficient communal vow of silence. The only human sound was song... A highly sensitive

psychological state was achieved in which the harmonious chanting would activate the body's chakras, and indeed affect the very cells. Sound thus becomes nutritive; it is objectively 'food', charging the body with the energy of universal harmonies... This is the purpose of sacred space.

Silence is unceasing Eloquence. It is the best language.

Ramana Maharshi

The ancient mystical usage of the word mountain literally meant retreat. So one could easily say that true solitude is a retreat into the mountain of one's own soul. In esoteric teachings, the mountain is a symbol of consciousness. It is both an obstacle to overcome as well as the accomplishment. One is going through it, with it, and into it, rather than trying to climb up and over it. Each stone of the mountain symbolizes another step along the journey. The stones we leave behind are the same stones that build our bridge into the future.

From the dawn of civilization there were sacred mountains calling to those who heard the call. Rites of passage into unknown paths led to horizons of unimagined beauty. One mountain chain after another was left behind and with each new mountain pass the journey began again. The external journey into such vast solitude with all its obstacles and challenges led back into the great source within. The sacred mountains within and without, evolving through time, became what one needed them to become. The Tibetans called it Shambhala, but deep within the consciousness of every culture one could find the same circle of mountains.

What castle could compare to this beauty? The brilliant yellow light of the dawn, the gentle moonlight – a dance of fire constantly changing the face of the mountain throughout the day and night. Who wouldn't want to retreat into such splendor?

Being alone for just a few days in the supportive atmosphere of nature can make a big difference in one's life. And for people who have a passion for mountains, just being there is enough... Former Canadian Ambassador JAMES GEORGE first fell in love with the French Alps when he was a student in Grenoble. This led to climbing mountains all over the world from the Himalayas to the fjords of Norway. But it was in Colorado that he found the mountains that became his special sacred space:

"One summer in Colorado I took a retreat for a couple of days, and I went up the mountain with a tent. Up there I was as deeply as I could be at that time in myself, in nature, in the emptiness of a space that had no pollution, no noise, no interruptions, no telephone, no people, no obligations. Nothing was required of me. I didn't even have to cook meals for myself because I was fasting, and since it was summer I didn't make a fire. The moon was my light.

There's a real privacy up there, when you're not activated by a stream of outer impressions. I was free to just be as the Indians say, in the most favorable inner/outer conditions I could find, for purifying my vision of life. There I could clarify the issues of my life, and sharpen the awareness of my presence in a way that was necessary before I could again return and participate.

Some people love the sea, and some need the mountains. I'm a mountain person... For me, they make a connection possible that doesn't happen so readily anywhere else I know. It's as if heaven and earth were a little closer at eight thousand feet, than they are at New York sea level... In between I am a link.

The advantage of being in high places is that I really feel high energies there. In this part of the Rocky Mountains called The Sangre de Cristo Range, there's a tradition from the earliest American Indian times, associating these particular mountains with healing retreats and vision quests. Almost anybody who comes there, feels the uplifting quality of these mountains.

When I was younger I had a passion for climbing anything I could see. I suppose there was some ego in it, the achievement of solo Alpine climbing. But when I was actually at the top of a peak, my strongest impression was a kind of euphoria that had nothing to do with ego... I felt myself at a kind of zero junction where ordinary time and space ends. Some totally different reality began. This was the sort of reality where totality is inexpressible. It wasn't a fantastic dreamscape. It was very real and it was such a strong emotional experience, that it would energize my being for many days after I came down...

For me, being in the mountains is an experience of feeling. I feel stillness, and I feel purity... No matter how sacred and beautiful the spaces, the retreat is of benefit only when I truly feel the relation between my inner landscape and the nature surrounding me. This means I drop that which is at the root of my tensions, the existential fears. Then a whole new well-spring of feeling can be opened, which I can experience as light and lightness. Then all my breath can circulate in a new kind of bodily emptiness. It's like the vehicle has been cleaned up.

Any inner exploration can be helped or hindered by the outer conditions. And certainly, what is most helpful in the mountains for me is that the air is of such purity. Just breathing it is a creative experience. It's better than the most wonderful gourmet meal. Here, the air is my food...

In a certain sense all space is sacred, and inner space is especially sacred. But when we're being drawn out all the time, no matter what surroundings we are in, we are removed from that which is sacred. Our *temenos*, our temple, our body, our ground of being is only partially inhabited. But when we can arrange to be connected to nature, in the solitude spot of our choice, it can enhance our inner journey. Then we may go more deeply inside. There is a special space in there, that is not the space of surface living. This is the sacred space within myself. For me, being in nature helps to make these inner connections stronger. When I'm in the mountain retreat, nothing is happening outside, it's all happening inside."

He has advanced beyond all horizons. There are no directions left in which he can travel. This is a country whose center is everywhere and whose circumference is nowhere. You do not find it by traveling but by standing still.

Thomas Merton

Each person retreats into the silence of sacred space in his or her own way. Through the gift of nature, through the gift of our ancestors who built monasteries and secret places, and through the gift of our own effort to remember who we are... we retreat.

HERBERT O'DRISCOLL, Episcopalian priest and author, shared his experience of being in sacred space. He talks about what retreating means to him, and how the sacred space of a monastery helped him during a time of crisis:

"Retreating is the way to taste real solitude, and solitude is very rich for me, because I go into what I call my inner country very easily and very quickly. I have no difficulty at all in internalizing. Most people have problems getting in, but my problem very often is to come out... Retreating is a way to be in communion with the universal to taste cosmic dimensions. But how do you do that?

Whether we like it or not, the entrance room into the universe is the ego. The only way into the universal, at least the channel door into the universe, is the personal. It is the way to sacred space, and it is the sacred space. I may not be able to directly taste the universal, but at least I must try.

For me it's natural to enter into an inner landscape, even while being involved with others. My inner world is teeming with images. It's teeming with intimations all the time. These are the hints, flashes, intermissions. It's what I consider the touches and flashes of God. And that is a blessing. For me, aloneness is very rich as an internal thing and sacred space can support this inner journey...

All over Ireland, there are hermit cells, from around about the seventh, eighth and ninth centuries. They are almost always built of stone, usually shaped almost like a beehive; there's nothing in them. You crawl into a low door and there you are inside.

These cells are in a very high place, yet you must enter by crawling... I remember when I had a very difficult decision to make, and I realized that one of those cells was not far away. It was a summer's day and I remember crawling in under the low opening and sitting on the gravel clay floor, and really reaching out and saying, 'I want to touch all the centuries of prayer and meditation, and perhaps sorrow and tears that have been in this place.' I wanted to draw on all that as grace to me, in making my decision. I thought, other people over thirteen centuries have had to do their deciding in this place. They have prayed for the presence of God. I remember feeling all those years of prayers, and thinking in my heart, I now pray that a link may be made for me. I sat there as a child of a long communion of saints.

I have often gone on retreat for three or four or five days but ordinarily I have not gone on solitary retreat. I've never needed to go *alone* alone for that's the way I taste my solitude. That's who I am. But, during that time of decision, I was quite alone in the hermit cell.

In a sense, time isn't as important as presence. Presence is not a time thing. Very often what is to us a very short period of time, can be in terms of depth and quality, in terms of reaching out for God, much time... It is said of St Anthony of The Desert, the fourth century hermit, that having not seen him for twenty years, at last they battered his door down, and that he came out and shared with them. Now that's the kind of thing that boggles the mind...

There's a lovely word in Russian Orthodox spirituality; the word is *poustina*. It means secret place. In Russian *poustina* means either a physical place that you go for retreat, or else it means the secret place within you. It means the hermitage within you. It means the place you go to be alone with the other. I find my richest retreat in my inner country. But it's hard to talk about.

It's not really easy for me to describe my retreat into the silence of sacred space. As Augustine once said, we only use words in talking about the things of God, because the alternative is silence... The only way I can tell you about my inner country is to say, be with me at a time when I am trying to communicate, because what is coming then are the things from that inner journey. It's like a traveler coming back after being away, and saying here is what I found. Here are the jewels, here are the ropes, here is the silver and gold that I found in that inner country... It's a way of sharing my angels.''

True solitude is the home of the person, false solitude the refuge of the individualist. Go into the desert not to escape other men but in order to find them in God.

Thomas Merton

Mushrooms and Misplaced Mystical Tales

In the *Wonderland garden*, where mischief, miracles and Alice ultimately meet, two great symbols of transformation set the tone for one of the most extraordinary mystical tales ever told. First of all, there is the friendly caterpillar who advises Alice on what to do about the mushroom. And then of course, there is the mushroom itself. Everyone knows that a caterpillar turns into a butterfly, and for ages the chrysalis process has been a charming metaphor of transformation. But what does a mushroom turn into, except for the ground?

A mushroom, as Alice discovered, can turn us into all kinds of new forms. But whether we shrink or expand, grow as tall as the sky, or become as short as a blade of grass, isn't as important as the process of turning inward — the spiritual conversion of turning toward and into the inner life. What really matters is this inner change, a changing of attitudes, spirit, perception. In this light, whole world views can be transformed in an instant.

The mystical experience has been described as: '*Becoming one with the ground.*' But are we under, above, or just in between? Are we the mushroom? Or are we Alice? How do you *see* it? Are you the one who eats the mushroom? Or are you the mushroom itself? Ultimately it's all a matter of perception, isn't it? Ultimately, it's all very mysterious. *Becoming one with the ground* has many, many nuances; that's why each experience is unique.

When heaven meets earth and earth meets heaven, when dark and light no longer create contrasts, when you know that living in and of the LIGHT is real, then you are into your own mystical path. The experience is great, like a great dinner. But how we digest it, how we transform it, that is something else.

Realms that we cannot grasp are like butterflies who refuse to be pinned down. Elusive, beautiful, free, in flight — it is something we feel we'll never quite capture. It is something we never quite understand. Until one day when we least expect it, we are given — even for a second — a window into a world beyond our normal imagination. And like Alice, we too become a part of a wondrous tale, maybe a misplaced mystical tale, but who cares, for it belongs to us!

In *Wonderland*, Alice never asked, Do butterflies play with caterpillars? But I have the feeling the thought crossed her mind.

And the grass becomes light
it is transfigured
yet unchanged.

St Symeon The New Theologian,
The Light of Tabor (Tenth Century)

The Mystical Experience

GOPI KRISHNA, a mystic from India, is a quiet legend in the spiritual world. He didn't go around guruizing, and like his contemporary Krishnamurti, he never tried to have disciples. Yet many people sought his teaching. "I am not a spiritual teacher," he would say, "I am just a human being." But then he added with a touch of humility and honesty, "I am not a normal human being like you or others because of the experience I had and the twelve years I suffered through charting the course of my inner journey."

As a young man, Krishna had a very profound mystical experience, and thereafter his life would never be the same. As he recalls: "I was meditating one morning in my usual way, and suddenly, when I least expected it, another energy entered my body, and I found myself immersed in a sea of light." He felt as if his entire soul was on fire, his body glowed with an energy far beyond the realms of scientific understanding. In short, he felt those energies running up and down his spine, and circulating throughout all the chakra centers. 'Liquid light,' as he called it, completely took him over, like a thunderstorm moving within him. Without asking for it, his *kundalini* was released. And this was just the beginning of many, many more experiences to come.

From then on, whether he liked it or not Gopi Krishna was on his own without the help of a spiritual teacher. For who could help him? As he put it, when one is flooded with the light in this kind of *Kundalini* experience, only grace and grace alone can come to the rescue!

Early on, he discovered that the answer to solving the riddle of the universe was inside him. But it would not be given without a fair price. His entire being became a laboratory of consciousness. This was the epitome of 'solo experiment'. For twelve long long years he suffered through the agony of *kundalini* overdose, (the shock of receiving too much light). And after surviving this incredible excursion on the inner planes, he came out to tell his story. It is one of humility, of courage, of moderation, but most of all it is the story of a soul's true faith in God.

Gopi Krishna had a definite vision about the next step in human evolution. He believed, ''the spiritual path would be a normal road for everyone to follow.'' He was convinced that the mystical experience would be the link between all people, and because of this shared perception, all conflicts stemming from different religious nomenclature would be dissolved. There would be a new kind of non-verbal communication based on the language of love and light. Therefore, everyone would be able to respect and understand each other, regardless of where they came from, what language they would speak, or what work they might do... When Gopi Krishna died, he held this dream in his heart... It is up to the future to decide.

During one of GOPI KRISHNA's rare visits to the United States, I had the opportunity to spend an entire day with him. After lunch, we were sitting in a room with a window facing the ocean. He looked out the window from time to time, gazing at the infinity ahead. Suddenly there was a silence, and after a while during this long pause where one digests the mood, I asked him, ''What do you see? How are you perceiving right this moment?''

''Do you mean with my senses?'' he asked, and I replied, ''You tell me.'' And so he did...

''What do I see? Perhaps more to the point, is *how* I see. I am not living in the same world as you and other beings. So right now, I see that there is a life energy everywhere. In my way I see a kind of intelligence, a life force that is full of subtle vibrations. In fact I am in a state where the body appears to be very removed, and what I am thinking or saying seems to be coming from a living source who surrounds me... So right now, my eye seems to feel like an appendage, something created by my body. But the actual thoughts, the feelings, and the ideas I express come from the void surrounding me, through the brain of course. I can perceive in detail the activity of every moment.

As you know, there is a lot of curiosity about the mystical eye, but perceptions are very personal. Therefore, I am not prepared to commit myself to any traditional view that is based on concepts such as the seven centers, seven planes of consciousness, or anything that is not verifiable. What I can say is this: human beings can attain through a higher level of consciousness a state where they can come in contact with the intelligence surrounding them. It's not for me to tell you whether spirits exist, or what happens to souls after death, that's for you to decide. However, what I am asserting is the beginning of a new science.

All great mystics and all great prophets have observed a

similar pattern. But this is only the first rung of a ladder. Some of them have had visionary experiences of angels, fairies, of demons, and many other forms. But the visions aren't as important as the common experience they shared. There are seven or eight characteristics which are common to mystical experience. For instance, the sensation of light, of infinity, of a cosmic personality, of deep emotion, a sense of surrender, humility. There is a sense of all cosmic knowledge as coming from another source. There are tears, deep humility, also a sense of a cosmic presence, which is either form or formless. After that comes the actual visionary experience. And that is diversified.

Some see Mohammed, the prophet of Islam. Some see Allah as described by Mohammed. Some see Brahmin as described by the Upanishads. Some see Christ as the Savior. Some see God according to their own picture and interpretation. I believe that the next higher stage of consciousness for humanity will include the mystical experience, but it will not be diversified and limited by specific beliefs. It will be a uniform state of consciousness. The future person will not assume that one group sees Krishna, another sees Christ, another Mohammed, another God. Each one will have a common and shared state of consciousness. Of course, people will not lose their individuality. They will still be unique and their thinking, their abstract reasoning, and theories may be different, but their consciousness will be the same.

During the time I suffered, I felt all alone in a disconnected way. But in the actual experience I had, I feel I was not and am not alone. The experience I had is fully confirmed by the Upanishads. It is confirmed by the highest Christian mystics. It is confirmed by Sufis. It is confirmed by Taoists. They also say that you cannot name the Tao, or describe the Tao. There are no visions. It is confirmed by mystics who had visions like Swedenborg, and others who didn't have visions.

But, I do not believe that at this stage we should differentiate between one kind of mystical experience and another. This will lead us nowhere. Then we will have to form sects and cults and creeds surrounding each mystic as is the case now. From my point of view we have to accept and to take mystical experiences as a new dimension of consciousness for human beings. We have to see what the real working model of it should be. There has to be a model that is applicable to all races and all sections of humanity. This should be a standard from which all individuals can test their own experience. For me, it is essential that the mystical experience becomes a science, and that humanity knows where it is going. Of course this has to be a new paradigm, based on very ancient principles, as well as direct personal experience. My aim is to prove scientifically that there is a link between spiritual illumination and biological evolution.

I believe that there is a difference between the biological system of a normal human being and one who has attained a higher level of consciousness. I believe that one can objectively prove that you will find differences in the blood, in the cerebral spinal fluid, in the brain, in the subtler levels of the brain. Science has very little knowledge about the brain. What science is just discovering, is the basic principle of kundalini, which is knowledge based on the ancient traditions dating back three thousand years. All those yogis who succeeded in yoga, were only performing experiments on consciousness and the mind, which modern science has not yet done. In order to reach those levels of deep understanding, they will have to perform the same experiments on themselves. As science advances, we will be able to detect the subtler planes of creation, way beyond the sub-nuclear particles. Imaging the invisible will become a normal kind of perception.

Without question, I feel that the great mystics of antiquity, and this includes all the women, especially the Saints, these people must have had a biological difference within the subtler levels of their own being, compared to a normal human being who hadn't yet reached that illuminated state. Also the great intellectuals like Einstein or Newton, they too were different. I believe that in principle, the higher an individual is in intellect, the more he or she has the potential to become mystical in temperament. But, they also must have good ideals of character.

The ideal human for me would be like a Ramakrishna having a scientific perception, or an Einstein having an illuminated experience. The ideal human of the future, would not be just a mystic, but an illuminated individual and scientist/intellectual. Combine this with the person of the noblest character, one who works for the benefit of all beings, and you have the future ideal.

Human beings are still in a state of biological evolution, so it is absolutely necessary to follow spiritual disciplines. But what is known as a spiritual path is actually a normal path for human beings. Human life has to be both spiritual and worldly if the evolutionary processes in the brain are to function normally and in a healthy way.

At the present time our brain is functioning in a lopsided manner and this is dangerous for us. We are developing too much intellect, and too little heart. That is why the world is in such a state of imbalance. We need to perceive not just with our senses and our intellect and abstract reason, but with our heart. From the point of view of evolution, the heart is the superior way to perceive. In order to be balanced, we need both intellect and heart — an equal development of each. The future person has to be a complete being in the course of his or her evolution. The future hope is to balance everything. With too much intellect, too much technology, and very little heart, the future person may very well be destroyed... But I have faith in a great change that is happening right now...

I believe that right now, at this very moment, there are hundreds of thousands of people all over the earth, who are spiritual in their humble way. These are simple unostentatious people in different aspects of life, who live noble lives, and who are perhaps more spiritual than those who claim to be spiritual teachers. My dream is to put spiritual knowledge into the hands of humanity, so that it is as normal as temporal knowledge. Everyone of us is a potential spiritual entity.''

It's not every day you meet someone who says: ''For me, death is the ultimate. I can't wait to die!'' But that's how film legend JOAN FONTAINE began talking about her incredible mystical experience. ''I have had what I consider three miracles in my life,'' she says. ''I have lived and died three times. That's why I'm not afraid of death.'' To disappear into the truth, as the Sufis would say, could sum up her captivating tale.

Joan Fontaine talked about angels, visions, and a magic creative moment. It was dramatic, larger than life, the stuff great films are made of. And she wasn't performing. This was a true story — her story. But how do you describe it? To spin this yarn, do you weave with magical ingredients and call it occult? Do you call it spiritual? Or, is it just a dream — a right brain fantasy? What do you call it, if you call it anything?

Mostly, it calls you — the silence, that peace, that overwhelming love. It is truly a misplaced mystical tale, and it is told by Joan Fontaine:

''When I was about ten, I had what I guess you could call an astral projection. It was an incredible experience. I went through my body, and went through my room, over my balcony, over the poplar trees, and I met white on white... It was like a negative backwards. It was white on white. Nobody there had any particular shape, but all of them were loving people. For me it was coming home. I had the most enormous sense, a familial sense of belonging... One person stepped forward then. It may sound idiotic but it's true.

There was a woman spokesperson, and she said:

You are accepted. You are acceptable . But there is something we'd like you to do. You can come now, but we'd like you to go back and do something else.

I said, yes, I would gladly do that — certainly! I felt the most extraordinary sense of love. I had more in that one moment, than I've ever had in anything else in my whole life... More comfort, more purpose, more solace, more anything. And that is the reason I am here today. Because I want to know what they wanted me to do. I haven't found out yet, but it could be anything. Maybe it's talking to you, it may be an influence, who knows. It may be just my meeting a taxi driver and saying hello. I don't know what the purpose is.

I believe in afterlife. Who knows where we go?.. There are thousands of planets, and thousands of similar other circumstances. I'm not talking about the Hindu perspective of reincarnation. I'm not even talking about limiting it to the earth. I don't think earth is the only planet with life and consciousness.

I believe we are here to learn and to take the consciousness of our experiences, our learning elsewhere. It's a preparation for the next step. *The whole point of life is death.* I know that because I have died, and it's so marvelous. It's the only way you can create something new. This is just nonsense down here — compared to what's ahead. Sometimes I wonder what I am still doing here. Maybe it is to share the goodwill, an essence of ourselves. It's a great mystery... But the point *is* the mystery of it all, and that's wonderful. The Church speaks of that constantly. I'm not a church-goer but I believe in those ten people who I saw, whoever they are, whatever it is...

I would say I was sort of a mystical/spiritual person. But I don't read about other mystics. I had the experience. Who am I going to read after that? When you have had an absolutely direct experience, you don't need anybody else... But, if you want a direct experience, you have to be alone. What is interesting is that I might not have had that experience if I had been hovered about with mothers and sisters and fathers and brothers. *Being alone* was the only way I could have met with Divine Wisdom.

I'm not sure how many people you are, or I am. I suggest we are many people and that the people I met in that vision were all of me. The welcome home committee were pieces of me... Maybe you and I are more than twelve people, certainly more than two people if you put all our mutual energy fields together. Anyway, it's such a tiny trip here on the earth, compared to what is next... I know there is an afterlife. But I've got, with luck, another twenty-five, thirty years here, so I may even find out why those ten mystical friends of mine asked me to stay here. And that might happen tomorrow. And it might happen to you too! Who knows; this is one stage of a journey.''

With a word as mysterious as mystical, it helps to re-define its meaning, but no matter which route we take, ultimately all definitions come back to the original route, the root of oneness. The mystic always lives inside the realms of a holistic universe, which in fact can't even be called a realm, because it is beyond the limitations of such a thought. DAVID SPANGLER knows a lot about these nuances, because he has been through and part of the mystical world from the time he was seven years old. For a very long time, he felt more at home in an 'altered state of consciousness (without the drugs)', and without even trying, an entire world of higher dimensions opened the door and let him in. As he said:

> "Most people grow up out of the earth, and reach out to heaven. It was like I grew the other way. Higher energy links and esoteric experiences seemed as normal to me as eating apple pie. What I call 'solitude', is getting in touch with that higher state of consciousness, and having lived with it now all those years, it's there for me when I need it, whether I am alone or with others. So today I feel that my task is to evermore learn how to communicate with people, so I can work on this planet in the spirit of love. For me, getting grounded is most important."

It's probably not an accident that after so many years of other-worldly experiences, David found Findhorn and Findhorn found David. This small spiritual community located in northern Scotland, famous for its gardens where plants grow out of sand and blossom in the snow, became a home away from home. In this miraculous environment where loving people worked in co-operation with nature, David received what he later called his 'transmissions'. *Links With Space* has three of these inner visions, and each one reflects another aspect of Divine Love. To describe the essence of these communications, is almost as impossible as trying to describe the mystical experience. One has to simply experience it, and in reading David's words, you not only see, but are brought into the level of both seeing and being. They are, like David, a combination of esoteric wisdom and new-age awareness. It is as though some science fiction writer of the future has love as his theme, and you can't help but feel he has a direct hot-line to all the angels.

For better or worse, David has been christened a 'New Age Prophet.' But he shies away from such labels and has a wonderful sense of humour and humility about his role. In helping/teaching others, he speaks mainly about love and being in touch with everyday ordinary life. For someone who has come from the 'stars' he comes across as very down-to-earth. In his presence, you feel extremely comfortable. And no wonder; for David, the mystical path means seeing God in everything and everyone. From the heavenly domains to the ground beneath the ground, all living beings are connected and part of the same Christ Energy Source of Love. In sharing his thoughts, David is a wonderful guide. He takes us on a journey inside his heart, and in the process we gain new insights about our own spiritual quest.

"When I was a child, the spiritual realms were more real to me than the physical realms. I would find my human perspective falling away and I would be in a state of *oneness*. The first time I had this kind of experience was when I was seven. I was in a car driving with my parents, and just like Bentov said, 'It was a kick in the pants by evolution.' It just happened. I was looking out the window, and one moment I was there, and the next moment I wasn't. There was a physiological sense of swelling up, like being pumped full of air and I know I had an out-of-the-body experience at that point. I remember being able to look down and see myself, but that didn't last that long. I felt as if my confidence was moving away from my human self, not only from my human form, but even from my human psychology. I was moving into a totally different kind of psychology.

Of course, I couldn't have verbalized any of this as a seven-year-old. I mentally didn't have the vocabulary for it. I just accepted this experience as something normal, but with it came a deep sense of understanding. After that, many more mystical encounters followed, and I just accepted them as a normal part of life. Perhaps that's why today, I don't feel the need to make such a big thing out of the *mystical experience of oneness*, it all seems so natural to me. Therefore, what I may communicate to others is that normality, and this helps them to become more relaxed in their own path.

In a sense you could say that I have grown from heaven to earth, and that most people grow from earth to heaven. But I don't feel that growing from heaven to earth, or from earth to heaven are very different, because both of those directions depend on a *conscious working with integration*. I suppose my entire teaching career revolves around this issue of trying to bridge those links. And what I find, more often than not, is that many people have misconceptions of what it means to be spiritual. They turn away from their everyday lives, and they get caught up in the glamour of the spiritual search. They forget about everything connected to daily life, and live in some kind of hermetic ivory tower. And that's not necessarily spiritual.

As far as I'm concerned, the mystical experience is essentially adopting an understanding that says I am responsible for the well-being and incarnation of everything around me. That means that everything without exception in my environment, whether it appears to be living or non-living from a human point of view, has an inner life and an inner potential trying to emerge. And my connection to all of this on a mystical level, is that I understand that I have a responsibility to help that emergence along. *It's like being a midwife*.

For example, if I have my working environment, then everything in that environment, whether it's a table or a chair, or the computer or my books, has an inherent life. And that life may be different from my own, but it still responds to being called forth. In a way, I help all these other forms give birth to themselves, and the way in which that is done is primarily through love.

The mystical connection is an act of loving and honoring all these forms, and trying to use them and relate to them in a way that honors that sense of their own intrinsic personhood, their own intrinsic life. It's the same philosophy that Martin Buber expressed in his book *I and Thou*. It's looking at everything in my environment as a Thou, instead of as an it... Then there's no separation between me and it.

The mystical point of view says that God is seeking to reveal himself (that is, to manifest) through each of us. So I am accountable to helping that unfoldment, in all the people I meet. When I say I am accountable, I mean I have a responsibility, and if I am true to the mystical path, I must relate to each person as a manifestation of God. This means that I am responsive and truly listen. Then a convergence happens, then I become part of them. This can happen between me and another person, or between me and a bowl of fruit. It could be anything.

This all seems true, whether one is going from heaven to earth, or from earth to heaven. Both routes seem to be basically the same to me. The only difference is that in my own case, I started a conscious search from the experience of the spiritual worlds being real, and because I had that perception, I related to the physical world as not having total reality. So my discipline has been to learn to honor and deal with the physical realms more fully.

For me the spiritual realms can be described in two ways: First of all, the spiritual realm is another dimension, which our physical senses don't perceive normally. That's the simplest definition. The other definition is that the spiritual realm is that relationship with the universe, in which God is present. The spiritual realms are the domains of God.

The way I first began to see the spiritual realms is by what I call the 'psychic trivia' route. I would look around, and I would see being, I would see form. I would see color that other people don't normally see. Now, all of that is 'psychic trivia' and there are thousands and thousands of people who see in that way. It is the equivalent of seeing auras. I don't see auras, but I see other things. I'll see images and colors and geometric symbols, yet I feel auras. If somebody comes around me, and I choose to do so, I can touch their aura and it has a texture to me. This is more than just perceiving and feeling the electro-magnetic field, but that is what it is. This is a perception of emanations that are beyond the five senses.

I don't think there is a spiritual organ of perception. It's like another sense but I don't know what to call it. Whatever phrase we use is meaningless without the experience. I can call it 'kything,' a phrase Madeline L'Engle made up for a series of novels that she wrote. And Robert Heinlein made up a word for it, he called it 'groking.' So we could make up our own words, but why try to name it?

However, there is a level of experience that comes from what I call psychic sensing, even though I don't have an actual name for the senses, it's still psychic sensing. The way I understand the meaning of psychic abilities is the following: Psychic abilities come from what is known as the psychic bodies, and there are different names for this. There is the etheric body, the astral body, and the subtle body. It is part of the human being that is connected to the physical form, and to our minds and feelings. But it is a distinct manifestation of energy, it's like another body. And even though it is separate, it is connected to us. Now, very little of my experience comes out of that. I don't consider myself psychic or clairvoyant. That's why I don't like to talk about it too much. Yet it certainly can be a part of the spiritual experience.

The other form of perception, different from '*psychic sensing*' is what I call '*soul perception.*' For me, this is equivalent to mystical experience. It is a perception in which I become part of, and one with, whatever is being perceived... There is a blending of identity.

This works on two levels. One is as background, and the other is my direct soul perception of it. For example, I'm sitting at my desk, and I'm writing and I'm aware peripherally of everything else in the room, but I'm not giving my attention to it, even though I'm aware of it. In a similar way, the soul perception is there, and I'm aware of my inner being participating in the flow and currents of life around me. I experience a feeling of background awareness, but what is that? Imagine what it would be like to be in a place in which you feel completely at home, very secure, surrounded by love, where it all is harmony. If you can remember your own experience like that, this is what I mean by the background experience. This is an experience that I know is always going on. It's a supportive experience. It's like being with loving parents who are taking care of you.

Now while I'm having that experience, my mind is focused on other things, on doing my everyday work. I'm aware of the 'background' but I'm not giving it my attention. It is an ongoing mystical experience. If I give it my full attention, if I turn my attention from other things, and put it wholly upon that awareness, then that awareness expands and it fills my heart!

Here is an example of how this [background experience] works:

Let's say that now I'm a child in my parents' home. I'm playing on the floor, and I'm aware of this feeling of being secure and cared for. This is a feeling of being at home, and a feeling of being relaxed at a very deep level. But now I decide to shift my attention from the toys on the floor to my parents. I look at the source of what I think is providing this home feeling. So when you ask me what do I do – I don't really do anything except take my attention away from the physical objects that I've been working with, and instead think and feel about this other awareness, this source.

I don't imagine light. I don't imagine a particular image. I don't try to give it a form because it doesn't have a form in that way. There is a feeling of love, and a feeling of connection there, of being part of my world, part of the wholeness of the world. Sometimes however, what comes through isn't always pleasant. Sometimes what comes through is an awareness of the pain in the world, and that can be as much a part of it as feeling warm and cosy. But whatever I experience, the joy or the pain in the world, I don't feel that I'm experiencing it all by myself. When I give my attention to this mystical side, I don't have a sense that I'm experiencing it on my own, that I, David Spangler, have to somehow cope with it, or do something about it, or enjoy it.

One reason why I don't work much with techniques, is that I find that technique can be a good way to get started, but I find that people in our culture seem to place too much reliance on technique. So in effect, as Krishnamurti said, at the end of a technique all you have is the technique. You've perfected the technique, but you still may not have that mystical experience you want. To me it's more important to use our daily habits as a way to channel our thoughts and feelings.

There are feelings that help to join our energies, rather than to fight them. And these are the keys to participating in the mystical/holistic union. What I recommend to people is that they work consciously, very deliberately, to observe in themselves and in their environment, how they work in relationship with others. What are the feelings and thoughts that come to mind when they do their work, when they live their lives. For example, you could ask yourself, how do I eat? How do I deal with my body? How do I react and interact with others? Then they can ask themselves, 'Do these feelings and thoughts that I have about others or about what I am doing, *enhance my sense of connection*, in my desire to want to be part of this other person, or part of this other thing? Or do these feelings put a block between us, do they separate us?' There really is no separation. But to change your attitudes about you and them, or you and it, you must go beyond what is called *astronomical separation*.

A very nice phrase to give us a new perspective is that *in a holistic universe, when I throw a stone in front of me, it hits me in the back of the head*. There is no separation. So, when I want to overcome astronomical distances, all I am saying to myself is, what do I have to give to this other person that I would like to come back to me. What do I want to put into this event that I want to come back to me, (just like the stone). In asking these questions, it's important to be very specific about it. Going beyond the appearances is also important, so they do not limit you.

I feel you cultivate the higher vibrations, those higher energy links, so that their connection will allow you to work, through service and relationship to and with others. It's one thing to talk about your spiritual ideals, it's another to face the person right in front of you, and to treat them as if they were your world, they were your God. So, a simple technique for the mystical path is to love other people, which means to respect them, to be courteous to them. This is where I must be willing to begin. I feel if I'm going to focus solely on meditative or 'spiritual' techniques, and in that process, I don't begin in relation to the world; then, in fact, I don't begin at all.

The mystical path is essentially a path that fosters compassion and connection in the sense of mutuality. And if I want to follow a mystical path, then it's a path that says that we all share the same source... and therefore I will relate to you, or I will relate to the things in my environment as part of a single home and family. On the mystical path, I will seek to try to understand what it is that is trying to unfold through this other person, or this event. What is God trying to do in and through this other person and how can I help?

Basically, for me, *the mystical path comes down to union with God through helping God's emergence with the world*. Therefore techniques, to me, become techniques that help us to work well with our earthly experience, and to draw out of that experience meaning and value and love and wholeness and all the things that represent God to us.

Are there other words for mysticism and mystic? I can think of three. There's lover, there's connection, there's empowerment. A mystic is someone who is a lover, a connector, someone who empowers. Those words relate to the mystical path for me, but I still think that mysticism is a good word. I personally don't try to find substitutes for it. It has served us well. It has been around for a long time, and in trying to find a substitute word for it, you may lose the essence of its meaning.

There are many people I consider great mystics. There's Meister Ekhardt, there's Jesus, there's Buddha. I think Einstein was a mystic. There's Rudolf Steiner and so many other people whose work and lives enhance my own mysticism. I feel that the mystical experience in the way I define it is the experience that is going to change the planet. The role of mysticism is a very important role for the person in the New Age to explore.''

Cosmic Consciousness

I once told Mother Serena that for my birthday I wanted to receive cosmic consciousness. ''Cosmic consciousness!'' she exclaimed, ''Do you realize what that means? This is awareness of the whole universe, this is the ability to see the entire cosmos as it is... If you could attain cosmic consciousness by your birthday, that indeed would be a miracle. If you could attain it after several lifetimes you would be blessed. This is what Christ had, and that is why he was in charge of the entire planet. What I think you mean is that you would like to attain peace of mind, and get to know the divine spark within you.'' ''Yes,'' I said, ''that is what I really mean, but I still wouldn't mind living in the light all the time!''

Being enlightened, of course, is on many levels. What is peace of mind to one, may be traffic to someone else. But absolute peace, to be one with God, is the ultimate healing experience. And once the door is opened, all stale perceptions of the past dissolve painlessly in the light. But trying to talk about experiences of the light is not easy. That's why we can be grateful for a very special book that has inspired many seekers of the truth.

Cosmic Consciousness by Richard Maurice Bucke (Citadel Press) is a fairy tale for all adults who are willing to believe that they are 'children of the light'. But this isn't just a make-believe story. It is a collection of incredible facts that lets you make your own conclusions. Bucke, who lived during the late nineteenth and early twentieth century was first and foremost a psychologist. He considered himself a detached observer of the experience he classified as *Cosmic Consciousness*.

Bucke's recipe for *Cosmic Consciousness* is based on his own personal experience of sudden illumination, plus his investigation into the lives of famous spiritual and religious leaders, great scientists and poets, and others who are unknown. He notes similarities between his subjects. For instance, in most of the cases the crucial age for illumination is between thirty-five and thirty-seven. This is when the cosmic egg cracks and lets in a divine spark of light. It is this moment that changes the lives of everyone touched. This is the breakthrough that gives peace of mind, a deep sense of solitude, and the ability to heal others.

In many of the cases, the person was either very sick or suicidal. They had given up hope to live. But all of them always had a conscious or unconscious interest in religion. When the light came to them, they each had instantaneous healings, and after that they gave the rest of their lives to selfless service, helping others.

What makes this book so controversial for members of organized religion, is that Bucke dares to list Christ, Buddha, and Mohammed along with various other unknown characters, some who have initials like A.J.W. Suddenly the three main deities of the modern world are included in a study with ordinary people, showing that they all have a similar pattern of evolution. On one level it may seem heretical, yet on another level, it is a great psychological service.

Finally, this whole question about illumination is taken off the pedestal reserved only for saints and brought down to earth. This book specifically points out how, *yes, the answer is indeed within*, and we aren't so different from the guru of our choice. It gives one the chance to realize that these people are the expanded actuality of our own dormant potential waiting to be awakened. They could be us!

Bucke's list includes a lot of my favorite sources like Swedenborg, Ramakrishna, Lao Tze, Pascal and Walt Whitman. But he also misses quite a few, especially women. Most of the ladies listed here have anonymous initials, but then again this is his list... But even so, it is an inspiring book, one to read with a sense of whimsy, yet one to consider very seriously.

Devotion ... A Way of Working

Work is rest for the one who loves!

Saint Teresa of Avila

By some route of coincidence, a fanciful moment of fate, I happened to get into a corner of my kitchen cupboard that had been long overlooked. I was trying to find a special bowl in order to store some freshly made avocado dip, but instead I found an old spice canister hiding behind a stack of rice bowls. Since I was already on the ladder, I thought: why not, let's see what's inside. I opened it, and the first thing I saw was this message: *Ask and ye shall receive*. I removed it carefully, this scrap of paper that had been sitting on top of what appeared to be laurel leaves, sage, cloves, and who knows what else! It had to be at least ten years since all this had been put together.

Now you may wonder what any of this has to do with devotion as a way of working, but don't worry, I'm getting to that as soon as I tell you what was on the other side of the paper. But before I tell you that, I have to confess that all day long I was aggravating myself about how I couldn't possibly properly introduce this final section to 'Solitude Nuances'. I kept thinking words could never describe what I really felt, and if they could, who was I to tell anyone about devotion, work, commitment, LOVE! To give myself a break I started to do some scut work in the kitchen; cleaning, sorting, cooking, escaping! And that's how I got into the cupboard and the other side of the message, which said:

See — the secret of working — Bhagavad Gita.

Was this a coincidence, or truly fate, or perhaps a bit of both? *Scut work as revelation* was one of those ideas that had lived with me as long as the message that lived amidst the spices. And there I was, standing on the ladder, looking for something I couldn't find, because the universe had to reveal something far more important. It is through the work that we find our work, and it is in the doing that we receive all we need to know. I climbed down from the ladder and spent the rest of the evening looking for my precious copy of the Bhagavad Gita. This I had to find, and in the course of looking for it, I ate the avocado dip, which settled the problem of not finding special bowls!

The Bhagavad Gita, also called the Message of the Master, is the great Hindu spiritual epic that devotes an entire section to 'The Secret of Work'. The inner workings, the spiritual practice of how to become a true servant of God, is what the entire epic is really all about. Devotion as a way of working, devotion as a way of being, is the real story within this story. The real work, the great and noble work, is to love God always, in ALL WAYS. The real secret of work is to simply *surrender*. Then and only then will you find your true devotion.

The prize for hard work is life!

Britton Chance

I never met anyone quite like BRITTON CHANCE. To say that he is one of our most dedicated and brilliant scientists — a scientist among scientists — is not enough. For Britton Chance is one of those rare human beings whose generosity of spirit and creative energy goes way beyond the circumference of his profession. His entire life work gives a whole new meaning to the definition of Renaissance man.

For him, devotion is not just a way of working; it is a way of being. Once he said something to me that became a living *mantra* for my own process of creativity. "Why anticipate the future?" he said. "The revelation is coming — why be greedy? — BE HERE NOW." For him, to be able to work creatively is both a blessing and a privilege. And now I'd like to share with you his wisdom about that which he knows best — the art of loving your work with all your heart, all your mind, and all your soul.

"There has to be a joy permeating the situation where devotion is an expression of joy and pleasure. Without that, there's very little. If my work didn't bring joy, it wouldn't be a natural outpouring of effort. But since I feel that way, there is joy in working, there is joy in discovery, and there is joy in sharing the fruits of discovery with others. If this process weren't a happy one, it seems to me that it wouldn't be very effective. And the joy comes from inside... deep down.

One has to rationalize that it isn't going to be every night that a great discovery is made. And that often, months or years of preparations go into that moment of discovery. So you could say, scut work is preparation for that moment.

Years of preparations may culminate in a discovery, and any individual element of that could be regarded to be scut work.

There's a lot of scut work you have to do every day, and that's probably the difference between the person who does nothing until they have a brilliant idea which flashes upon them, or the others, who have an idea, and then strive for its culmination, its verification, its identification. So there's a big difference between the so-called stroke of genius, which you read about in books, and the real *scientific serendipity* which comes from days, months, and years of work...

For me, work is not an end in itself; the *end* is to push back the borders of knowledge. The point of work is to get you to that ultimate goal, which is increased knowledge, *revealed knowledge*. Those are the kinds of truth I'm interested in, and the lasting truth, the *real truth*, requires WORK. There are no short cuts... In terms of your work, or what you do, it doesn't matter what you are committed to, as long as you are committed...

In a sense, all true work and true commitment is service. In this sense we are all servants of God. However, idealism might suggest to dedicate one's work to God and nobody else. But that is an ego trip that I can scarcely afford. My work is dedicated to humanity in hopes that medical science may be useful for all of us. Idealistically, throwing oneself into one's activities at the feet of God is a wonderful thing. But it's also true that one is attempting to work for humanity at the same time. So I insist that the two things coexist. Perhaps, as I will reiterate, it is an ego trip that this is only dedicated to God. But doing one's work with the idea that 'God' means you are doing it for the welfare of everyone is very different. It seems to me that that's the way the New Testament works. In fact, one can only read from scriptures that to do it for humanity is to do it for God...

Solo experimentation, which I truly love to do, enhances my creativity, and I believe that dedication to creativity is very important. But without devotion, there is no creative solitude. For me, devotion is a way of working. Dedication and devotion are sufficiently similar, but devotion has in it a more emotional approach. Dedication could be a cold abstract dedication, while devotion says: your heart is in it. When we give our heart to God, our heart is in our work.

The key to *doing it* is perhaps more devotion as well as more dedication. In knowing this, we've made a plan for work. We've identified the ingredients, and if there are not enough of the right ingredients, you don't get a good tasting soup. So if you are devoted, you will do whatever it is you are doing with the utmost of your abilities. Beyond that, we can't ask anybody to perform.

If you ask me why am I devoted to my work, it's because

there's joy in working. And then if you ask me, but what if I stopped working, how would I feel? I'd say, well I wouldn't stop working, because there's joy in working. For me, because work is joy, joy isn't work! And I refuse to live without joy.''

Service must be its own and sole reward.

Mahatma Gandhi, *On Myself*

DEAN JAMES PARKS MORTON, whose caring and persistent guidance put the activities of the Cathedral of St John the Divine into global perspective, sees work on many levels. For him, the interweaving of all these levels is what the new age of holistic thinking represents. Ecology, planetary responsibilities, individual and collective awareness, solitude, and religion are all interconnected. What you do alone in your kitchen is just as important as a whole congregation getting together to discuss planetary survival:

''Everything is truly, radically interrelated. This is a perception that the Zen masters have known forever, that the Christians in the desert have known forever, that the Jewish mystics have known forever. So it's not a new thing. But the scale of issues, and what's happening now, thanks to the acceleration through technological processes of the last century, have made these mystical philosophical understandings today, sort of A.B.C.'s for school children. In this day and age, the esoteric stuff must be recognized as very explicit stuff, and if people don't deal at this level, they miss the whole point. But more and more people are beginning to realize this — 'saving the planet' is not just a cliché.

Assuming the personal risk of doing something about it, that kind of drive is what makes the religious person what he or she is; this is what commitment *is*. *It's perception of task*. All of this came together in my solitude — the perception of the task. Once it does come together for you — sort of like knowing the sun is there — you henceforth can't act like it is not there. The structure of your existence is now changed by that which is now laid upon you, and you have to act accordingly.

Facing your commitment doesn't happen all in one day. It grows and it deepens. You start out with something and you learn more and more about it, and more and more things that I knew are now being confirmed on different levels in different ways. The basic intuitions are being proved by disciplines I never thought much about. Even though I didn't know a lot about math, I perceived systems of mathematics as verifying these perceptions. Without question, individual and collective perceptions of task have greatly altered the way we do our work and live our lives.

A great glory of this time is that ways of thinking have changed. Before, philosophies perceived as mutually exclusive, are now being seen as complementary. This is very much of our time. We're at the end of the ages when everything was divided and understood separately. Now we are at a time of true interconnection. That we are able to recognize that and even put a name to it is sort of like Adam and Eve in the Garden of Eden naming the animals. Perceiving it, recognizing it, and calling it by name — this is what gives us the basic structure of the *ecological age as age*. Ecology is really the interdependence and communion of different systems that now are inhering and coinhering within each other. This is the age that all of this is now coming together, and that's great.''

Perceptions of the universe have changed, and so have we. In a world where one stitch interweaves with the whole tapestry, everything is integrated. Whatever work we do is absolutely related to the whole, be it running the largest Gothic cathedral in the world, like creative catalyst Dean Morton, or cleaning out our kitchen sink — in the truly *Zen and the art of cleaning up* spirit! In fact, some people enjoy doing the 'dirty work'. For them, cleaning up is meditation. As each particle of dust disappears, another bit of ego is swept away. Call it *the path of the hands,* call it the path of the heart, it is really one and the same.

In Paris during the late seventeenth century, a lay brother worked in the kitchen of a Carmelite monastery. There 'he found heaven on earth among the pots and pans of the institutions kitchen.' Brother Lawrence, as he came to be known, left behind a legacy that is called 'the practice of the presence of God'. Through this humble teaching, we learn great truths. The secret of devotion, the secret of happiness, is the real recipe our Carmelite cook shares:

WE CAN DO LITTLE THINGS FOR GOD

The time of action is not different from that of prayer. I enjoy God with as great tranquility in the hurry of my kitchen, where frequently many people call upon me at the same time for different things, as if I was on my knees at the holy sacrament. We can do little things for God. I put my little egg-cake into the frying pan for the love of God. When it is done, and if I have nothing else to call me, I prostrate myself on the ground, and I adore my God who assists me in everything by His grace; after which I rise up more contented than a king. When I can do nothing else, it is enough for me to pick up but a straw from the ground for the love of God.

Brother Lawrence, *The Practice of the Presence of God*

Commit thy works unto the Lord
and thy thoughts shall be established.

Proverbs 16:3

Who are we doing *it* for?… Sometimes it's confusing to know if it is the will of God, or our own little wills that spur us on. Learning to make these distinctions sort themselves out and become clear as we continue to pursue the path of devotion. Through the work we find the work, but we must do it, do it, do it, even when we don't know why! Scut work is the work we love to avoid the most because it is the most boring, the most lonely, and often the most unsatisfying kind of work. But this is the work that, if well done, separates the angels from the animals. This is the work — if done consciously in service for a higher spirit — that becomes the foundation of our real faith and devotion.

Krishnamurti offers the following advice:

For many people the most difficult thing in the world is to learn to mind their own business: but that is exactly what you must do. Because you try to take up the higher work, you must not forget your ordinary duties, for until they are done you are not free for other service. You should undertake no new worldly duties; but those which you have already taken upon you, you must perfectly fulfil — all clear and reasonable duties which you yourself recognize, that is, not imaginary duties which others try to impose upon you. If you are to be His, you must do ordinary work better than others, not worse, because you must do that also for his sake.

Knowing you have no choice is the beginning of freedom...
When I write, it does it.

Dorothy Norman, on creative discipline

DOROTHY NORMAN, whose salon of intellectual luminaries included the likes of Indira Gandhi, Joseph Campbell, Nancy Wilson Ross, D.T. Suzuki, Heinrich Zimmer, Ananda K. Coomaraswamy, and so many others, is first and foremost remembered and appreciated for her long collaboration with one of the greatest photographers of the twentieth century. The modern art movement as we know it today might not exist the way it does, if by chance, years ago, Dorothy Norman had not walked into the studio of Alfred Stieglitz.

For many years they shared a unique relationship. She was his student, his patron, and he was for her a great master who taught her the meaning of life and work. As she said, "He never really tried to teach me anything, and yet through him I learned everything!" I asked her if she could say what it was that made him work the way he did, could she capture the essence of his incredible spirit, and she smiled, reflected a moment, and said one word: "LOVE."

DOROTHY NORMAN on *Alfred Stieglitz*

"He was a great spirit, a great poet... He was a great *amateur*. He did everything through love. That was the way he photographed. He had no tricks, he knew everything from the inside. He knew you from the inside. He was the most intuitive person, and yet at the same time he had a wisdom that came out of examining life every inch of the way. He was constantly talking his life out loud...

For his funeral, Stieglitz said, 'I want no words, no music, no flowers!'... He talked about hitting not only the center of the target, but *the center of the center* of the target, and then the point even beyond that. That's the way he photographed, and that's what most people didn't understand. It was the difference between his photographs and those of others, the difference between his life and that of others. He never tried to sell anything, he never took anything for himself. He never tried to analyze anything, to analyze it out of existence. When he photographed something it was always the point beyond the possible or the reaching beyond the possible, that he wanted to put down. His work is so ethereal because it is *so* real.

Why he mattered to me is why we came together, because

nothing happened at Stieglitz's that could have happened any-where else. Picasso happened. Cézanne happened. *It happened.*

Stieglitz was like a magnetic force who magnetized people and art toward him. He never went out to find anything! He photographed the sky because it was there and he loved what he saw. He said, *'When I photograph I make love.'* He always said that if he didn't have an art gallery, the same thing would happen if he had a peanut stand..."

BUCKMINSTER FULLER

No one should have to worry about how they will earn their living; they should be able to do what they truly love.

JOHN CAGE

"Solitude for me is the opportunity to work. And my work is done by means of chance operations or other disciplines, so that my work is a continual revelation of discovery of things that were not in my mind.

Solitude, or being alone in itself, without the work, is some-thing I wouldn't prefer. I like to work. If I'm in a circumstance where I'm not doing any work, then I do something else like it.

For instance, I look for mushrooms, or I look at the situation in which I find myself... If I'm standing in line in the supermarket, which is another kind of solitude, I ask, how can I spend my time there without just being impatient? And the way to do it is by paying attention to the environment.

The way you do that is by working with it, as though you were at a concert, or as though you were in a museum, *looking and listening,* which is what Thoreau did all of his life. He did no other work than to pay attention to his environment. And then he wrote it down. That's all he did. That was his work. He had no other employment... True, he had a few odd jobs with Emerson, but they weren't serious.

For Thoreau, doing his work was like play because he identified himself with nature. He said, I am sorrow, I am ice. It was what he was. It is very poetic, too... It's like Rilke not knowing he was himself the tree he was looking at... Rilke was very intent on being alone. He went out of his way to do it, just like Thoreau... Eric Satie was another great solitary soul... I think that anyone who is doing any work is, in part at least, intent upon being alone to do it.

How I feel about solitude is how I feel about work. I enjoy it...

Sometimes I have a solitude in which I don't yet know how to use it. I may get into some kind of project where I'm still baffled or puzzled and I can't immediately use the time... So then I play something like a cat with myself, pretending that the mouse is not there, or that I'm not here, and that the mouse has a certain freedom.

The key to creativity, for me, is to act like the cat, as though I was not having the problem. And then suddenly some mysterious thing happens, and the problem is solved... It's a kind of Zen game... I learned this from Alan Watts, as a matter of fact. He pointed out that problems were often solved by not paying attention to them — that if you paid attention to them, they remained unsolved. But if you turned your attention away from the problem, it would solve itself...

So I'm speaking about a solitude that is useless, because you don't yet know how to solve the problem... So how do you solve it? You solve it by pretending that you're not paying attention to the problem... You do something else. Then suddenly the solution to the problem appears, and then you can use the solitude more efficiently. But being efficient in solitude isn't everything. I also like to play. I play chess, and chess is very near solitude, because the two people don't talk together, and they don't even play at the same time. Each person in a chess game plays by himself.

...I spend my day alone, except when people arrange to see me. I'm not exactly a hermit, even though I like to work alone a lot. But if people didn't come to see me, as they do, I probably would, after a while, go out of my way to see people... Yet I would spend most of my time doing my work, and I have to be alone. But I don't really feel alone because the work is actually not for me. It's for all those other people. I like to think of them as a great community of unknowns. Essentially we are all a community of solitary spirits.''

NANCY WILSON ROSS, ON WORK

It is most important and least understood. In the Zen monastery of Po-Chang, there is a saying: A day of no work... a day of no food.

JOSEPH CAMPBELL

"Creative solitude and work go together. Even though solitude isn't something that has ever concerned me, I have been in solitude for years, because of the work... And in working I have compelled myself to renounce going out, and staying home getting the work done... But I don't consider myself a very solitary person. I'm a very gregarious person, but I've spent a great deal of time in solitude... During those years of the Depression, when I didn't have a job and was up in the woods, I was alone and reading. I'd go out in the evening for dinner with friends when I was invited, but I was basically alone, and would stay home and cook something and work...

If I had to choose between being alone, or being with people I select, I'd rather be with people... But when it comes to my work, in terms of my creative process, I want to do it alone. I like doing it alone. I can write my own book and then I'm in control of what it says... I don't like to go with a whole pack of people to have my ideas put out... I guess I am solitary in terms of ideas, even though I've had some very good collaborations. There's no doubt about it, my nourishment is really my work... The secret is to love your work, and then it will work for you."

The storyteller tells his story... "Who says solitude needs special food?" he asks. And then, ISAAC BASHEVIS SINGER, who has just won the Nobel Prize for literature, continues to say: "What kind of food do you need for cooking solitude? There isn't such a kind of food. Solitude in itself is the nourishment." Then he pauses a long, long time. He removes his very dark sunglasses, rubs his eyes, puts his hand on his chin, and peers directly into my question. "Young lady," he says, "not that I usually give advice, but if I were you I would change the title of your book. There isn't such a thing as food for solitude, but then again maybe there is, and a lot of people will like it... My work is my food for solitude. But I don't write to be alone. It's the opposite. When I'm alone I write, which means I still speak to somebody."

Singer, who has charmed so many people with his gift of storytelling, does not want to admit that he spends a lot of time alone, because he doesn't equate creative solitude — working alone — as being alone. For him, solitude in itself is not an ideal, but rather "a means to reach either truth or creativity."

The Yiddish novelist and storyteller, who for years wrote for the

Jewish *Daily Forward* and *The New Yorker*, has suddenly become an international celebrity at the age of seventy-four. Everyone wants to meet him to talk about the Nobel Prize. A part of him enjoys it, but the other part needs to be alone. He says: "There are times like now that I need to be alone. Now, I wouldn't mind a lot of solitude," he says, "after a lot of communication with people, you need solitude, you have to have it."

ISAAC BASHEVIS SINGER *talks about what nourishes his creative Process.*

"What feeds me is life. The best food for creativity, for my writing, is life. The very essence, the very food for spiritual development, is the life which we can observe. Observing human life is the real gold mine for literature, for painting, for all creativity. It is especially interesting to observe the love life of people as much as you can. The love life of people is a kind of law, a kind of learning which is never exhausted. No matter how much you learn about it, you get new things all the time. And this is what the masters of literature really did. They learned from life.

What there is to learn from myself is very easy because I'm always with myself. I remember more or less what I went through. But I see that what's to learn about other people is more difficult. The real masters of great literature always observed others. Homer, the father of all literature, learned from the life of his time. To be able to write *Madame Bovary*, Flaubert did not look only into his own soul. He had also to look at others. The same thing is true of Dostoyevsky, about Gogol. They were all great observers of life. They ate life like a cow eats grass.

I too like to eat up life. My curiosity for human life never stops... For me, solitude is good, if it works for your creative process. Solitude is good after you're full with what you know. Then you have to be alone and be able to digest it. If you lock yourself up between four walls, and your spirit is empty, and you know only yourself, you will not be able to produce much. But if you are full of the lives of other people, then you can bear solitude, and it's even good for you, because too much of this nourishment is also not good, like in everything else. So being alone is good.

...Loneliness in itself, without the work, is isolation. A person who doesn't speak to anybody, or read anything, or write anything, is completely isolated. Such kind of isolation is very difficult for a human being to bear. You have to be very strong to bear this kind of loneliness.

...But even when I'm alone, working, I feel very connected with the world, with everything. It's the connection that matters... I combat my loneliness with action, by working. For me, action is the best way to change loneliness.

...For loneliness to be transformed into something else, you have to be a creative person. So it may be good for a very creative person to be lonely. I can stand much more loneliness than most people because I was always doing creative work. I was reading, and when you read you're not lonely any more. You are connected with people. You hear people speaking to you, not directly, but in the words. And when I'm writing, even though I'm alone I'm certainly not lonely. When I'm writing I speak to people. Creativity is communication.''

He who would find God must accept discipline.

Sirach 32:14

Are we alone in order to create, or do we create in order to be alone? Creating solitude — creative solitude — where do the boundaries begin and end? For sculptor LOUISE NEVELSON these questions addressed the very essence of her way of working. She was a larger than life character, endearingly eccentric, at times outrageous, at times totally understated. And everything she made, everything she did, expressed this glorious energy, an energy that she grew and cultivated herself:

''I believe in *the intelligence of labor*. Work is very important to me. In working, everything is done with great awareness, awareness of life. I am that life, and I am the one who creates my life, whatever it is... I am always in myself no matter where I am! My work reveals myself to me. When I am working I create my own energy. I project the world that is out there. When I am working I feel that the electricity is plugged into my life, I feel that humanity's electricity is projected into the world. I believe we create our own energy. So when I pick up a cup I try to pick it up with awareness. Martha Graham truly knows how to move — everything she does, she does with awareness — and I try to live the same way myself.

...I don't really have a public, I think I project it. I project my work. I work for myself, and then this work presents me to myself... I understand my solitude through my work. I know I am living when I am working!''

What characterizes a creative person? Great talent isn't the answer.
It is the courage to work without talent, energy to work without fear.
That is the labor of faith. When we can work and labor in
thanksgiving, that is the test.

Brother David Steindl-Rast

ROSALYN TURECK, who has brought Bach into the hearts of a whole
new generation of admirers through her brilliant piano concerts,
said, "I should really be worrying about my hands when I'm in the
kitchen, but I don't. Besides, who else can prepare this melon exactly
the way I like it?"

For Rosalyn Tureck, doing it on your own is an understatement.
When she was just four years old, she sat down one day and began
to play the piano. Musical prodigies are one thing, but persistent,
creative, and devoted lifelong workers are something else. From that
moment on, Rosalyn Tureck would no longer belong to herself, for
within her stirred an idea that she and only she could bring to
fruition. Years and years passed, and all along it was clear that she
had received a gift from somewhere other than normal realms. But it
wasn't until she was seventeen that she received the great revelation
of her life, the insight that was a complete turning point in her career.
This began her lifelong love affair with Johann Sebastian Bach. From
then on she lived, she breathed, she worked and worked for this one
moment — a revelation, a giant insight, that someone else might have
certainly enjoyed, and then said, thank you. But for Rosalyn Tureck,
her work and lifelong practice *is* the thank you.

I can still taste the melon she served — impeccably sliced, a
generous portion, sweeter than most crenshaw, perfectly ripe — like
the fruition of her particular kind of devotion.

"Some people say to me that my work seems like breathing
because I love it so much... But it isn't as though I couldn't work.
As long as I have my mentality, I would work, even if I couldn't
rush physically around the world... It's not possible to stop the
brain if you've got one! It moves. If you've got a spirit that's alive,
you don't stop work. And you never retire, that's just laughable.

Some people make such a big thing out of work, but I have
always wondered why that's such a discovery... Ever since I
breathed I worked. You may say that I was *called*, but there is a
certain cultural aspect to it. I was surrounded by people who
thought this way... Work was just taken for granted... You didn't
think about whether you should do it or not, you just did it...

All the great creative things happen, whether you let them or not, for when it happens it happens. I think that a more accurate way of saying it is, when you are ready these things happen.

We have a way of saying, if you allow yourself, or if you open yourself to it, and all that kind of thing. And I suppose there's something in that, when you are ready to relax inside. But the human being, each individual, is so complex that if you say, *if you allow yourself*, I wonder, which area is going to relax? You haven't got the keys to all those millions and billions of things inside.

But if it happens, it happens in solitude, because everything important happens in solitude. That means everything important happens in your inner self. That doesn't mean that you can't love somebody else, but that love comes from your inner self... And that is the inner self which I interpret as meaning solitude in this sense... *Because solitude is everything, and everything that is inner is solitude*.

...How do insights work? For me, revelations have nothing to do with action. There is no activity. There is not even mental activity. When I had my 'Bach revelation' it was like being in the void, but when I came to, it was all there. I didn't have to get excited, and think this or think that. My mind wasn't going so fast that I couldn't even begin to keep up with it. That's how I live almost all the time. But it wasn't like that...

It was simply all there. It was peaceful. It was serene. It was complete. I knew everything... It's so total that you don't even have to make comparisons to what you know, or didn't know before. Everything I needed was there, present with me. I was alone with solitude itself. Only in looking back, I say I could never return.

I had entered a new world, and once you enter that new world, you can't go back. The image that I have is of this small door in a garden wall. You open that small door, and you go into an infinite immensity, not measurable. How can you turn back and go into the garden? You can't... But if you are a creative person, you never look back. You can't wait. You can't go back. You have to go on to the new creative ideas.

You may wonder, can you equate the difference between your love of work, and the love of a person? Do you measure it, and can you measure it? Is there a different level of experience, where you feel more ecstatic about your work than a person, or the other way around?

I never measured it. But as you were asking me about loving my work and all that kind of thing, I was thinking, there are so many different levels to my work. And love and relationships also occur on so many different levels.

I believe it's possible to have an intimate relationship, but extremely rare, and extremely difficult. But so is art extremely difficult. I think that one tries to develop a relationship with a human being who has to be on the same wavelength, so that you can experience an ecstasy of the inner life together... I have had beautiful experiences like these in my life. But I feel I'm capable of having them more and more, because I'm always just beginning... I feel as though I'm beginning a new life now.''

GLORIA VANDERBILT:

I see the creative process as becoming part of some great force. The creative process — the life process — is one for me. I do believe that I am part of something that is larger. I also believe that there are people who are on the side of the angels, and people who are not. And the people who are on the side of the angels are the people who give love, create love, create beauty, create goodness itself.

Ruth Gordon said the most extraordinary thing about creative success. She said, 'It takes courage, it takes believing in it, it takes rising above it, it takes work. It takes you liking me, and me liking you. It takes the dreaming soul of the human race, that wants it to go right, that's never stopped dreaming.'

This is like a prayer for me. It's so important to me. This is my spiritual food for solitude... And the idea of God, the creative process, is like life itself... It all works together.''

The Cosmic Patience becomes, in part, our patience, for after all God is at work in the world. It is not we alone who are at work in the world, frantically finishing a work to be offered to God. Life from the center is a life of unhurried peace and power. It is simple. It is serene. It is amazing. It is triumphant. It is radiant. It takes no time, but it occupies all our time.

Thomas R. Kelly *(Quaker contemplative), A Testament of Devotion*

Think of the gods, that the gods may think of you! Ask that ye may receive! From food, creatures are nourished and grown; from rain cometh the food; from the gods comes the rain in response to the desires and demands of man; and the desires and demands of man are forms of action; and the actions proceed from the One... All-pervading Life...

The Bhagavad Gita

Place your burden at the feet of the Lord of the universe who accomplishes *everything. Remain all the time steadfast in the heart, in the Transcendental Absolute. God knows the past, present, and future. He will determine the future for you and accomplish the work. What is to be done will be done at the proper time. Don't worry. Abide in the heart and surrender your acts to the Divine.*

Ramana Maharshi

Believe in the works, not in the words; words are an empty shell, but the works show you the master.

Toil, a Divine Commandment, in Paracelsus, Selected Writings

According to eternal immutable great laws —
we must all complete the circle of our existence.

Goethe, *Divinity*

REFLECTIONS

holding onto nothing
  i let it go.
    holding onto nothing
      it knew where to flow.

why do you think in terms of fitting?
  doesn't the ocean fit inside the shell?
      just be.
      let God
      enter you.

the mountain became a speck of dust in my eye.
  a tear drop away and I could see.
holding onto nothing I let it go,
  fear, loneliness, incompletion.
a lifetime of such karma dissolving
  in one humble intimate moment.
if this is what it means to surrender
  why have I waited so long?

Epilogue

Contemplating contemplation
  I asked a silent question
I kept asking and asking until —
  I asked: what more can I say?
The greatest reason for being alone
  is no reason at all.

  yesterday's food
    yesterday's mood,
      yesterday's solitude.
        That was yesterday —

  BEGIN NOW

About the Author

FRANCINE SCHIFF is a pioneer in Cable Television. She guest hosted an Emmy Award TV program. She then went on to produce, moderate and write her highly acclaimed *The Talk Show*, which was the first nationally sponsored Cable TV series in the USA.

As artist in residence at the Cathedral of St John the Divine, she reflected her own vision of spiritual ecology by producing and moderating *Energy Links*, an international media program.

From this very public work, Francine retreated into several years of spiritual solitude, out of which emerged this book in which she combines her remarkable talents as interviewer–journalist with her direct experience of contemplative life.

She makes her home in New York City, where she writes, teaches, and continues her work as *spiritual/catalyst*. She is currently working on *Thinking Hearts*, a TV and radio series she founded to raise consciousness about creative and spiritual life.

Who's Who in
Food for Solitude

Abbreviated biographical sketches of the people interviewed

BIBI ANDERSSON — Actress, best known for her roles in the films of Ingmar Bergman including *Persona*, *The Seventh Seal*, and *Wild Strawberries*. She also played the part of the psychiatrist in *I Never Promised You a Rose Garden*, a film based on Joanne Greenberg's novel and directed by Anthony Page. pp. 17–18, 53, 77–8, 103, 113, 145

JENNY ANDERSSON — Bibi Andersson's daughter, six years old at the time of the interview, now in her late teens. pp. 18–19

GREGORY BATESON — Anthropologist/philosopher, whose Bali studies with his wife Margaret Mead broke new ground for anthropology; author of *Steps to An Ecology of Mind*, *Mind & Nature: A Necessary Unity*, and (with his daughter Mary C. Bateson) *Angel's Fear: Towards an Epistemology of the Sacred*. pp. 7–8, 37, 105

POLLY BERGEN — Actress whose credits include many roles on ''Playhouse 90'' and in ''The Helen Morgan Story'' on television. She was a panelist on ''To Tell the Truth.'' pp. 14–15, 24

JERRY BROWN — Governor of California from 1975 to 1983; attorney and chairman of the California Democratic Party; also known for his spiritual lifestyle, including extensive time spent in a Zen monastery and deep involvement in environmental issues. pp. 37, 112

JOHN CAGE — Avant-garde composer and conductor, considered one of the greatest composers of the twentieth century, author of several books including *Silence: Lectures & Writing* and *Themes & Variations*. pp. 117–21, 254–5

JOSEPH CAMPBELL — Noted mythologist, longtime professor at Sarah Lawrence College, author or editor of numerous books including the classic *The Hero With a Thousand Faces*, a series of books on *The Masks of God*, *The Mythic Image* (with M.J. Abadie), and *Skeleton Key to Finnegans Wake* (with Henry Morton Robinson). He also did a notable series of programs on mythology for PBS. pp. 38, 76, 105, 256

BRITTON CHANCE — Scientist, considered a legend in medical science; foreign member of the Royal Society, and award-winning biochemist and biophysicist, with more than 9,000 citations, noted for his enzyme work. Director of the Johnson Research Foundation at the University of Pennyslvania from 1949 to 1983. His work shaped what we now know as the fields of biochemistry and biophysics. He is also a pioneer in nuclear magnetic resonance research. He was a Gold Medal winner for yachting in the 1952 Olympics. pp. 12, 52, 104, 224, 248–50

BARRY COMMONER — Environmentalist, activist, editor (with others) of *Energy & Human Welfare* (three volumes). He participated, with Margaret Mead and Robert Redford in 'Sun Day', a major event at the Cathedral of St John the Divine promoting solar energy. pp. 32–4, 75–6

JOAN FONTAINE — Already a film legend by the time she was twenty-five, her name conjures up all kinds of images for us. She won the Academy award in 1941 for her role in *Suspicion* (with Cary Grant). She starred in over forty other Hollywood films, including *Damsel in Distress* (Fred Astaire's first film) and *Jane Eyre*. pp. 16, 35, 80, 223, 235–7

BUCKMINSTER FULLER — Architect, designer, philosopher, teacher; innovator noted for his geodesic dome and dymaxion car. Fuller coined the phrase 'spaceship earth'. His many books include *Critical Path*, *Operating Manual for Spaceship Earth*, *Intuition*, and *Synergetics: Explorations in the Geometry of Thinking*. pp. 5, 254

JAMES GEORGE — Former Canadian ambassador to India, Iran, Sri Lanka, Nepal, and the Gulf States; director of the Threshold Foundation in England, and president of the Sadat Peace Foundation. He initiated the movement of Tibetan refugees to Canada in cooperation with his friend the Dalai Lama. pp. 225–7

TENZIN GYATSO, THE 14TH DALAI LAMA — The spiritual leader and temporal head of the Tibetan government in exile in India, and winner of the 1989 Nobel Peace Prize; author of numerous books including *Kindness, Clarity, and Insight*, and his recently published autobiography, *Freedom in Exile*. pp. 9, 58–60

MARY HEMINGWAY — Writer and last wife of Ernest Hemingway. She was custodian for her late husband's extensive literary legacy, and was the author herself of *How It Was*. She has been active in efforts to save whales and other environmental issues. pp. 30–31, 53

GEOFFREY HOLDER — Dancer, actor, choreographer, director, born in Trinidad, later came to New York. Holder was a solo dancer with the Metropolitan Opera, then formed his own dance company in 1950. He won Tony awards in 1975 both as director and as costume designer for *The Wiz* on Broadway. He also was a Guggenheim Fellow in painting in 1957. p. 77

JIM JENSON — With WCBS-TV in New York City for twenty-six years, twenty-five of those years as news anchorperson; he is now senior correspondent for WCBS-TV and hosts a commentary program, "Sunday Edition." p. 76

GOPI KRISHNA — Indian mystic who founded the Research Institute for Kundalini at Nishat, and who has cooperated with scientists in investigations of the physiological bridge to higher consciousness. After seventeen years of meditation, he had an unexpected experience of awakening of Kundalini energy. His many books include *The Mystic Experience, Kundalini: The Evolutionary Energy in Man, Kundalini for the New Age*, and *Higher Consciousness: The Evolutionary Thrust of Kundalini*. pp. 177–8, 231–5

JOHN LILLY — New Age explorer best known for his dolphin research and his experiments with sensory deprivation flotation tanks. His books include *The Center of the Cyclone: An Autobiography of Inner Space* and *Communication Between Man & Dolphin: The Possibilities of Talking with Other Species*. pp. 10, 38

ROLLO MAY — Existential psychologist, whose pioneering efforts led to changes in the psychotherapy profession allowing psychologists to become psychoanalysts without a medical degree. Author of the international best-seller *Love & Will* and numerous other books, including *The Art of Counseling, The Courage to Create, The Meaning of Existence, Power & Innocence*, and *Man's Search for Himself*. pp. 22, 36, 72–3

EUGENE MCCARTHY — Former US Senator (Minnesota), presidential candidate, writer/poet, and teacher. In his presidential bids he paved the path for serious independent third-party candidacies. His books include collections of political essays and memoirs, an illustrated children's book (*Mr Raccoon & His Friends*) and a collection of poetry (*Other Things & the Aardvark*). His most recent book is *The View from Rappahannock* (1989). pp. 40–41, 54

EDGAR MITCHELL — Astronaut who participated in the first moon landing and who conducted the first mental telepathy experiments from outer space; founder and chairman of the Institute of Noetic Sciences. He also narrated the film, *The Ultimate Mystery*. pp. 55–6

JAMES PARKS MORTON — Episcopal priest, architect, Dean of the Cathedral of St John the Divine in New York City since 1972, and a leading figure in the ecumenical religious community. He has been a spiritual catalyst for environmental issues on a global scale, and was responsible for the development of the cathedral's innovative artist-in-residence program, which has fostered many projects including providing impetus for the completion of the cathedral. pp. 250–51

LOUISE NEVELSON — Russian-born American sculptor, best known for her large abstract wood sculptures, including *Sky Cathedral* (1958) at the Museum of Modern Art. *Night Presence IV*, a 1972 steel sculpture, was given to New York City. p. 258

EDWIN NEWMAN — News commentator, with NBC since 1952; served as NBC bureau chief in London, Rome, and Paris, news commentator, narrator of numerous TV specials, moderator of presidential debates, syndicated columnist, author of several books, including *Strictly Speaking*. Newman won seven Emmy awards and a Peabody award. pp. 3–4

JULIE NEWMAR — Actress and dancer, Tony award winner for the Broadway play *The Marriage Go-Round* (with Claudette Colbert and Charles Boyer). Her film debut was in *Seven Brides for Seven Brothers*, and she played Catwoman in the original "Batman" TV series. pp. 10, 29, 134–5, 145–6

LEONARD NIMOY — Actor, screenwriter, and film director, best known for his role as Spock on *Star Trek* (both the television series and the films). He also played Paris in "Mission Impossible" as well as numerous stage roles including the part of the psychiatrist in *Equus* on Broadway. Nimoy is also a poet. pp. 75, 107

DOROTHY NORMAN — Writer and patron of the arts, known especially for her long collaboration with photographer Alfred Stieglitz. Her books include *Encounters: A Memoir, America & Alfred Stieglitz* (editor), *Beyond a Portrait* (with Stieglitz), *Alfred Stieglitz* (compiler) in the Masters of Photography Series, and *The Heroic Encounter* in the Bollingen series. pp. 75, 253–4

HERBERT O'DRISCOLL — Episcopal priest, lecturer, writer, dean of Christ Church Cathedral in Vancouver, Canada since 1968. He has had a series of weekly radio talks, and is the author of several books including *Crossroads: Times of Decision for People of God*. pp. 228–9

IRA PROGOFF — Depth psychologist and founder/director of Dialogue House in New York and the National Intensive Journal program which he created in 1966. As a Bollingen Fellow he studied with C.G. Jung in Switzerland in the early 1950s and shortly afterward with D.T. Suzuki. Author of *Jung, Synchronicity, & Human Destiny*, *Depth Psychology & Modern Man*, *The Well & the Cathedral*, *The Star-Cross*, and numerous other books on psychology and journal-keeping. He also translated and provided a commentary for *The Cloud of Unknowing*. pp. 11, 52–3, 74, 112, 216, 219–22

KYGONGLA RATO — Tibetan Buddhist teacher, who divides his time between India and New York City where he has been founding director of the Tibet Center since 1976. A close associate of the Dalai Lama, he also is the author of *My Life and Lives: The Story of a Tibetan Incarnation*, which was edited and includes a foreword by Joseph Campbell. p. 13

NANCY WILSON ROSS — Novelist and social historian; longtime student of Asian life and thought whose non-fiction books have included *The World of Zen* and *Three Ways of Asian Wisdom: Hinduism, Buddhism, Zen*. pp. 2, 39, 49, 157–8, 255

MOTHER SERENA — Spiritual healer for more than seventy years, who early on embraced and helped to initiate the 'New Age' in the twentieth century. She was a long-time leader of the original Rosicrucian Society in America, beginning in 1916. pp. 3, 20, 167–72, 245

ISAAC BASHEVIS SINGER — Yiddish writer who won the Nobel prize for literature in 1978; noted for his many humorous stories, several of which were made into major movies. pp. 256–8

PAOLO SOLERI — Visionary architect and creator of Arcosanti, a 'city of the future', whose concept of 'arcology', blends architecture and ecology. His books include *Arcosanti: An Urban Laboratory?* and *Technology & Cosmogenesis*. pp. 37, 104

DAVID SPANGLER — Co-director of the Findhorn Community in Scotland and later founder of the Lorian Association. David's writings, lectures, and workshops helped to pioneer a whole new energy in the field of esoteric education. Before it was fashionable he spoke about consciousness, planetary peace, and spiritual ecology. His books include *Revelation: The Birth of a New Age*, *The Findhorn Garden*, and *Links with Space*. pp. 111, 238–44

BROTHER DAVID STEINDL-RAST — Benedictine monk known especially for his work in bridging Eastern and Western thought, and author of several books, including *A Listening Heart* and *Gratefulness: The Heart of Prayer*. pp. 189, 204–13, 216

GLORIA STEINEM — Writer, feminist, and founder/editor of *MS.* magazine. Her books include a collection of essays and a portrait of Marilyn Monroe, *Marilyn*. pp. 22, 36

FRANCES STELOFF — Literary legend, founder of the Gotham Book Mart, an important center that nurtured and supported many influential literary figures through most of the twentieth century.In her seventy-year career she also devoted herself to bringing metaphysics into the world at large. pp. 2, 80, 86, 138–40

WILLIAM IRWIN THOMPSON — Cultural historian and author of several influential books, including *Passages About Earth, Darkness and Scattered Light*, and *Imaginary Landscape*. He was a founder of the Lindisfarne Association, a contemplative community in the heart of New York City and Crestone, Colorado. pp. 39, 56–8, 178–9, 216–18

ROSALYN TURECK — Concert pianist, harpsichordist, and clavichordist. She has been called 'the high priestess of Bach'. Her work as a scholar and educator is reflected in five honorary degrees including an honorary doctorate from Oxford University, making her the fourth woman in its long history to be so honored. She is founder of the Bach-Tureck Institute, where she gives master classes and holds symposia. pp. 37, 106, 114, 259–61

GLORIA VANDERBILT — Artist, actress, fashion designer, and poet/playwright, has won numerous awards. She has had many one-woman art shows and her parts included roles in *Picnic* and *Peter Pan* on Broadway. She has also designed stationery and greeting cards, fabrics and clothing, china and glassware. pp. 74, 108–9, 112, 261

DIANA VREELAND — A legend in the fashion industry, and founder of the Fashion Institute at the Metropolitan Museum of Art. She was fashion editor at *Harper's Bazaar* from 1939 to 1962, and editor-in-chief of *Vogue* from 1962 to 1971. pp. 6, 74, 102–3, 113, 190

ANDY WARHOL — A leading figure in the Pop Art movement, best known for his Campbell soup cans and portraits of Marilyn Monroe. He was also a producer of avant-garde films and founder of *Interview* magazine. p. 103

TOM WOLFE — Best-selling author and social commentator, an iconoclastic journalist whose book *The Painted Word* (first published in *Harper's Bazaar*) stirred up the art world. His many books have included *The Right Stuff* and *The Bonfire of the Vanities*, both of which have been made into major motion pictures. pp. 38, 89